MUSEUM

THE BASICS

Museum and Gallery Studies: The Basics is an accessible guide for the student approaching Museum and Gallery Studies for the first time. Taking a global view, it covers the key ideas, approaches and contentious issues in the field. Balancing theory and practice, the book addresses important questions such as:

- What are museums and galleries?
- Who decides which kinds of objects are worthy of collection?
- How are museums and galleries funded?
- What ethical concerns do practitioners need to consider?
- How is the field of Museum and Gallery Studies developing?

This user-friendly text is an essential read for anyone wishing to work within museums and galleries, or seeking to understand academic debates in the field.

Rhiannon Mason is Professor of Heritage and Cultural Studies and Head of the School of Arts and Cultures at Newcastle University, UK. Her teaching and research focuses on the role of heritage and memory institutions in mediating public understandings of people's histories, cultures and identities.

Alistair Robinson is Director of the Northern Gallery for Contemporary Art, having held positions at the Victoria & Albert Museum and the National Museum of Photography Film & Television. He is undertaking research into museums of modern art collecting contemporary art.

Emma Coffield is an Early Career Academic Fellow in Media, Culture, Heritage (MCH) at Newcastle University, UK, and leads the MA in Art Museum and Gallery Studies. Her research focuses on contemporary art history, production and display, and the spatial politics of artistic practice.

THE BASICS

For a full list of titles in this series, please visit www.routledge.com/
The-Basics/book-series/B

MUSEUM AND GALLERY STUDIES

THE BASICS

Rhiannon Mason, Alistair Robinson
and Emma Coffield

LONDON AND NEW YORK

First published 2018
by Routledge
2 Park Square, Milton Park, Abingdon, Oxon OX14 4RN

and by Routledge
711 Third Avenue, New York, NY 10017

Routledge is an imprint of the Taylor & Francis Group, an informa business

© 2018 Rhiannon Mason, Alistair Robinson and Emma Coffield

British Library Cataloguing-in-Publication Data
A catalogue record for this book is available from the British Library

Library of Congress Cataloging-in-Publication Data
A catalog record for this title has been requested

ISBN: 978-0-415-83454-4 (hbk)
ISBN: 978-0-415-83455-1 (pbk)
ISBN: 978-1-315-14857-1 (ebk)

Typeset in Bembo and Scala Sans
by Book Now Ltd, London

CONTENTS

ILLUSTRATIONS

FIGURES

TABLES

ACKNOWLEDGEMENTS

This book represents the shared thinking and practice around museums and galleries in which we have been engaged, both independently and collaboratively, for the past two decades. Our perspectives owe much to our experiences of teaching on the Masters and PhD programmes in Museum, Gallery and Heritage Studies at Newcastle University. Our ideas have been tested, challenged and developed through discussions with our students and colleagues in this context. Similarly, our collaborations with colleagues on research projects and publications have further shaped our own understandings of the field.

Most importantly, our fascination with museums and galleries has been enriched and sustained through the collective enthusiasm for our subject that defines the community of museum, gallery and heritage scholars, practitioners and students at Newcastle. At the same time, academics at other museum, gallery and heritage HE departments and institutions in the UK, and beyond, have also shaped our thinking. We recognize that ours is a very rich, interdisciplinary and cooperative field of study.

We would like to thank the reviewers at proposal and draft stage who provided us with such constructive and thoughtful feedback. Thanks also to the team at Routledge for their support and endless patience throughout the long process of bringing this project to completion.

Specifically, we would like to thank the following people for their input: Joanne Sayner who read an early draft, Katherina Massing who helped us understand the linguistic issues around terms such as museum and gallery in the Chinese context, Susannah Eckersley who similarly informed our understanding of the terms in the German context, Chris Whitehead who greatly informed our understanding of museum and gallery history, as well as how to critically think about display, Bethany Rex who contributed to our review of international museum definitions, Peter Davis who both inspired and encouraged us, as well as introducing us to a much broader, international understanding of museological thinking and practice, and Areti Galani for teaching us so much about Digital Heritage over the years. Our thanks also go to Zelda Baveystock, Gerard Corsane, Elizabeth Crooke, Simon Knell, Viv Golding, Katherine Lloyd, Suzanne McLeod, Wayne Modest, Andrew Newman, Aron Mazel, Bryony Onciul, Richard Sandell, Peter Stone, Iain Watson, Sheila Watson, Iain Wheeldon, Helen White, Conal McCarthy, and Andrea Witcomb for many stimulating discussions around museums, heritage and galleries over the years. Any errors remain our own responsibility.

Our thanks also go to the following museums and galleries who gave their permission for us to include the images and tables in this book: Tower Museum, Derry; British Museum, London; Tate Gallery, London; DCMS; Kelvingrove Museum and Art Gallery, Glasgow; Bowes Museum, County Durham; V&A Museum, London; Great North Museum, Hancock, Newcastle; National Museum of African-American History and Culture, Washington.

INTRODUCTION

What are museums and galleries for? Why do societies have them? What's the point of them? How much power and influence do they have over the way people understand the past, present and future and what responsibilities does this bring? How do they communicate ideas and values through their collections, displays and interpretation? What public roles do and should they play? Who are they for? Who do they represent and, crucially, who do they *not* represent and why? Does it matter if they don't represent everyone and their cultures and histories? Is it even possible to represent everyone and everything? Are museums political or are they neutral spaces?

Should the public pay for museums and galleries collectively through general taxation, or should people pay on entrance through ticketing, as with sports matches or theatre visits? Should museums and galleries be expected to rely on the generosity or needs of private donors and corporate sponsors to support them? What are the ethical implications of the financial arrangements which underpin museums and galleries? This book, and the field of museum and gallery studies, addresses these questions among many others.

In Europe, museums and galleries have been in existence since the seventeenth century (see Chapter 2) and are a 'part of the landscape' in almost every medium or large city. Elsewhere in the world, as in China and the Persian Gulf, there is a 'museum boom' going on right now, where museums and galleries are being built in great numbers and with great expense. In many parts of the world, we are so used to having museums and galleries that it is easy to take their existence and importance for granted. However, it is important to ask ourselves why societies and governments worldwide have taken hundreds of millions of objects out of commercial circulation to keep ownership of them in 'public' hands. Building an institution like a museum or gallery is a major financial burden. It usually requires a huge form of 'capital expenditure' where a vast sum of money must be found and not used on any other urgent requirement. Maintaining an institution like a museum or a gallery is disproportionately expensive to other spaces. They require special air-conditioning and environmental controls, security, storage, conservation and, of course, staff to look after everything. Museums and galleries have high fixed costs while having relatively few opportunities to raise the funds to cover them; this means they are always reliant on financial support from donors, patrons or the state. Most importantly, the whole idea of the traditional museum or gallery is that it has a responsibility to house, protect and conserve its collections *forever*. This is not only a philosophical responsibility but a financial commitment in perpetuity.

Seen in this light, we might conclude that museums are absurd undertakings and historical anomalies left over from an earlier time. After all, is impossible to arrest the decay or change that all objects inevitably experience with age. On the other hand, if so many societies have been prepared to invest such enormous resources in preserving all these things for the future, then this does suggest that those objects, and the institutions in which they live, have been and continue to be incredibly important to humans in many places and over many generations. So, for this reason, if nothing else, they deserve serious attention. We have to ask ourselves, why have so many societies decided that it is worth sacrificing so much of their collective resources in order to keep and to show objects to each other? What is it about these institutions and their practices of collecting, preserving and interpreting that makes so many societies convinced that they are an essential part of our collective public life?

WHAT THIS BOOK WILL DO

This book explores these fundamental questions by providing an introductory overview of the field of museum and gallery studies, and establishing some of the key debates and parameters of this fascinating and interdisciplinary field of study. We will also look at policy and practice in museum and gallery work. The term 'museum and gallery studies' refers to the formal academic examination of just about any aspect of what museums and galleries are and do. It encompasses the study of the institutions themselves and how they operate. Just as museums and galleries themselves encompass many different academic disciplines from art history, natural sciences, human history, ethnography, geology, to archaeology, so museum and gallery studies also draw on many different intellectual currents, traditions and debates.

In this respect, this book is taking on a very difficult challenge. Let us be clear; there is no one standard kind of museum or gallery because they come in such different shapes and sizes and all with their own histories, logics and peculiarities. Even the briefest look at what cities and countries hold in trust will reveal a dazzling diversity of archaeological and anthropological artefacts; fine art, paintings, photographs, sculptures; decorative arts and designs; natural history, materials from the natural sciences; and artefacts that relate to social history, history and 'culture' in the wider sense of that word. We absolutely recognise the tremendous diversity of the collections held by museums and galleries and the disciplines to which they relate. So, we are not attempting to write the definite, singular account of museums and galleries worldwide. It cannot be done, and it is their individuality which makes them so interesting. What we are attempting to do in this book is to provide an insight into the kinds of issues, challenges and features which many museums and galleries will have in common and to provide a framework for thinking about these institutions in all their many forms.

In recognition of the potentially enormous scope of our topic, we have decided to place particular emphasis on how public museums and galleries tell stories of human history, and of histories of art. This decision is partly because these are our specialisms but also because this allows us to look at many of the areas where there have been debates and controversies in recent museum and gallery studies. We have adopted an international approach while recognising that our knowledge is most extensive of the Anglophone literature on museums and galleries. While the parameters we have adopted mean that we will inevitably not cover all possible ways of looking at the field of museum and gallery studies, many of the principles and issues we discuss are also applicable to other disciplines, other collections, or different institutions to those examples given here.

WHO IS THIS BOOK FOR?

Put simply, this book is for anyone interested in the questions posed above and anyone who has visited a museum or art gallery and wanted to know about what they do, how they work and why they exist. If you have never visited a museum or a gallery, we hope this book will inspire you to discover them for yourselves and think about them in a new way. Our book is also for those people who have wondered what it might be like to work in museums and galleries. Our book is not a training manual – those already exist – but it will provide an insight into the kind of activities that make up 'museum and gallery-work', and the challenges and pleasures involved. Crucially, we will consider why this work matters to societies in the present day, but also why it has mattered in the past, and why it will – we firmly believe – continue to matter for the future generations yet to come.

At the end of each chapter we have provided suggestions for further reading. In many cases, these suggestions are edited books which contain many articles by different scholars. These kinds of publications are an excellent next step into developing your understanding of museum and gallery studies because they offer a range of perspectives from different countries and because the introductory section will typically provide an overview of key issues and authors in that particular topic. We recommend to always begin with the introductory overview to build up a sense of the parameters and most important debates in the 'field' of study. This broad overview can then be developed by pursuing particular areas of interest in more depth. At the back of the book you will find all the references and weblinks for each chapter. These also provide further sources to explore.

WHAT ARE MUSEUM AND GALLERY STUDIES?

Museum and gallery studies look at all the different ways we can understand museums and galleries. These range from their day-to-day business to the symbolic roles they play in, and for, societies. One crucial fact is that it is an interdisciplinary field which draws on ideas from other academic areas. This is because it is a relatively new field compared to some fields of academic enquiry. It is also because as a domain of academic study, it is expanding rapidly, internationally. This is, in part, because many more academics from a wide range of disciplines are becoming interested in museums and galleries and what they represent and do. It is also because of the extraordinary expansion of high-profile museums and art galleries world-wide in recent years, particularly since the 1980s. Another reason for the proliferation of museum and gallery studies courses and publications comes from the variety of institutions they encompass, as we have already suggested. Museums and galleries can range from so-called 'universal' museums like the Louvre and British Museum (Figure 0.1) through to idiosyncratic, personal collections

Figure 0.1 The Great Court, British Museum, London.

and brand-new collections. Scholars' approaches are diverse, in part, because of the sheer diversity of subjects they are discussing.

The field of study therefore encompasses topics such as visitors' types of behaviour: how visitors move through exhibit spaces, what attracts their attention and ignites curiosity. It also includes how nations' galleries build or cement public expressions of national identity, how they are part of political processes of 'state formation', and how they actually create rather than merely attract a 'public'. Scholars study museums and galleries in terms of how they function in the present, as well as what roles they served in the past.

Terminology is important: we define fields in academic life through processes of what gets called 'naming and framing', as we will explore. The precise names given to this field of study are different in different countries, in part as they draw on varying traditions of thought. 'Museum and gallery studies' is an Anglophone term that encompasses both 'academic theory' and 'practice' (what professionals do every day), although we argue that they should be seen as inseparable. Museum and gallery studies are taught and researched in universities but museums and galleries equally produce, share and authorise new knowledge through their collecting, displays, research and publishing activities. Academic study, curating and indeed managerial administration all require reflective thought and new ideas about *why* museums and galleries exist, who they are for, as well as how they should be run.

MUSEUM AND GALLERY STUDIES AROUND THE WORLD

In French-speaking countries and other Western European countries like Italy, a distinction is often made between the two terms 'museology' and 'museography' that suggests a difference between practical and theoretical study. Museography usually refers to the "practical or applied aspect of museology", meaning exhibition design, conservation, and collections management amongst other areas (Desvallées and Mairesse 2010: 52). To complicate matters, Desvallées and Mairesse note that in Central and Eastern Europe, what French speakers call 'museography' would be referred to as 'applied museology' or what English speakers would describe as "museum practice" (2010: 52). From an international perspective, they argue that 'museology' or 'museum studies' can take at least five definitions. We share their preference for the most expansive of these, which they explain as comprising "all the efforts at theorisation and critical thinking about the museal field" in their totality (2010: 56). What has become called 'new museology' since the 1970s is an important, distinct development in the discipline which we deal with below (see Chapter 1).

There are some further differentials. 'Museum studies' is now well established as an academic discipline and in several countries (e.g. UK, US, Sweden, Australia, New Zealand) there are university departments which specialise in it. 'Gallery studies', though, are less common and more often untaken inside university departments for art history, fine art, museum studies, visual culture, or cultural studies, rather than existing separately. Here we need to give some clarification. When we use the term 'gallery', here we mean *public* art galleries and art museums, as well as exhibition spaces or centres which specialise in temporary exhibitions rather than holding permanent collections or displays. This understanding of the term 'gallery' is standard in the UK but does not translate into other languages or cultures, as we discuss below. Ordinarily, gallery studies do not focus upon commercial galleries, even though in practice the commercial art market and public galleries cannot be separated. In the Anglophone literature, gallery studies has often discussed issues like the ways public galleries help create systems of value, in cultural and financial terms.

'Heritage studies' is an adjacent, overlapping field of study to 'museum and gallery studies'. While it is essential to understanding the relationships between museum and gallery studies, on one hand, and heritage studies on the other, this book will not attempt to cover heritage studies for reasons which will become clear in Chapter 1.

In the context of British universities, 'museum and gallery studies' usually refers to an academic discipline that is pursued at postgraduate rather than undergraduate level, after the completion of a first degree in a subject like archaeology, history or art (fine art practice or art history). Many of these postgraduate programmes can be described as quasi-vocational, in the sense that they are undertaken by students as a stepping-stone towards a career in a museum or gallery, or in academic research. Many museum and gallery studies departments effectively therefore have two roles or allegiances. One is to the academic and critical study of institutions and their practices. The second is to ensuring students become aware of what practical and everyday kinds of knowledge are needed to work in museums successfully even though these can, and must, be 'theorised' in various ways. Just as 'theory' and 'practice' are intertwined, these programmes are often both intellectual and vocational, providing a route by which museum and gallery professionals of the future are equipped, both practically and theoretically, to undertake particular jobs.

However, such programmes of study are not the only route by which professionals enter the sector. Many will begin their academic and working lives by studying disciplines such as art history, history, the natural sciences, archaeology and ethnography and enter the profession without a museum studies or gallery studies background, learning their craft on the job. It has long been the case, however, that in Europe, and in Britain especially, work in museums and galleries is often paid far less than other graduate-level professions, and this is a significant structural factor limiting the diversity of people who go into museum professions. In countries like the UK, there is a long-standing and important debate about the routes by which people can access the museum and galley profession, and indeed, the barriers which many face. In response some organisations have offered traineeships and apprenticeships to attract under-represented groups, particularly from ethnic minority backgrounds. Universities have similarly been involved in such initiatives. To find out more, look for debates about entry into the profession on the UK's Museum Association website.

'THEORY' AND 'PRACTICE'?

As suggested above, it is our view that the terms 'theory' and 'practice' can be misleading because one cannot be separated from the other. The process of studying makes us aware that what we imagine is 'natural', 'normal' or 'obvious' is seldom that, and that those things that seem simply 'right' or 'good practice' can be put under question or amended. We also suggest that there is a false opposition between activities that are basically intellectual and those that are practical. The 'materials' that museum and gallery professionals work with, just like academics, artists, historians and archaeologists, include ideas, artefacts and codes of professional practice. Ideas that often get described as 'theoretical' are crucial to museum studies and work, and inform our understanding of how museums function. Understanding different ideas is essential in thinking through what professional practice is for, and what it is built upon.

We need to reiterate that there is not a single body of 'museum theory' even though particular texts have sustained scholars' interest and provided key turning points in creating new areas of debate. Museum and gallery studies are interesting to us precisely because we have to draw upon ideas from different areas – and unite them. Such work draws on ideas and writings in multiple fields including cultural studies, philosophy, art history, archaeology, tourism and leisure studies, economics, anthropology, ethnography, sociology and linguistics. This is a challenge, and has many pitfalls to avoid. But if we genuinely want to conceptualise the roles that museums and galleries play in public life, we need to ask several complex questions, and these often necessarily relate to other areas. For example, in order to think about museums and galleries as 'public' institutions we need to refer to political theorists' competing ideas of what 'the public sphere' is and does. We need to know how this concept differs from merely 'public space'. We need to know why some scholars consider museums as part of an 'ideological state apparatus' which conditions citizens, aligns them into a system of belief, and impresses upon them the power of the state. Most people begin by thinking that museums and galleries are intrinsically 'good', whatever they do, or however they do it. Often enough these institutions are imagined to have an intrinsic moral good inbuilt in them, as they uphold the values of 'great art' or even 'civilisation', but our job is to ask how we arrived at these value judgements and think about why this might be the case. It is important to take a position ourselves and decide how autonomous museums are, or can be, from wider governing ideologies. Here, as throughout this book, we draw attention to where ideas have been problematised or debated by placing them inside inverted commas.

WHY STUDY MUSEUMS AND GALLERIES?

There are many reasons to study museums and galleries. As Donald Preziosi (1998) has argued, museums not only disseminate but *produce* 'knowledge'. In many instances, national museums have something like a monopoly in their field in their own territory. They provide the official public account of one area or history. This lends them a special public authority and prestige, and despite the mass availability of 'information', digital images and every kind of diversion or entertainment, museums and galleries are more visited than ever (see Tables 0.1 and 0.2). This is particularly true of the world's major cities. For example, ALVA, the Association of Leading Visitor Attractions in the UK reported that 65,218,272 people visited attractions in London in 2015, an increase of 7.5% on the previous year, and that all of the UK's top 10 most visited attractions were in London (ALVA 2015).

It is not simply the numbers of visitors which make these institutions significant as an object of study, but also what we can call the visiting *patterns* that become visible on analysis. Also important are the institutional responses to such patterns. When Tate Modern in London (Figure 0.2) staged an exhibition of the work of the artist Henri Matisse in 2014, it was seen by 3,907 visitors per day: half a million visitors in just five months. Following its showing in London, it toured to the Museum of Modern Art in New York, where more than another half a million visitors saw it (Miller 2015). The exhibition was extended due to excessive demand (Tate 2014). What is particularly striking is that demand for the Tate exhibition was sufficiently strong that the exhibition was kept open through the

Table 0.1 Visitor figures for London's top four most visited museums

Institution	Location	Visitors in 2015
British Museum	London	6.8 million
National Gallery	London	5.9 million
Natural History Museum	London	5.3 million
Tate Modern	London	4.7 million

Source: ALVA (2016).

Table 0.2 Most visited art galleries in the world in 2015

Institution	*Location*	*Visitors in 2015*
Louvre[a]	Paris	8.6 million
British Museum	London	6.8 million
Metropolitan Museum of Art	New York	6.5 million
Vatican City	Vatican City	6.0 million
National Gallery	London	5.9 million
National Palace Museum	Taipei	5.2 million
Tate Modern	London	4.7 million
National Gallery of Art	Washington, DC	4.0 million
State Hermitage Museum	St Petersburg	3.6 million
Musée d'Orsay	Paris	3.4 million

Source: Art Newspaper (2016).

Note:

a It should be noted that the Louvre's visitor figures fell in 2015. In 2014, a total of 9.2 million people visited it. This drop in international tourist numbers has been attributed to the terrorist attacks in Paris during 2015.

night on the last weekend to provide non-stop entry over thirty-six hours. Are there other institutions that could possibly attract such devotion in this way? This night-time 'special' opening has been repeated with other exhibitions. Perhaps even more unusual is the subsequent tour of the exhibition broadcast to over 200 UK cinemas named *Matisse Live* and seen by 15,000 cinema-goers (initially). This number continues to grow as the broadcast is shown again. We have chosen this example because the patterns of visiting and experiencing museums and galleries is changing. The museum is becoming a "transmedia" institution working on different media "platforms" of which the gallery space is only one (Kidd 2014). As this example demonstrates, high numbers of visitors to museums and art galleries has become a recognisable, international phenomenon in many societies. Why?

The boom in people visiting museums and galleries can be linked to broader demographic trends, like the growth of a middle-class in many countries keen to consume cultural tourism. It has been argued that 'post-industrial' economies are characterised by such factors as

Figure 0.2 Tate Modern, Bankside, London.

© Tate, London 2017.

a rise in tourism, by widespread access to higher education, and by rising disposable incomes, although this might also be said – at least for some sections of the society – to be true for rapidly industrialising countries, like China. In both contexts, we can argue that museums have become 'beacons' for civic and national governments to attract international tourists and inward investment. As such, they have become understood as means by which cities and governments can 'regenerate' areas. For example, the term 'the Bilbao effect' became popular around 2000 to describe how a museum, in this instance the Guggenheim Bilbao, has been used to 'rebrand' an entire city rather than just one part of it (Plaza 2006). At the same time, there are critics who point to the limits of culture-led regeneration approaches and argue that the effect is too limited and often result primarily in low-paid, job creation in the hospitality sector rather than providing an industrial strategy which can benefit a wider-cross section of the economy and population. As this demonstrates, the study of museums and galleries can provide insight into wider changes and trends in societies.

By looking closely at museums and galleries in different international contexts we can also find out about how states and governments understand and deploy culture to achieve various politics goals, both internal and external. In rapidly growing economies like China, there is not only a drive to create museums and galleries for emerging international and domestic tourist markets but also to assert cultural, political and economic power. Vickers, for example, noted in 2007 that the Chinese government planned to build 3,000 new museums, whether to encourage tourism, to attract investment, or for "training in patriotic education" (Zhao cited in Vickers 2007: 369). This target has already been exceeded (see Chapter 4). As well as providing patriotic education for their citizens, the governments in countries like China also see museums and galleries as valuable players in international relations and cultural diplomacy.

CULTURE AS 'SOFT POWER'

The use of museums and galleries as a form of what has been called 'soft power' in international relations is both widespread and long-standing. Joseph Nye defines 'soft power' as: "the ability to get what you want through attraction rather than coercion and payments. It arises from the attractiveness of a country's culture, political ideals and policies" (Nye, 2004: x). Indeed, we can say that national self-promotion has been a central reason in the establishment of such institutions from the very outset. Not only do museums and galleries serve as ambassadors for their nations by promoting them to other countries, they also provide unifying symbols for nations at home, particularly after or as part of a struggle towards political independence. In Eastern Europe, for example, countries like Estonia and Poland have sought to re-establish their own distinct national cultural identities after the dissolution of the Soviet Union in 1991 through new national museum projects. Similarly, in Scotland, a new national museum was opened in Edinburgh in 1998 at the same time that political devolution was taking place and a newly independent Scottish Parliament was being established. In Spain, the Museum of the History of Catalonia in Barcelona (est. 1996) is similarly strongly associated with Catalonia's claims to cultural and political independence. In Taiwan a new National Museum of Taiwan History opened in the city of Tainan in 2011 with a specific focus on the history and culture of Taiwan as distinct from China. This is significant given that the political autonomy and separateness of Taiwan continues to be contested by the Chinese government. In all of these situations, what is at stake is the story of who the people 'are' and their claim – accepted or reputed – to political independence and cultural distinctiveness. Each of these museums is inevitably charged with great political significance, whether or not its staff or visitors might want it to be.

As we can see here, the importance that museums and galleries have in promoting a nation, a people or a city on an international stage can scarcely be overstated. 'Culture', in this sense, is about symbols. A national museum or gallery is a large, expensive and permanent symbol of a city or nation's place in the world, its self-image, its aspirations or its sheer power. This is a global phenomenon. Whereas many of the traditional, famous museums and galleries are to be found in European countries, some of the most recent investments in such symbolic projects can be seen in the Persian Gulf. The United Arab Emirates (UAE), for example, are investing very large sums of money in new national museums and art galleries, sometimes employing Western architects to create 'signature' buildings whose adventurous or unorthodox designs are intended to be photogenic, and so seen in reproduction around the world. The aim is for the UAE to become an international destination for a particularly wealthy class of cultural tourist. The Louvre Abu Dhabi is another high-profile example; it is part of an 'island' of museums where a new national history museum, maritime museum, performing arts centre and biennale park will all be built. Similarly, Sharjah in the UAE opened its own Museum of Islamic Civilisation in 2008. It is completing a new national art gallery, and has launched the Sharjah Biennial, an international art exhibition. Qatar has employed French architect Jean Nouvel to remodel its national museum, and in 2008 opened a brand new Museum of Islamic Art in Doha.

Such enterprises are vastly expensive (see Chapter 4) and they clearly indicate the value political leaders continue to place upon museums' symbolic and 'ambassadorial' roles as well as their educational and economic ones. At the same time, we need to remember that museums come in many sizes and have diverse functions. In the UK, for example, independent and community-run museums operate alongside those receiving large-scale public subsidies. In the UK, there are over 2,500 museums and galleries, the vast majority of which are small-scale. In reality, a tiny number attract a disproportionate amount of press coverage, and often resources (Museums Association 2014).

CONCLUSION

Public museums and galleries have been created, generation after generation, for diverse reasons. The reasons for their existence, or their success, have often changed, or been reattributed, over time. Common to them, however, is the belief that museums and galleries are an important carrier of a society or group's collective memory, and that they are crucial to advancing our understanding of ourselves, others and the world around us. Because they address fundamental questions about who we are or who others think we are, the political motivations attached to museums and galleries are crucial to understand. We all have a stake in how societies represent us or 'others' (as we will discuss in the next chapter), our histories and our collective achievements. We also have a stake in whether museums narrate these histories 'in the round' and account for the parts of our history we cannot be proud of, or the ideas our predecessors believed which we no longer subscribe to. Given the importance accorded to these institutions in societies and the strength of recent interest in museums and galleries from politicians and publics alike, they are essential topics of study in making sense of who we have become, and the ways in which the world is ordered.

REFERENCES

Kidd, J. (2014) *Museums in the New Mediascape: Transmedia, Participation, Ethics.* Farnham: Ashgate.

Nye, J. (2004) *Soft Power: The Means to Success in World Politics.* New York: Public Affairs / Perseus Books Group.

Plaza, B. (2006) 'The return on investment of the Guggenheim Museum Bilbao'. *International Journal of Urban and Regional Research* 30(2): 452–467.

Preziosi, D. (1998) *The Art of Art History: A Critical Anthology.* Oxford: Oxford University Press.

Vickers, E. (2007) 'Museums and nationalism in contemporary China.' *Compare: A Journal of Comparative Education* 37(3): 365–382.

WEBSITES

Art Newspaper (2016) 'Visitor figures 2015: Jeff Koons is the toast of Paris and Bilbao'. *The Art Newspaper: Special Reports* 31 March. URL: http://theartnewspaper.com/reports/jeff-koons-is-the-toast-of-paris-and-bilbao/

Association of Leading Visitor Attractions (ALVA) (2015) 'Visits made in 2015 to visitor attractions in membership with ALVA'. URL: http://www.alva.org.uk/details.cfm?p=606

Desvallées, A. and F. Mairesse (eds) (2010) *Key Concepts in Museology.* International Council of Museums. URL: http://icom.museum/fileadmin/user_upload/pdf/Key_Concepts_of_Museology/Museologie_Anglais_BD.pdf

Miller, M.H. (2015) 'Half a million people have seen MoMA's Matisse cut-outs show'. Art News 7 January. URL: http://www.artnews.com/2015/01/07/half-a-million-people-have-seen-momas-matisse-cut-outs-show/

Museums Association (2014) 'Frequently asked questions'. URL: http://www.museumsassociation.org/about/frequently-asked-questions

Tate (2014) 'Matisse is Tate's most successful exhibition ever'. URL: http://www.tate.org.uk/about/press-office/press-releases/matisse-tates-most-successful-exhibition-ever

FURTHER READING

Carbonell, B.M. (2012) *Museum Studies: An Anthology of Contexts, Second Edition.* Malden, MA and Oxford: Wiley-Blackwell.

Corsane, G. (ed.) (2005) *Heritage, Museums and Galleries: An Introductory Reader.* London and New York: Routledge.

Knell, S., J. MacLeod and S. Watson (eds) (2007) *Museum Revolutions: How Museums Change and Are Changed.* London and New York: Routledge.

Macdonald, S. (2011) *A Companion to Museum Studies.* Chichester: Blackwell.

McClellan, A. (2003) *Art and Its Publics: Museum Studies at the Millennium.* Malden, MA and Oxford: Blackwell.

FIRST PRINCIPLES

WHAT IS A MUSEUM OR GALLERY?

Most of us will have a fairly clear idea in our heads of what a museum or gallery is and does. So it may come as a surprise to learn that these terms are the subject of regular scrutiny and debate by bodies such as the Museums Association (UK) and ICOM (International Council of Museums), by national governments, and those who study or teach museum and gallery studies. One reason for this ongoing debate is that there has been an enormous expansion in the numbers and types of museums around the world from the second half of the twentieth century. To take a deliberately extreme contrast: the same term 'museum' is used to refer to an institution like the British Museum (Figure 1.1), established in London in 1753, and which holds eight million objects, and the Pencil Museum in Cumbria, also in the UK, which has collected pencils since 1980. The latter is a real registered museum. Given the differences in scale, topic and focus we might ask what if anything they have in common as museums. Can we define any shared 'core' characteristics or purposes? As a starting point, the *Oxford English Dictionary* (2008) gives the definition that a museum is only "a building used for storage and exhibiting objects of historical, scientific, or cultural interest".

Figure 1.1 The frontage of the British Museum.
© The Trustees of the British Museum.

Notice that the emphasis here is on the museum as a physical space, as a 'container' for its 'contents'. There is very limited indication here beyond the idea of 'interest' as to why institutions collect, at whose expense, or for whose benefit. If we look instead to definitions produced by the museum sector itself, we can find more help in thinking through the roles and purposes of museums. The UK Museums Association's definition (Boylan 1992: 11) takes "public benefit" as a prerequisite for providing accreditation to institutions: "A museum is an institution which collects, documents, prepares, exhibits and interprets material evidence and associated information for the public benefit".

Such definitions are periodically revised. Looking at these changes can give some insight into debates and preoccupations in the sector and more widely. In 1998 the above definition was revised to be: "Museums enable people to explore collections for inspiration, learning and enjoyment. They are institutions that collect, safeguard and make accessible artefacts and specimens, which they hold in trust for society" (Museums Association 2016). Notice how this latter definition reorders the idea of a museum by putting the visitor or user first in the definition. The 'internal' activities that museum staff undertake are not the first item mentioned. The museum's role as a store-house or container preserving things for posterity has become secondary. Some have argued that those activities are now seen as means to other ends. "People", understood here as the general public are repositioned as the centre of the museum's actions and priorities. (It is worth noting that in some countries, like the UK, the general public are understood to own the objects both philosophically and legally; this is not the case in all countries.) This shift towards a more visitor-oriented role is indicative of changes in museum thinking and practice in many countries around the world. Kenneth Hudson describes this change of emphasis in the role of museums as a "revolution – the word is not an exaggeration – in museum philosophy and in its practical applications" (1998: 48) that has taken place since the 1970s.

This "revolution" entails a much greater awareness of the political and politicised nature of museums. It requires paying greater attention to questions of power relations that are central to museums. The idea of the museum as 'neutral' space which is simply for 'everyone' whatever it does, and of a so-called 'general' public undifferentiated by class, education, ethnicity or other criteria have all been challenged. Those who began this revolution insist that museums should pay attention to the *effects* they have on individuals and communities, and not simply care for their objects. This idea involves a shift away from the idea of museum as *container*, *shrine* or *temple* to the museum as *forum*, *contact zone, platform or social activist* (Sandell and Nightingale 2012). This is not to suggest that objects are not important, but that greater attention ought to be paid to representation of varied people's histories and cultures; and indeed to people representing their own histories rather than being spoken about by others. As a consequence, terms such as 'inclusion', and 'empowerment', and 'participation' or 'co-production' have entered museums professionals' vocabulary in many countries, although they may be interpreted or acted upon in many varied ways. Needless to say, different institutions in different places face varied demands on them. For example, the South African Museums Association (SAMA) created a definition in 1999 that places emphasis squarely on museums' social and political roles:

> Museums are dynamic and accountable public institutions which both shape and manifest the consciousness, identities and understandings of communities and individuals in relation to their natural, historical and cultural environments, through collection, documentation, conservation, research and communication programmes that are responsive to the needs of society.
>
> (SAMA 2013)

This fundamental shift in thinking about museums has been widely discussed. It can be neatly summed up by the title of an article by Stephen Weil (1999): "From being *about* something to being *for* somebody: The on-going transformation of the American museum". A number of the ideas described above are also associated with what has been termed the 'new museology'.

'NEW MUSEOLOGY'

The 'new museology' is often associated in Anglophone museum and gallery studies with Peter Vergo's edited 1989 book of that name. He described "a state of widespread dissatisfaction with the 'old museology' … what is wrong with the 'old' museology is that it is too much about museum *methods* and too little about the role of museums within society" (Vergo 1989: 3; Marstine 2005). In fact, as museologist Peter Davis notes, the ideas around this 'new' museology had predecessors in many different parts of the world since as far back as the 1950s in the US. He notes similar debates in the UK and France in the 1980s, and in ICOM (International Council of Museums) conferences in the 1970s and 1980s. The ICOM debates led to the establishment of MINOM (the International Movement for a New Museology) in 1985 in Lisbon, Portugal, at the second International New Museology Workshop. This had been inspired by the Quebec Declaration of 1984 that set out the "Basic Principles of a New Museology" and that declaration, in turn, identified its origins in discussions about a new museology back in 1975 in Santiago, Chile (MINOM 2014). This long, convoluted history is retold to demonstrate that across the world, over the course of a generation, numerous professionals and academics desired changes: changes in how museums work and who they work for.

What is called 'new museology' in English has also been called 'sociomuseology', 'critical museum theory' or 'new museum theory', in other languages or contexts. The debates are also closely related to debates about 'ecomuseology' and 'community museology' (Davis 1999). While each is distinct, all these movements share similar concerns about the role of museums and galleries in society, and the power they have to influence understandings of the past and the future. A central critique of this movement has been that telling 'official' stories only really tells the *dominant* social group's ideas and histories, and marginalises others. There is an old adage that 'history is told by the victors' but, in effect, new museology has argued that the stories of the present are also told by the 'victors' in the sense that they are typically the stories of those who are most powerful, or the biggest group in society. New museology argues that the cultures, histories and identities of the varied groups who make up each society tend to be less well accounted for.

For many concerned with the ideas of new museology another central question is whether museums and galleries can have a positive, social impact. Can museums foster productive debate, bring people together in their very differences, address prejudice, even improve wellbeing? Taken together, as Davis puts it, the "new museology could be seen as shorthand for the radical reassessment of the roles of museums in society" (1999: 54).

Anthony Shelton (2013: 7) provides another framework for thinking about new museology when he argues there is "not one but three museologies". "Operational museology": Shelton uses this term to describe *how* things are done within museum teams, and the organisation of professional knowledge including protocols and codes of practice, as well as organisational structures, and regulatory systems. "Critical museology": Shelton uses this to describe the critique of 'operational' museology, addressing *why* museum practice has the patterns it does. A 'critical' museology asks what agency museum practice has in the world, and what forms of power it enables or requires. Understood in this way, we see museums as *producers of culture* and as such, embedded in pre-existing power relations rather than 'autonomous' actors. "Praxiological museology": is linked to artistic ideas of 'institutional critique' that challenge museums' orthodoxies by revealing the implicit politics that have become invisible through repetition and seeming 'normal'.

As Shelton makes clear there are many ways in which conventional understandings of museums, and what they do, have been challenged in recent years. The idea that museums and galleries preserve and work with material cultures – tangible, ownable, often unique and portable commodities, remains probably the single, strongest image of what defines a museum. However, even this has been complicated in recent years, as we will see. For example, the attention paid to 'intangible cultural heritage', to non-European indigenous heritage practices and to oral history and personal testimonies has diversified many people's understanding of what museums can do. At the same time, the enormous increase in the use and potential of digital and social media has also begun to change how people engage with museums. Many museums now count online visits as well as 'physical visits'. In order to really grasp these current debates about what museums do and are for, we need to go back in time to consider their origins and development.

ORIGINS OF MUSEUMS

The most common history told about the development of museums is that they are a European invention, and that they developed out of early, private, Renaissance collections (Hooper-Greenhill 1992). Royal and aristocratic 'cabinets of curiosity', 'Wunderkammern' and 'Kunstkammern' of the sixteenth and seventeenth centuries are usually seen as the distant antecedents of art and natural history museums. 'Wunderkammern' translates literally as 'wonder-cabinet', where 'cabinet' could describe a whole room as much as an individual display case, while 'Kunstkammern' means cabinet of art (Bennett 1995: 73). These rooms were mostly privately owned, although they could sometimes be visited by permission of the owner. The very ideas of both 'the public' and 'public' institutions in the way we would understand them today did not exist at this time. The purpose of these collections was to show the knowledge and wealth of the owner but also to inspire awe and amazement at the rarity and novelty of the assembled objects, both natural and made by humankind. In particular, collectors commissioned explorers to bring back such wonders from the 'New World' as European explorers were beginning at this time to travel further into parts of the globe previously unknown to them. This meant that early collections could include objects as diverse as shells, animals, birds, but also artefacts associated with humans – weapons, decorative objects and, later on, other humans themselves.

The creation of 'public' institutions as we would begin to recognise them, with collections ordered along 'scientific' and scholarly lines familiar to many contemporary societies effectively began in eighteenth-century Europe (Davis 1999). The classical museum is very broadly associated with 'Enlightenment' ideas of rationalisation and scientific forms of classification (although the 'Enlightenment' is itself a complex and contested term which scholars debate). For example, the introduction in the 1750s of 'binomial nomenclature' – a system for classifying and naming species and genus – by the Swedish botanist, Carl Linnaeus, transformed the way that the natural world was understood to be organised. It provided a whole new way of thinking about classificatory and taxonomic systems for organising, differentiating and relating specimens in museums which is still in operation today.

In terms of thinking about the public nature of these institutions, we cannot overstate how any use of the term 'public' needs to be historically specific. In eighteenth-century Europe, in practice the term did not mean much more than 'the minority who owned property': namely the wealthy and literate higher social groups. The British Museum, established by act of Parliament in 1753, was indeed the world's first national, public museum and "granted free admission to all studious and curious persons" as the museum observes (British Museum 2016).

However, in practice, this meant primarily for use only by scholars and 'gentlemen' – and even then on request only. Gaining entrance originally required a letter of introduction from an authority figure (Crow 1985). According to the museum's own account of its history, 'Visitor numbers have grown from around 5,000 a year in the eighteenth century to nearly 6 million today' (British Museum 2016). It was in the nineteenth century that access to this institution became more widely understood, as part of a broader shift which can be seen in a number of European countries, albeit with variations.

THE LOUVRE: A TURNING POINT

Central to this history of the public museum is the Louvre in Paris. The French Revolution of 1789 led directly to the transformation in 1793 of the King's private collection in the Palais du Louvre into a fully public museum, belonging to the French people. This marked a decisive turning point, though it did not elicit an immediate transformation elsewhere. Most importantly, it set a precedent that new museums across Europe could and should be open to all citizens of the nation state. It instilled the idea that spaces shared by different groups might be one means of creating a sense of belonging to the nation for its citizens. When the South Kensington Museum in London (now the Victoria & Albert Museum) opened in 1857, social campaigners soon argued that its opening hours should be arranged so that even ordinary working people could visit. This was not an accident: there had been revolutions across many European states in 1848 overthrowing old elites.

One underlying and much-discussed aim of new thinking around museums by both social reformers and politicians was precisely to allow different social groups to see each other, in order to promote acceptable models of behaviour and to expose the lower echelons of society to the improving effects of culture, as understood at that time. The overall aim appears to have been to create 'social emulation' where 'lower' groups would try to copy their 'superiors' and be both socially and spiritually improved by their visit (Duncan 1995). Exposure to art and culture, it was thought by social reformers at this time, could have a spiritually uplifting effect and if working men could be persuaded to visit with their wives and children, it was imagined that this would also have an improving and 'softening' effect. It is difficult now to even imagine the stark extremities of difference between people's appearances, education and life expectations of that time but the lives of working people and the growing and educated middle classes could not have been more different. Poverty, disease, no access to healthcare, poor or abject housing conditions, short life expectancy, very hazardous working conditions, little or no access to education, limited or no political representation, and grinding hardship characterised the daily lives of the majority of working people across the industrialising world.

In this context, museums were seen as prime social spaces by which governments could 'civilise', improve and educate their populations. There is evidence that museums were widely understood by many social strata as providing a form of education. Universal free education through schooling is a relatively recent invention in many European countries and comes after access to public museums in countries like Britain. It was this widespread recognition of the educational value of museums that led both to public subscription campaigns and to the introduction of public contributions through general taxation in 1845, in order to raise the money to create public museums. The result of this history in the UK is the broadly accepted status of museums as institutions that have the educational benefit of a 'wide public' at their heart.

This is not to say that we should think of museums as being wholly benign institutions. In the nineteenth century, some governments and social reformers in Britain explicitly saw museums and art galleries as one means of managing an enormously expanding urban population, especially in London, which became the world's biggest city during the nineteenth century. In many cities in Britain, museums were expressly seen by their advocates as a way to align working-class audiences with the elites, and distract them from drink and radical politics at the same time (Bennett 1995). The development of public museums, in this case, was therefore closely related to ideas about control and management of the population at times of potential crisis. In other cases, leaders or governments have viewed museums and galleries as useful ways to make bold or aggressive statements of civic confidence and wealth. As Carol Duncan (1995) has argued, museums and galleries at this time were also seen as a means of projecting governing groups' self-image as the heirs to Greece or Rome, and having the historic mission of leading the world by governing an empire. When we study the histories of museums it is common to see different rationales like this in operation at the same time.

MUSEUM DEVELOPMENT: NATIONALISM
AND COLONIALISM

The creation of new museums in the nineteenth century was undoubtedly also driven by competition between European nations and the rise of nationalism in an age of empire. These developments encouraged many European governments to foster and promote the idea of their nation's distinctiveness, or even unique historical destiny. This might sound exaggerated but at the beginning of the nineteenth century, modern countries including Germany and Italy were not unified states; France was at war with much of Europe; and many governments feared, or even expected revolution 'from below'. Rioting and civil protest was increasingly common as populations became more urbanised and as working peoples began to organise themselves into political movements. In this context, encouraging people to identify with the idea of their nation-state, and to now see themselves as citizens of it, became an imperative in the face of both external war and internal threat. There were few tools at their disposal to positively unify peoples. As described above, the various social classes lived such radically different lives that it was not a given that they would have readily identified with each other as all being part of one nation. The many processes of nation-building and features of national citizenship which we take for granted today were not yet in place prior to the latter part of the nineteenth century. For example, passports as we know them today were not enforced until the early twentieth century, at the time of the First World War in Britain. Prior to this so few could travel internationally, either regularly or voluntarily that it had not been deemed necessary. For all these reasons, the history of European museums must be understood in parallel with the rise of nationalist movements and broader processes of nation-formation, including ideas around national folk culture (Mason 2007).

Nation-building at this time in many Western European countries went hand-in-hand with colonialism. Nineteenth-century civic museums were often built from the wealth created from colonial and industrial expansion into overseas territories which were acquired through treaties or seized through force (MacKenzie 2009). In many cases the material results of colonial encounters, involving violence, exploitation, or subjection of colonial peoples, fed directly into European national and local museums and their development. Objects were also obtained through European museum-sponsored collecting expeditions on a vast scale around the world, especially in Africa. Shelton observes that one estimate reckoned that "by the mid-1960s, there were more than 1,500,000 ethnographic items in US museums alone, and 4,500,000 in the world as a whole" (Shelton 2011: 68).

Objects and human remains were 'acquired' for museum collections sometimes legally, sometimes not. What is problematic is that even those acquisitions which were considered to have been acquired through legal means at that time may now, according to some, have been illegal or unethical. This is particularly the case where the acquiring country at the time was a colonial power and where the descendants of the colonised people may now reject the legal and ethical right of their former colonisers to exercise that power. One of the most well-known and controversial examples is that of the Parthenon or Elgin Marbles, elements of which currently reside in the British Museum and the Louvre but which is claimed by the Acropolis Museum in Athens.

These kinds of examples illustrate how what is legal in one historical and political context does not necessarily always remain so, and that what is legal and what is ethical are not necessarily the same thing. European museums also hold human remains from these colonial times and this is often considered particularly offensive by those people's descendants. In 2016, for example, it was revealed that the Prussian Cultural Heritage Foundation which runs Germany's state museums currently holds in Berlin 4,600 human skulls collected for research between 1885 and 1920. More than 1,000 of these are from Rwanda and 60 from Tanzania; both countries were part of the Germany East Africa Colony from 1885 to 1918. It is thought that these skulls came from African people killed by German troops in colonial wars and that the skulls were subsequently sent back to Germany for so-called 'racial' scientific experimentation (Deutsche Welle 2016). As this example illustrates, the legacies of the relationships between European museums and their states' colonial histories can still be seen in many museums today, explicitly or otherwise.

Unsurprisingly, this history has resulted in sharp ethical dilemmas for numerous museums and art galleries in the twentieth and twenty-first centuries. Some museums' colonial legacies remain sharply divisive, as above. In South Africa, Australia, New Zealand and North America, museums have been criticised heavily for previously reproducing and bolstering colonial ways of thinking about different cultures in their display and collecting practices. Consequently, many have sought to rethink their displays and decolonise their institutions. What has been particularly problematic is those instances where museums collected human remains from 'indigenous' peoples for display alongside inanimate objects or examples of the natural world. In the process, some museums had presented indigenous people as though they were part of a timeless, 'primitive' or crude 'nature', opposed to the 'culture' of so-called 'civilised' modern races. Many indigenous peoples have expressed their anger at this kind of representation and campaigned for the return of their ancestors' remains and cultural property. In North America the legal framework of NAGPRA (Native American Graves Protection and Repatriation Act) was drawn up in 1990 to manage such processes (National Park Service 2016). At the same time, the concept and definition of 'indigenous' is not straightforward. It varies from country to country, according to diverse histories and legal arrangements. Human remains, looted property, and colonial relations remain highly contentious aspects of many museums and galleries even today. Understanding the interrelationship between nationalism, colonialism and the histories of museums and galleries is an essential part of understanding the place and politics of these institutions in contemporary societies.

DO ALL CULTURES HAVE MUSEUMS?

Public museums like the British Museum and Louvre are European inventions but there are museums all around the world. Nicolas Thomas reminds us how countries such as Argentina, Brazil and Chile created their own 'national art and natural history museums from 1818 onwards' (Thomas 2016: 25). He also notes that museums were created in India (the Indian Museum in Kolkata dates from 1814), in Egypt (the Egyptian Museum of Antiquities was created in 1835) and in Japan (from the 1870s) (ibid.). In part, the spread of the Western European model of museums to other parts of the globe happened because European colonisation led to these kinds of museums being 'exported' as a cultural form. Consequently, many former colonial countries have European-style museums originally created by the colonisers, rather than created either out of, or for, 'local' cultural traditions.

As with the nineteenth-century idea of 'improving' the so-called lower classes in countries like Britain, similar attitudes towards 'improving' foreign peoples were equally applied at the time of the creation of these colonial museums. These museums were intended to show the locals what they should aspire to be, to impress upon them the sophistication of their colonisers and thereby justify the 'natural right' of the colonisers to be in charge. It is perhaps difficult to overstate how completely hierarchical the dominant theories about race and social organisation were, especially in the nineteenth and early twentieth century. In some cases, this extended well into the latter part of the twentieth century. Ashley Sheriff has written about the use of museums in South Africa noting that:

> In fact, black Africans were (re)presented in natural history museum spaces as lower species of early humans not quite ontologically separate from indigenous flora and fauna. During the era of apartheid, which officially began in 1948, many South African museum exhibitions fervently codified the status quo of white privilege and power under the colonial regime.
>
> (Sheriff 2014: 2)

It was only with the end of Apartheid in 1994 that museums in South Africa began to be decolonised. In cases like South Africa, many of the current museums still occupy the same buildings previously used for these colonial museums, which can present considerable challenges for reinterpretation.

While the European model of museums can therefore be found worldwide, it has become increasingly recognised by museum and heritage scholars that many cultures have had their own different practices of collecting and displaying significant cultural artefacts. Recent museum-studies scholarship has begun to also recognise how indigenous peoples have their own long-standing, different and complex traditions for recognising and valuing important objects. As part of this process, such scholars are drawing attention to the importance of intangible heritage practices. In Canada, for example, First-Nations people like the Blackfoot take important objects and place these into bundles. Along with ritualised performances of song, dance and storytelling, these form a central part of their collective ceremonies and the transmission of cultural knowledge from one generation to another (Onciul 2015). In Australia, Aboriginal peoples have a tradition of 'keeping places' which can range from very small display and collection spaces up to purpose-built cultural centres. In Australia, the public recognition of the importance of these indigenous practices can now be seen in governmental policy statements. It is also recognised by the Australian government that some communities believe that collective memory is the most appropriate 'repository' for knowledge, and that this resides in the community's elders (Australian Government Department of the Environment 2001). The Australian Museums Association recognises both the European and indigenous aboriginal Australian traditions in its following definition:

> The Museums Australia Constitution (2002) defines a 'museum' as an institution with the following characteristics:
>
> *A museum helps people understand the world by using objects and ideas to interpret the past and present and explore the future. A museum preserves and researches collections, and makes objects and information accessible in actual and virtual environments. Museums are established in the public interest as permanent, not-for-profit organisations that contribute long-term value to communities.*
>
> Museums Australia recognises that museums of science, history and art may be designated by many other names (including Gallery and Keeping Place). In addition, the following may qualify as museums for the purposes of this definition:
>
> (a) natural, archaeological and ethnographic monuments and sites and historical monuments and sites of a museum nature that acquire, conserve and communicate material evidence of people and their environment;
>
> (b) institutions holding collections of and displaying specimens of plants and animals, such as botanical and zoological gardens, herbaria, aquaria and vivaria;

(c) science centres;

(d) Cultural centres and other entities that facilitate the preservation, continuation and management of tangible or intangible heritage resources (living heritage and digital creative activity);

(e) such other institutions as the [Museums Australia National] Council consider as having some or all of the characteristics of a museum.

(Museums Australia 2002)

This new recognition of parallel traditions and divergent practices of valuing cultural heritage brings novel museological challenges. Increasingly, museums in postcolonial countries are being called upon to bring together the European or Western and indigenous cultural practices, so as to find ways to value them differently and develop a new kind of indigenous museology. Different solutions and approaches to dealing both with artefacts and more abstract concepts like time are required (see Chapter 2). Whereas Western museums are based on an inviolable principle of preserving objects in perpetuity, indigenous communities may wish 'their' object to degrade naturally, or to be ritually destroyed (Onciul 2015).

CAN ANYONE CALL ANY SPACE 'A MUSEUM'?

Given the variety of things which can be called a museum in the definition above, we need to ask ourselves if there are limits to what a museum can be. Let us look again at some other national definitions:

Museums are a public or private institution which collects, preserves, analyses and exhibit objects of cultural and natural heritage.

(Republic of Kenya 2006, The National Museums and Heritage Act, cited in Karega-Munene 2011)

Today, the core competencies of a museum – gather, preserve, research, exhibit and communicate – constitute the foundation for museum work.

(German Museums Association 2017a)

[Museums are] organizations with the purpose of collecting and preserving (including nurturing) materials related to history, the arts, folk customs, industry, natural science, etc., exhibiting them, providing them for use by the general public on the basis of educational considerations, conducting necessary work in order to contribute to education, research, recreation, etc., and in addition undertaking surveys and research relating to these materials.

> (Museum Act (Japan), Act No. 285 of 1951, last amended
> by Act No. 50, 11 June 2008; Japanese Association
> of Museums 2008)

According to these definitions there are many examples of collections of material evidence and associated information which have been put together by enthusiastic individuals which would qualify as museums. In some instances individuals have called their collection a museum. However, in many parts of the world to be officially recognised as a museum by a national funding body or a museums association, there are principles and agreed 'industry standards' that have to be met. This can be seen in the following US definition:

Museum means a public or private non-profit institution which is organized on a permanent basis for essentially educational or aesthetic purposes and which, using a professional staff:

– Owns or uses tangible objects, either animate or inanimate;
– Cares for these objects; and
– Exhibits them to the general public on a regular basis.

- An institution which exhibits objects to the general public for at least 120 days a year shall be deemed to meet this requirement
- An institution which exhibits objects by appointment may meet this requirement if it can establish, in the light of the facts under all the relevant circumstances, that this method of exhibition does not unreasonably restrict the accessibility of the institution's exhibits to the general public.

> (Office of the Federal Register (US) 2011)

In this last example, it is clear that being open and accessible to the public is seen to be a defining feature of what makes something officially 'a museum'. In many countries, for example, the UK, the US and Australia, the relevant museums associations also run a national system of museum accreditation or registration to which museums and galleries apply. Accreditation schemes set recognised standards for how a museum is organised, managed, staffed and funded and how collections and buildings are cared for. This matters because institutions with accreditation can apply to receive public funding or loans of objects and artworks from other museums and galleries. Without accreditation, many funders will not provide support or trust that an institution has the necessary policies and practices that others do.

It is also possible for an institution to forfeit its accreditation as a punishment for breaking the rules of the profession. In 2014 the Delaware Art Museum in the US lost its accreditation after it sold off a famous pre-Raphaelite painting. The US's National Association of Art Museum Directors "advised its members to stop loaning works to the Delaware Art Museum and collaborating on exhibitions" (Fishman 2014). To lose accreditation is to risk gaining pariah status amongst peers. Selling off artefacts and artworks is seen in many places as a cardinal sin; in others less so. It is viewed negatively because it marks a fundamental breach of the museum's special status of caring for objects on behalf of the public, and holding them in trust, in perpetuity.

As this example illustrates, the relationship between ownership, ethics and the law is complex when 'deaccessioning' is concerned (removing an object from the principal collections). To date there is no single international accreditation standard, although all ICOM members agree to uphold their code of ethics which sets out minimum standards about professional practice. Museum ethics is a particularly contentious and complex area of museum studies practice and research in its own right (Marstine 2005).

WHAT IS AN ART GALLERY? WHAT IS AN ART MUSEUM OR MUSEUM OF ART?

As with the term 'museum' the words 'gallery', 'art gallery' and 'art museum' are used in different ways by different people and societies. It is important to remember that many museums that collect natural history specimens, social history and archaeology also do house collections of art. Some of these museums can be described as 'encyclopaedic' in their scope. This means they collect across disciplinary boundaries – acquiring artefacts relating to natural history, ethnography, archaeology, and art. Similarly, historic houses, stately homes, churches and palaces often have art collections. An institution which collects only art may call itself specifically an 'art museum' or a 'gallery'. Most official national and international definitions of 'museums' also include art collections, public galleries and contemporary art centres, as seen in these two examples:

> Australia operates under the ICOM definition of a museum, which is inclusive of: museums, art museums, public galleries, keeping places, contemporary art spaces, craft councils, artist run initiatives, botanical gardens, herbaria, zoos, historic houses, monuments and historic sites.
>
> (Museums Australia 1998)

> Founded in 1917, the German Museums Association is the national organization for all museums and museum professionals. It represents art museums as well as museums of history, cultural history and natural history, museums of technology as well as those on specific topics.
>
> (German Museums Association 2017b)

To give an actual example, GoMA in Glasgow, Scotland, is officially, according to its title, a gallery of modern art but it has a collection of contemporary art and is also part of a museum service: Glasgow Museums in Scotland. This cross-over between the two terms 'museum' and 'gallery' stems partly from their usage over the period in which European museums developed. The word 'galleria' in the early Renaissance referred to a long, narrow space, often with windows on one side where paintings and antiquities were displayed together. In aristocratic palaces these were places to walk and converse. Reflecting that early Renaissance use, the modern word 'gallery' can also mean either an institution, or else the individual rooms within a museum, irrespective of what kinds of objects are shown.

In the UK today, the word 'gallery' can mean multiple things: a commercial gallery which sells art to private collectors, as well as a public 'art museum' as it would be called elsewhere. For example, Dulwich Picture Gallery in London shows historical collections of paintings and would almost certainly be named as an 'art museum' in other English-speaking countries. The term 'art museum' is seldom used in the UK, whilst being standard practice in the US. In the UK, 'gallery' can also refer to a space showing *either* contemporary art or historical art; and to *either* a permanent collection or a temporary exhibition space. If an 'art gallery' or 'centre for contemporary art' has no collection then according to most definitions it is not a museum. However, such institutions often have archives that house collections of documents about their work. In much contemporary art, there is little if any gap between a document and an 'original' work, so that the difference between an 'archive' and a 'collection' has narrowed to almost zero. Many kinds of artworks are only made to be seen once or are intentionally temporary, like performance, so documentation is the only way they can be known. Other works are made 'on demand' or can be remade without any requirement for storage, so that exhibitions galleries could easily become museums and vice versa.

As we have outlined, terminology varies from country to country and according to different languages. In Germany, for example, there are three different and distinct terms to capture how art is exhibited and/or collected for the public: 'Kunsthaus' (art-house), 'Kunsthalle' (art-hall), and 'Kunstmuseum' (art-museum). Traditionally, the division between 'Kunsthalle' and 'Kunstmuseum' was the division between a contemporary art centre and a museum with a permanent collection, although these distinctions are now, in practice, often blurred. A 'Gemaeldegalerie', like the one in Berlin, is a permanent museum of art – akin to Dulwich Picture Gallery in its role. So PS1 in New York, Palais de Tokyo in Paris, and the Serpentine Gallery in London are amongst their cities' principal 'kunsthallen' whereas the Metropolitan, Louvre and National Gallery, and MoMA, Centre Pompidou and Tate are those countries' largest museums of art respectively.

In China what might be called 'traditional art' (in other words, not contemporary) can be displayed alongside archaeological, historical and ethnographic material and these institutions are called 'bowuguan' which equates to 'museum' in English. An example of this would be the Shanghai Museum. There is a different Chinese word 'meishuguan' for what would be called in English a 'museum of fine arts or national art gallery' but these museums may also include other kinds of object such as ethnology, for example, the National Art Museum of Beijing. In many Chinese institutions, the traditional distinction between institutions with, and without, permanent collections is not as clear.

State-run museums that specifically focus on contemporary art are also a relatively new phenomenon in China, although there have been privately funded initiatives of great scale. Museums specialising in contemporary art may include the word for contemporary in their title ('dangdai', connoting 'contemporary era'; or 'xiandai' connoting 'modern'), but not necessarily. Another term that may be used in relation to contemporary art is 'hualang' ('gallery'). While institutions dedicated to contemporary art may be a relatively new development, the speed of development is extraordinary. For example, the Rockbund Contemporary Art Museum in Shanghai opened in 2010, describes itself as: "the first contemporary art museum in China that is fully devoted to supporting contemporary art production and creativity" (Rockbund 2016). Numerous other examples have followed in the time it has taken to research and write this book.

As the English, German and Chinese examples demonstrate, the naming practices reflect the complexity of the cultural ecology in different countries, and the principles by which it is subdivided, and supported by different institutions and funders. Moreover, as views about what has sufficient value to be collected change, so do the boundaries between domains. It is worth remembering that the names of institutions themselves are seldom changed even if their remits change or values shift. So, an institution that may have started its life as one kind of space could change its approach without necessarily changing its name.

HOW MANY DIFFERENT KINDS OF MUSEUMS AND GALLERIES ARE THERE?

Museums and galleries take diverse forms, but they can be classified according to different criteria. Ambrose and Paine, for example, categorise them according to several ideas: the nature of their collections; their management; their geographical scope; their audiences; and the way they exhibit their collections (2012: 10). To this we would add their sources of wealth or capital stock, income and status. Some museums and galleries can be almost entirely 'publicly funded'. Their income is entirely or almost wholly provided by the state from money raised by taxes. Alternatively, they can be 'independently' funded, meaning their income can be self-generated through trading (entry charges, cafes, shops, corporate hire), donations from wealthy private individuals including their own trustees and trusts, and from corporate sponsorship. This is more usual in the US than in the UK or many other European countries: a famous example would be the Museum of Modern Art in New York.

In Europe most public museums look to grants from government bodies, trusts and foundations to provide awards of money for time-limited specific projects. The balance between different sources of income – or how they interact or lever one another – is important. Few museums can afford to rely on one funder, but operate a 'mixed economy' combining several, or even innumerable different sources of income, each with different agendas (see Chapter 4).

The funding basis of the museum or gallery goes hand in hand with the system of management and governance of the institution. It has important political and ethical implications. For example, in the UK those national museums and galleries which are publicly funded by the central governments of the four nations (England, Scotland, Northern Ireland and Wales) have been expected to provide free access to their permanent collections since 2001 as a condition of their funding. Yet, the museums in each of the four capital cities, namely London, Edinburgh, Belfast and Cardiff, have different access to private donors, and to the numbers of both tourists and local visitors from whom they can hope to generate income. A look at the list of private and corporate funders of Tate in London contained in their annual reports shows that the largest 'world cities' like London have immense sources of surplus private capital flowing through them which finds its way into public institutions. In this respect, geography has a direct bearing on the scale and scope of museums and their activities in more ways than might be immediately obvious.

In some countries a distinction is made between areas of the museum that are free and those that are charging. Sometimes the temporary exhibitions are charging spaces, and sometimes the permanent collections are. As an alternative model, the Metropolitan Museum of Art, New York, charges a $25 'recommended' entry fee, but this includes access to all of their special exhibitions. A museum's charging regime has implications for museums including shaping its visitors' habits. Put simply, it influences who visits and who doesn't. In many state-funded museums, it is closely related to cultural policy measures to increase and diversify audiences along lines of both ethnicity, socio-economic status, educational background and 'cultural capital' (see Chapter 3). Again, income targets influence, whilst not determining what kinds of programme institutions are likely to programme – even if some exhibitions can cross-subsidise others.

Museums and galleries can, of course, also be classified in terms of their scale and remit, and by who owns or manages their collections. The two are not always the same. In the UK, for example, museums and galleries are usually classified as either national (state level), local authority (funded by the regional government body), university (owned and managed by individual universities), independent (owned by charities or independent bodies) or regimental (managed by the army). The UK's museum sector can also be understood to extend to unoccupied royal palaces, historic sites and properties (for example stately homes) which also hold museum-type collections and are managed by charities or bodies such as the National Trust and English Heritage, or Historic Scotland or Historic Wales (Museums Association 2016).

Unsurprisingly, the scope of an institution's collections tends to reflect the funding and ownership arrangements. It is perfectly possible in the UK for collections in smaller cities to be identified or 'designated' as being of national significance. It is also possible for one organisation to legally own the collections or 'hold them in trust' for the public and for another to manage the museum or gallery in terms of its day-to-day operations. This happens for practical or historic reasons. For example, a collection may be owned by a small charitable group who created it in the nineteenth century but this collection may now be part of a museum administered by another body because legal ownership has never been transferred. Collections are built cumulatively often over generations, and single institutions can encompass multiple collections. As we will see, reducing the size of a collection, and therefore reducing ongoing costs, is much more difficult for a museum than almost any other type of organisation.

Some museums and galleries are also part of larger, multi-site families, networks or franchises. In the UK, there are several large organisations with sites around different parts of the country – for example, Tate includes Tate Modern and Tate Britain in London, and Tate Liverpool and Tate St. Ives. Some art museums have international offshoots: the Guggenheim Foundation has institutions in New York, Venice, Bilbao and Abu Dhabi.

WHAT ARE MUSEUMS AND GALLERIES FOR?

As the range of funding sources is extensive, so too is the range of functions and uses which societies or funders expect of their museums and galleries. The basic function of an art gallery might apparently be simply to present art objects or experiences, in the same way that a museum's primary role is to house, preserve and display historical artefacts. Nevertheless, museums and galleries can be seen to play, or have played, incredibly diverse roles as indicated below. It is important to note that some of these may seem historical and anachronistic and would not necessarily be widely endorsed now, or receive universal acclaim across the world.

Let us start with a list of purposes a museum or gallery may have, and which major museums and galleries certainly have had at some point in their history:

- To tell us about the past by presenting artefacts from it or reconstructions of it;
- To tell us about ourselves as parts of collectives, as nations, communities, or a species;
- To educate people about specific places, individuals, events and ideas;
- To unite, and to develop a collective memory and historical consciousness to build national identity, by educating people about a nation's past;
- To create or consolidate a body or 'canon' of 'official' knowledge such as a received history of fine art;
- To protect and conserve things of special importance for future generations;

- To show what people valued in previous times and places and tell us why;
- To celebrate the power and wealth of individuals, groups, cities or nations, in order to make manifest their social status and/or dominance;
- To show how we are different or similar from people across time;
- To show how we are different or similar across space through cross-cultural comparisons;
- To create, perpetuate and reinforce traditions of thought and belief – by making a worldview manifest (or else countering it);
- To give voice to people/s and foster ideas of citizenship;
- To deliver present-day government policy agendas, whether of social inclusion, diversity, wellbeing, happiness, multiculturalism or regeneration;
- To act as a 'forum' for debate through objects and discussion, or in conflict zones to provide a neutral or 'safe space' for such debate;
- To display demonstrations of skill, craftsmanship, or technological or technical achievement;
- To memorialise and create dedicated spaces for acknowledging individual people, places or events that have finished, been lost, or transformed;
- To tell us about things we are likely to have forgotten or never knew; to draw attention to 'hidden histories';
- To allow 'forgetting' or else avoid confrontations with past events;
- To construct knowledge, ways of knowing the world, create and give status to canons of authorised knowledge;
- To give expression to what it is possible to think, do or be;
- To regulate and 'police' social and cultural norms as manifest in material culture practices;
- To reform us and to 'improve' our state of being;
- To delineate and claim the limits of a territory, identity and history for nation- or community-building purposes; where territorial claims are disputed;
- To give form and space to a collective sense of past, present and future and contribute to society's sense of memory and identity across generations and communities;

- To facilitate economic regeneration, especially of post-industrial areas;
- To build cultural tourism;
- To rebrand a city and change public perceptions about a place, an individual, a company or a nation;
- To create a sense of place; as part of a place-making project.

As this list indicates, museum and gallery studies are a major emerging field precisely because of the diversity of the areas they encompasses and touch upon. Since the philosophical 'revolution' of the new museology, and the parallel development of 'New Public Management' principles in OECD countries (Organisation for Economic Cooperation and Development) expectations of museums have changed – and intensified in order to justify their public subsidy amongst other deserving candidates (Scott 2013).

For some academics and museum professionals this means that museums and galleries should aim to be agents of social change by, for example, positively tackling prejudice (Sandell and Nightingale 2012). This can be controversial: some figures have vociferously argued for museums' autonomy and re-emphasising the value of their collections (Cuno 2012). What audiences expect of museums and galleries is equally varied as we will see in Chapter 3.

WHY DO SOCIETIES HAVE MUSEUMS AND GALLERIES?

Let us return to our initial question. Museums can cost hundreds of millions of dollars, euros, pounds (or other currencies) to build. They also cost very large amounts of money to run – and their costs seldom if ever get smaller over time, because collections seldom if ever shrink substantially. They also have an environmental cost given their specific storage and conservation requirements (see Chapter 2). So why do we go to the effort of preserving or creating museums and art galleries or their equivalents? There are some figures who have argued that we should privatise state-run museums or 'contract out' their role as it would be more financially efficient and make cost-savings to taxpayers.

The reasons why societies persist in creating and maintain muse-ums and galleries are contained in that list of purposes outlined above. Nation-building, economic regeneration, fostering patriotism, edu-cating the citizenry; these are just some of the reasons which we explore in detail throughout the following chapters. However, one further thing all societies are doing when they engage with heritage as represented within museums and galleries in the broadest sense is building collective memory and a sense of shared identity based on a shared sense of the past. Some societies and groups will engage in this process of building historical consciousness more explicitly than others; in some cases it will be part of a governmental agenda – for example, the Chinese government has been clear that museums are for patriotic education and cultural diplomacy. In other cases, muse-ums and galleries can be a by-product of a different intention, for example, regeneration of post-industrial cityscapes which simultane-ously provides a new opportunity for a museum to tell the history of that city, as in case of the new national Museum of Liverpool in the Albert Docks regeneration area in the UK. Either way, Peter Seixas argues that societies engage in practices of building a sense of shared historical consciousness because of what it enables them to do not just in the present but in the future too:

> A common past, preserved through institutions, traditions, and sym-bols, is a crucial instrument – perhaps the crucial instrument – in the construction of collective identities in the present . . . . Belief in a shared past opens the possibility for commitments to collective missions in the future.
>
> (Seixas, 2004: 5)

An example of this can be found in the commemoration pro-cesses around the terrorist attacks of 9/11 in New York, and the new memorial and museum built into the very site of the destroyed World Trade Centre. Such spaces provide a focus and a permanent reminder of events.

Although many tend to think that museums are 'about' the past, one of the most important roles of museums and galleries is to enable members of society to think about how their present was shaped and what kind of society we might wish to be part of in the future. At the same time, we need to remember that people learn about 'the past', and receive information, myths or misinformation about it, through diverse media: books, television, newspapers, online, word of mouth, their schooling, families, rituals, folk stories and customs, architecture places and monuments, antiques and other kinds of material culture such as maps or archival documents, and art forms of all kinds. Our idea of 'the past' or 'history' is formed through a complex and often contradictory composite of sources; museums and galleries are just one source among many, although they often enjoy high status and trust compared to other forms.

Different cultures, and indeed social groups, value some sources more than others, whether oral knowledge and rituals or written records. In Western European cultures, 'heritage' as embodied in museums, galleries and physical heritage sites is often variously associated with being official, institutional, collective, formal, public and tangible. It is generally accorded a high status and high levels of public trust because of this. Heritage need not always be tangible though. In recent years, the museum and gallery sector in many countries like the UK have also embraced personal histories, individual stories and incorporated different forms into their displays and interpretation like film, oral histories, sound, photography and digital media, as part of the collecting of everyday life.

In some other cultures, any close association between official bodies like national museums, art galleries and the national government is viewed in negative terms. On the one hand, there can be no 'neutral' perspective on the past, but – in some contexts – there are reasonable perceptions that stories have been manipulated or told so selectively as to be unreliable. In such situations, unofficial accounts and personal or community memories may be seen as the real source of authority and reliability. The question of whose histories, cultures, and whose knowledges come to be valued is always necessarily 'political' – in the sense of being related to questions of power – but in many parts of the world, museums, galleries and their staff today will generally want to avoid being overtly *politicised* for fear of being seen as propagandist and biased. This distinction is crucial because it underpins public perceptions of trustworthiness.

PUBLIC TRUST

We have already introduced the idea that museums and galleries hold their collections 'in trust' for the public. We can also speak of 'public trust', in the sense of the public having faith in the authority of institutions as reliable, trustworthy, or merely independent of other vested interests or sources of power. What establishes 'trust' is seldom simple and often a matter of perceptions.

In some instances, in studies over recent decades visitors have claimed to place a greater trust in museums than, say, in media like television or newspapers that are known to be connected to sources of power including corporate ownership or political affiliations. The UK's Museums Association (MA) published a report about public attitudes to museums which stated: 'museums are in a rare position of being trusted to provide accurate and reliable information in a national conversation increasingly dominated by bias and vested interest' (Museums Association 2013). Though there is more research available on public trust and museums than on art museums or galleries, a US study found similar conclusions to those of the MA:

> When members of the general public were asked to rank the trustworthiness of a variety of sources of information about the past, they placed museums above any other choice, giving them an 8.4 on a ten-point scale, with 10 being the highest.
>
> (Rosenzweig and Thelen 1998: 21–23)

HERITAGE

In this chapter we have usually employed the word 'heritage' to designate a particular sector separate to museums and galleries. It is appropriate at this point to briefly address how it is used within the sector and without. We are aware that 'heritage' is also used as an overarching term which encompasses museums and galleries into a single area both in practice and in academic literature; currently there is much overlap between heritage, museum and galleries studies but also some divergences. (For example, heritage studies in the UK has recently been considerably influenced by the discipline of cultural geography and its particular theoretical trends.) 'Heritage' also includes things outside of formal cultural heritage institutions and not all heritages are commensurate with Western ways of thinking or standards of preservation. While many cultures assume that museums are the right and proper places to present *material* heritage this is not a universal view. Tangible and material heritage is far from the only sort: how we preserve, present, or conceptualise 'intangible heritage' has increasingly been of interest to scholars. In recent years, UNESCO (the United Nations Educational, Scientific and Cultural Organization) has placed considerable emphasis on intangible heritage as opposed to tangible heritage by which they mean the physical, built and material heritage. Intangible heritage – also known as 'living cultural heritage' – is defined by UNESCO to mean: "Oral traditions and expressions, including language as a vehicle of the intangible cultural heritage; performing arts; social practices, rituals and festive events; knowledge and practices concerning nature and the universe; traditional craftsmanship" (UNESCO 2012).

UNESCO's (2003) Declaration for the Safeguarding of Intangible Cultural Heritage states:

1 The "intangible cultural heritage" means the practices, representations, expressions, knowledge, skills – as well as the instruments, objects, artefacts and cultural spaces associated therewith – that communities, groups and, in some cases, individuals recognize as part of their cultural heritage. This intangible cultural heritage, transmitted from generation to generation, is constantly recreated by communities and groups in response to their environment, their interaction with nature and their history, and provides them with a sense of identity and continuity, thus promoting respect for cultural diversity and human creativity. For the purposes of this Convention, consideration will be given solely to such intangible cultural heritage as is compatible with existing international human rights instruments, as well as with the requirements of mutual respect among communities, groups and individuals, and of sustainable development.

2 The "intangible cultural heritage", as defined in paragraph 1 above, is manifested inter alia in the following domains:

(a) oral traditions and expressions, including language as a vehicle of the intangible cultural heritage;

    (b) performing arts;

    (c) social practices, rituals and festive events;

    (d) knowledge and practices concerning nature and the universe;

    (e) traditional craftsmanship.

In contrast with the above, the narrowest, most traditional use of the term 'heritage' in English is to mean: 'the material culture of previous elites'. In Europe, heritage can be popularly taken to mean historic buildings or archaeological sites alone, but be aware that this meaning is not uncritically accepted in scholarly literature. Again, heritage is often understood as political in the sense that what societies have materially inherited frequently still belongs to, or is correctly associated with elites, even if it is now owned by the state.

Heritage is also used more broadly to mean what individuals and societies value or have 'inherited' from the past. In this usage it includes and exceeds what we find in museums, galleries or individual heritage sites – e.g. the national heritage of France or the concept of 'world heritage'. Yet, if we accept that 'intangible heritage' is a valuable term, then the problem is that such an idea of 'heritage' excludes almost nothing and can be interpreted unhelpfully broadly. Almost nothing exists only in the present, especially if it is conceived of as a 'practice': everything has some sort of genealogy. The kinds of things that we 'inherit' as intangible heritage include our language, customs, rituals, 'tacit knowledge' and many other kinds of behaviours and interactions.

HERITAGE AS INSTITUTION, ADJECTIVE OR TRADITION

One use of the word heritage can be to refer to the *institutions* and the 'cultural products' themselves contained within those institutions – in other words, both art galleries and the art in them. The crucial thing is that, whilst there are forms of heritage that have world-wide significance, ultimately any type of heritage always 'belongs' to someone. The predecessors of one ethnic and social group or another either created or continued it. So the questions here are *whose* heritage something is claimed to be, and who *lays claim* to it.

There are ambiguities, of course. An art museum in Germany can hold works by French artists who worked in Britain. This raises the point that the domain of fine art, perhaps more than any other, has been seen both in terms of 'national' schools and in terms of its 'universal' historical importance. For example, the British Museum holds important examples of Benin's artistic traditions, although these may also be presented by some people as part of a 'world heritage'. Aside from the issue of 'whose' they are, should the Museum's Benin bronzes be seen as 'art' or 'heritage' or both? Who decides – people in Benin, visitors or curators? Societies that have been subject to colonial regimes or hold different indigenous value-systems can also differ fundamentally to European ones in attitudes to 'heritage'. Some languages make specific distinctions between different kinds of heritage and their management (Kockel and Craith 2007: 1-3).

Another way we may increasingly encounter the term 'heritage' in society is as an *adjective* to denote a set of values, often associated with tradition, wholesomeness, stability, authority, authenticity, community and being 'natural'. For some, the terms heritage and tradition are used interchangeably, creating an implicitly conservative ideal where continuity is an intrinsic good. Therefore, a fundamental question in assessing ideas about heritage and narrating histories in museums is how we evaluate concepts of change and continuity. Privileging 'change' over 'continuity' implies one set of values and vice versa. Put in extreme broad-brush terms, political and social conservatives have emphasised the value of cultural continuity. Most humanities academics have privileged change, both in social history and in stories of art. Dramatic changes in particular receive special attention. This remains true even though historians such as Ferdinand Braudel have emphasised the different 'speeds' of change at which different processes take place and different types of adaptation are negotiated.

Some museum studies scholars have looked to those celebrating radical change, such as the philosophers of history Walter Benjamin and Michel Foucault. Both attempted to rethink the very ideas of 'history' and 'heritage' by drawing our attention to the value of abrupt breaches and discontinuities rather than continuities. They argued against seeing history as a single linear sequence in which all 'heritage' is to be treasured whatever values it embodied when it was first created. Likewise, both figures saw historians' jobs as finding those things in the past that have been suppressed or ignored, or that remain unspoken. For Benjamin, the historian's imperative was "to blast open the continuum of history" in the face of "the 'eternal' image of the past . . . . In every era the attempt must be made anew to wrest tradition away from a conformism that is about to over-power it" (1999: 254).

ELITE OR 'EVERYONE'S' HERITAGE

These intellectual positions suggest that the veneration of certain kinds of elite material heritage encourage forms of conservative poli-tics, or even a subservience or unwitting deference towards modern-day elites. It is important to recognise the gap between the 'aesthetic' appreciation of some types of material heritage, and the imaginative understanding of the lived history of which they were part and par-cel. Many Europeans happily enjoy visiting 'stately homes' or large 'historic houses'. Yet, we do so in the knowledge that the historic system of property ownership that concentrated almost all wealth in 0.001% of the population is not one we want back. Most of our predecessors were in the 99.99% and were not landowners but serv-ants, workers or peasants. The point here is not only critic Robert Hewison's much-debated polemic that some parts of "the heritage industry" sell a saccharine, nostalgic, airbrushed and false view of history (Hewison 1987). It is also that few people visit ordinary indi-viduals' houses because they seldom ever owned anything of perma-nence, and few of their life-stories, memories or possessions could or would have been preserved or written about. The exception here is the tradition of folk museums which does preserve the material evi-dence of ordinary people's lives and vernacular housing but these are typically shown to illustrate particular national or regional cultures so that the histories of individuals within those groups remain absent.

In Europe, in particular, control over society's material heritage, its history, and even its collective memory, has been largely wielded by elites until very recently. In recent years, there has been a grow-ing official recognition in some countries that many other kinds of heritages have value, whether preserved in material artefacts and buildings or not. We can think about our own personal 'heritage' in terms of family history, place(s), language(s) and cultural identity, in relation to bigger stories about types of artefacts and practices. The degree to which an individual can choose which heritages to identify with, and whether they can have that claim recognised by others, relates to questions of power and influence. Gaining recognition for a broader spectrum of heritage, of course, requires collective action but has been taken forward, in some instances, by official bodies with some surprising results. For example, Historic England, which is the national statutory body charged with managing England's 'heritage' has developed a scheme called 'local listing'. Listing, in their words, is

> the term given to the practice of listing buildings, scheduling monuments, registering parks, gardens and battlefields, and protecting wreck sites. Listing allows us to highlight what is significant about a building or site, and helps to make sure that any future changes to it do not result in the loss of its significance.
>
> (Historic England 2017)

Local listing "helps to raise the profile of local heritage by identifying heritage assets that are of greatest importance to local people" (Historic England). So, as well as listing traditional historic sites of national importance which we would expect, like battlefields, monuments, churches and stately homes, the local listing scheme works to identify much more everyday sites which are important to the local community.

As the above suggests that 'heritage' can be defined at different scales, even at the same time. It can be considered as very localised and identified with a specific group – e.g. the heritage of 'my' community or family. Equally it can be understood as World Heritage and therefore belonging to us all – e.g. some heritage is designated as having universal value by UNESCO. Whether the same heritage can be claimed by different groups for different purposes (e.g. can my heritage also be your heritage if we identify with different groups?) and whether it can be both universal and also particular at the same time (e.g. belongs to Italy and also belongs to humanity, past, present and future) is the source of much debate in heritage studies. For example, the Universal Museum idea argues that such museums hold their collections for the whole of humanity – present and future – not just one specific group. However, material culture can generally only be in one place at one time and most of the Universal Museums are located in, and held by, former European powers who 'acquired' some of their collections through processes of colonisation. In both practical and philosophical terms this means that some nation-states and parts of the world (e.g. Europe) have much more access to so-called universal heritage than others. As all of the above suggests, 'heritage' is always closely linked to questions of identity, power and politics.

CONCLUSION

This chapter has explored some first principles in thinking about museums and galleries. What should now be evident is the extent to which people's understanding and perceptions of these institutions will vary significantly according to their own political, cultural, linguistic and historical contexts. This is particularly evident, for example, when we are looking at museums and galleries from the perspective of European colonising powers as opposed to those who were on the receiving end of colonial collecting practices. This chapter also demonstrates how the concept of the museum and gallery is a shifting one and the subject of intense debate in many countries around the world. This is a theme which will reoccur throughout the book. A third key point to take away from this chapter is the vital importance of engaging with the histories of museums and galleries and their collections. We cannot overstate how critical it is to understand how individual institutions were developed and the wider contexts within which they and their collections were formed. These pasts are still very much present within the institutions as we see them today. They are written – both metaphorically and literally – into their architecture, their spaces, their collections, their missions, their staffing structures, and the ways in which they think and act as institutions. A historically and critically informed understanding of museums and galleries is the key not only to appreciating why they are like they are today, but also to having the sense of perspective to think for oneself how they might be different in the future. Having laid this foundation for understanding what museums and galleries are and what roles they may perform in societies, the next chapter will focus on two of the essential features of museum and gallery practice: collecting and curating.

REFERENCES

Ambrose, T. and C. Paine (2012) *Museum Basics*. 3rd edition. London: Routledge.

Benjamin, W. (1999) 'Theses on the philosophy of history', in *Illuminations*, trans. H. Zorn. London: Pimlico, 245–255 (first published 1968).

Bennett, T. (1995) *The Birth of the Museum*. London and New York: Routledge.

Boylan, P. (ed.) (1992). *Museums 2000: Politics, People, Professionals and Profit*. London: Routledge.

Crow, T. (1985) *Painters and Public Life in Eighteenth Century Paris*. New Haven, CT and London: Yale University Press.

Cuno, J. (ed.) (2012) *Whose Culture? The Promise of Museums and the Debate over Antiquities*. Princeton, NJ: Princeton University Press.

Davis, P. (1999) *Ecomuseums: A Sense of Place*. Leicester: Leicester University Press.

Duncan, C. (1995) *Civilising Rituals: Inside Public Art Museums*. London and New York: Routledge.

Hewison, R. (1987) *The Heritage Industry: Britain in a Climate of Decline*. London: Methuen.

Hooper-Greenhill, E. (1992) *Museums and the Shaping of Knowledge*. London and New York: Routledge.

Hudson, K. (1998) 'The museum refuses to stand still'. *Museum International* (Paris: UNESCO), 50(1): 43–50.

Karega-Munene (2011) 'Museums in Kenya: Spaces for selecting, ordering and erasing memories of identity and nationhood'. *African Studies*, 70(2): 224–245.

Kockel, U. and M.N. Craith (eds) (2007) *Cultural Heritages as Reflexive Traditions*. Basingstoke: Palgrave Macmillan.

MacKenzie, J.M. (2009) *Museums and Empire: Natural History, Human Cultures and Colonial Identities*. Manchester: Manchester University Press.

Marstine, J. (ed.) (2005) *New Museum Theory and Practice: An Introduction*. Malden, MA and Oxford: Blackwell.

Mason, R. (2007) *Museums, Nations, Identities: Wales and Its National Museums*. Cardiff: University of Wales Press.

Office of the Federal Register (US) (ed.) (2011) 'Definition of a museum'. *Code of Federal Regulations, Title 45, Public Welfare, PT. 5000–1199*. Washington, DC: US Superintendent of Documents, 493–494.

Onciul, B.A. (2015) *Museums, Heritage and Indigenous Voice Decolonizing Engagement*. London and New York: Routledge.

Rosenzweig, R. and D. Thelen (1998) *The Presence of the Past*. New York: Columbia University Press.

Sandell, R. and E. Nightingale (2012) *Museums, Equality and Social Justice*. London and New York: Routledge.

Scott, C. (ed.) (2013) *Museums and Public Value: Creating Sustainable Futures*. Farnham: Ashgate.

Seixas, P. (2004) *Theorizing Historical Consciousness*. Toronto and London: University of Toronto Press.

Shelton, A. (2011) 'Museums and anthropologies: Practices and narratives', in S. Macdonald (ed.), *A Companion to Museum Studies*. Oxford: Blackwell, 64–80 (first pub. 2006).

Shelton, A. (2013) 'Critical museology: A manifesto'. *Museum Worlds: Advances in Research*, 1: 7–23.

Thomas, N. (2016) *The Return of Curiosity: What Museums Are Good for in the 21st Century*. London: Reaktion Books.

Vergo, P. (1989) *The New Museology*. London: Reaktion Books.

Weil, S.E. (1999) 'From being *about* something to being *for* somebody: The ongoing transformation of the American museum'. *Daedalus*, 128(3): 229–258.

WEBSITES

Australian Government Department of the Environment (2001) 'State of the Environment Report 2001'. URL: http://www.environment.gov.au/science/soe

British Museum (2016) 'History of the British Museum'. URL: https://www.britishmuseum.org/about_us/the_museums_story/general_history.aspx

Deutsche Welle (2016) 'Over a 1,000 skulls from Germany's colonies still sitting in Berlin'. URL: http://www.dw.com/en/over-1000-skulls-from-germanys-colonies-still-sitting-in-berlin/a-36488751

Fishman, M. (2014) 'Delaware Art Museum loses accreditation'. *The News Journal* 19 June. URL: http://www.delawareonline.com/story/life/2014/06/18/museum-directors-sanction-delaware-art-museum/10757111/

German Museums Association (2017a) URL: http://www.museumsbund.de/wp-content/uploads/2017/03/dmb-satzung-2016.pdf

German Museums Association (2017b) URL: http://www.museumsbund.de/themen/das-museum/

Historic England (2017) 'What is listing?'. URL: https://historicengland.org.uk/listing/what-is-designation/

International Movement for a New Museology (MINOM) (2014) 'About us'. URL: http://www.minom-icom.net/about-us

Japanese Association of Museums (2008) 'Present status of museums in Japan'. URL: http://www.mext.go.jp/component/a_menu/education/detail/__ics Files/afieldfile/2012/03/27/1312941_1.pdf

Museums Association (2013) 'What the public thinks'. URL: http://www.museumsassociation.org/museums2020/11122012-what-the-public-thinks

Museums Association (2016) 'FAQs'. URL: http://www.museumsassociation.org/about/frequently-asked-questions#.U6qa65RdXTo

Museums Australia (1998) 'What is a museum?'. URL: http://www.museums australia.org.au/site/about_museums.php

Museums Australia (2002) 'Constitution'. URL: https://www.museumsaustralia. org.au/membership/organisation

National Park Service, US Department of the Interior (2016) 'Native American Graves Protection and Repatriation Act [NAGPRA]: Law, regulations, and guidance'. URL: http://www.nps.gov/nagpra/MANDATES/INDEX.HTM

Rockbund Museum of Contemporary Art (2016) 'About: Mission'. URL: http://www.rockbundartmuseum.org/en/page/detail/474cr

Sheriff, A. (2014) 'Symbolic restitution: Post-Apartheid changes to the South African heritage sector. 1994–2012.' *Electronic Journal of Africana Bibliography*. URL: http://ir.uiowa.edu.cgo/viewcontent.cgi?article-1019&context_ejab

South African Museums Association (SAMA) (2013) 'Constitution'. URL: http://sama.za.net/home-page/samab-journal/

United Nations Educational, Social and Cultural Organization (UNESCO) (2003) 'Convention for the Safeguarding of the Intangible Cultural Heritage 2003'. URL: http://portal.unesco.org/en/ev.php-URL_ID=17716&URL_DO=DO_TOPIC&URL_SECTION=201.html#RESERVES

United Nations Educational, Social and Cultural Organization (UNESCO) (2012) 'Definition of intangible heritage'. URL: http://www.unesco.org/services/documentation/archives/multimedia/?id_page=13&PHPSESSID=99724b4d60dc8523d54275ad8d077092

FURTHER READING

Altshuler, B. (2008). *Salon to Biennial: Exhibitions that Made Art History*, Volume 1: 1863–1959. New York and London: Phaidon.

Aronsson, P. and G. Elgenius (eds) (2015). *National Museums and Nation-Building in Europe 1750–2010: Mobilization and Legitimacy, Continuity and Change.* London and New York: Routledge.

Barker, E. (1999) *Contemporary Cultures of Display*. New Haven, CT and London: Yale University Press.

Bennett, T. (1995) *The Birth of the Museum*. London and New York: Routledge.

McClellan, A. (2008) *The Art Museum from Boullée to Bilbao*. Berkeley, CA: University of California Press.

Stefano, M. L. and P. Davis (2017) *The Routledge Companion to Intangible Cultural Heritage*. London and New York: Routledge.

Witcomb, A. (2003) *Reimagining the Museum: Beyond the Mausoleum*. London and New York: Routledge.

2

COLLECTING AND COLLECTIONS

CURATING AND COLLECTING

Collecting would seem to be the fundamental common denominator between all museums, if not the basis of what makes them what they are. The noun 'curator' is believed to be derived from the Latin 'curare', meaning to 'take care', to act as an overseer or manager of an implied collection of valued objects. In museums, the label still often means the keeper of a segment of cultural heritage, for example, archaeology. Collecting might seem at first glance to be a neutral and reactive act but the reality is far more complicated and interesting. The history of collecting in museums and galleries is itself an important sub-field of research (Knell 2004).

How do museum and gallery professionals collectively set about deciding what to collect, how to collect, what not to collect, how to organise their collections and how to justify these decisions? How does the collecting of one institution relate to another? Should museums and galleries all aim to collect the same things in their respective places or should they establish different remits and direct visitors to look to different institutions to provide different things? In history museums we might ask if it is important to collect the same item in different museums in different locations in recognition that the story of its usage is place- and often person-specific. This leads us to consider whether we are collecting the object itself, or the stories attached to the objects or both. If we are collecting objects with their own histories and people's memories of them how does this affect the way we decide what to collect and how we go through the processes of acquisition and documentation? To what extent is a museum or gallery's collecting practices determined and shaped by the institution's history and previous collecting habits? How and why do some objects enter or – more rarely – leave museums?

These questions have been further complicated by the unprecedented expansion of mass-produced objects and globalised consumer capitalism during the latter part of the twentieth-century. In a world of ever-expanding production where the material culture of our lives vastly exceeds our ability and need to keep track of it, it becomes ever more challenging for museums and galleries to decide what will 'stand the test of time' and should be part of the historical record.

Figure 2.1 Spirit-preserved specimens in the Collection of the Natural History Society of Northumbria.

© Dan Gordon, Tyne and Wear Archives and Museums.

Underpinning this is the question of how can museums can imagine and 'predict' what they will need to have collected from the present in order to create a convincing account of the present for our future selves. What is likely to be attainable and preservable? The presentation of public culture and history involves such moral, political, philosophical and scholarly dilemmas and choices. However, before addressing these problems we should address what we might mean by the 'past' and 'present'.

COLLECTING THE PAST

Museums and galleries, like newspapers and history textbooks, aim to be institutions 'of record': that is to say, to be the reference sources for trustworthy, authoritative, official accounts of their subject. The name 'museum' implies that what that institution does is to 'collect the past' but in these three words are several knotty intellectual and practical problems.

To begin with, 'the past' and 'history' are different things. We define the former as what came before us in time: the sum total of every individual, action, event, idea, process and artefact to date. A history is, or should be, a carefully crafted story abstracted from that overwhelming totality. It has to have a focus, and therefore to exclude much. A history is a *narrative account* ordinarily told in words, which usually concentrates on one area of time and of space. Every such story must have a perspective or point of view. It has to respond to the histories that came before it and define that area of time and space. The only material for making written histories is language. Language has limitations and fallibilities. The stories we can build with it are also subject to the existing narrative structures and forms that our particular culture has developed. We can adapt, but not completely invent new narrative forms without losing the ability to communicate.

Unlike written histories, museums tell their histories in architectural space through words that are alongside and make sense of objects, images and various other types of display apparatus that direct and prompt us in various ways. As we will see, displays are multi-dimensional and multi-sensory: physical, spatial, aural, sometimes emotional and affecting, always embodied. Another way that museum histories differ from written histories is in the way that people engage with them. Visitors inhabit these spatialised histories by the way they move through displays. Out of the vast range of objects and display media, visitors choose to look at and examine specific things or topics based on what they personally find significant or worthy of attention for a whole host of idiosyncratic reasons. The importance of this aspect of the museum experience has led some museum researchers to describe museums as "free choice learning environments" (Falk and Dierking 2016).

Despite these differences, museums and galleries share many of the professional codes with the academic discipline of history and are influenced by trends in academic research. Their ways of conceptualising historiography (the practice and methods of making history) overlap. Museums and galleries necessarily have to conceptualise a history of their subject or medium, however implicitly. Museum and gallery professionals need to have a view on which histories might be as yet missing from their collections. They need to know which displays and exhibitions need to be amended as our view of the past and the present-day changes.

Curators are in effect akin to 'public historians' for their specialism: that is, historians whose work addresses a wider audience rather than their peers, and other specialists or academics alone. The artefacts, materials and ideas they deal with are the ones they believe to have (or believe will have) a *lasting* public value.

RECONCEPTUALISING THE DISCIPLINE OF 'HISTORY'

There are some fundamental aspects to traditional Western historical thought that are relevant for thinking about the way that museums and galleries construct our understanding of the past. For example, periodisation – conceiving of how time has been ordered, and should be categorised into segments – is one unavoidable aspect of their work. It is common to public museums' and academics' work alike. Any story has a timescale, whether about art, social history, ethnography or natural history. A central concept like this has been the source of much debate varying across fields. The professions of academic history, art history and even the practice of natural sciences have been reconceptualised since the 1960s.

One recent idea of particular relevance to museums is the increasing recognition by historians of the co-existence of multiple histories inside each discipline. History, it is now widely recognised, was for a long time told from the perspective of the 'victors' and elites at the expense of other possible accounts. The accent by contemporary historians is increasingly now on pluralised accounts, whether told from the point of view of different interest groups, positions or alternative historical traditions.

Some museums have adapted accordingly. There are now a significant number of museums or exhibitions dedicated to those whose histories were previously marginalised; the Te Papa Tongarewa Museum of New Zealand which was developed during the 1990s and opened in 1998, for example, was developed on the principle of biculturalism to 'be a partnership between Tangata Whenua (Māori, the indigenous people of New Zealand) and Tangata Tiriti (people in New Zealand by right of the Treaty of Waitangi)' (Te Papa 2015). Similarly, the newest addition to the Smithsonian Institution's family of museums in Washington, DC, opened in 2016 is the National Museum of African American History and Culture which describes its mission as follows (see also chapter 6):

> Equally important is the opportunity to help all Americans see just how central African American history is for all of us. The museum will use African American history and culture as a lens into what it means to be an American.
>
> (bmorenews 2016)

In 1992 the Musée d'Art Américain de Giverny opened; when it changed from being run by the Terra Foundation for the Arts to local government it changed name in 2006. Its new name is the Museum of Impressionisms, with its subject in the plural. The "geographical diversity" and multiple "streams" of Impressionist painting, rather than just its 'canonical' artists, are its specialist area (Givernet 2016).

It is not only the subject of previously marginalised histories which is now recognised but also the mode of historical thinking in the sense that it is now recognised that that many Aboriginal and native American cultures have different historiographical traditions. In countries like Australia and New Zealand some museums are attempting to work with these alternative concepts of time and history in exhibition design and interpretation.

A second fundamental, which we will return to below, is what geographic scale and imagined scope we imagine our specialist disciplinary history to have. There is no simple or single answer to how we might understand the relations between the 'local' and the 'global', and where conceptual boundaries can be drawn. Can and should museums be responsible for representing their city, their nation, or artefacts from or about the largest and loosest geopolitical unit (for example, 'the West') or without boundaries? How can one make secure judgements, rather than assumptions, about what is on one side of a boundary and the other? After all, transnational and even transcontinental trade in ideas as much as commodities has been central to almost every nation-state's story, whichever way we tell it.

How can museum professionals negotiate such complex terrain? On the one hand, we can all recognise that no individual scholar or curator could conceivably have expertise across every time period, nor every geographical territory. On the other, no serious art museum or history museum can conceive of its mission responsibly without considering what 'globalisation' means for it now and in the future. It is worth noting here that the terms used in academic life that affect museums are complex and changing. Two decades ago, the term 'postcolonial' was perhaps more habitually used to describe international relations, and continues to have considerable purchase. Today, the ideas, in the plural, associated with 'globalisation' and transnationalism have assumed almost a ubiquity in the academic humanities.

ACKNOWLEDGING YOUR OWN STANDPOINT

Differentiating between types of relation to the past is crucial. It reminds us there is no professionally or politically neutral position for any museum to take, in any field. It also reminds us that we all come with preconceptions about how history is constituted, whatever academic discipline we call our own. How does this affect museums? To take one example, European and American art museums traditionally conveyed 'the story of art' to non-specialists in a manner akin to that told by the art historian E. H. Gombrich in his book of that name. Gombrich's book was written for teenagers in a simple, accessible way and has become the most popular art history book in Britain. In some versions of art history, it is as though particular countries have a special focus as if passing on a kind of 'baton' of greatness in a relay race. An example of this can be seen in historic floorplans of the National Gallery, London, which are organised by national 'school'. In its then outpost the Tate Gallery, the British national collection of twentieth-century art from other countries was labelled that of 'modern foreign pictures', even after 1945. The clear separation between 'native' artists and 'foreign' ones now seems startling, as does the reduction of art to 'pictures'.

This approach of organising the world of art into a simplified, single linear sequence came under sustained criticism after the Second World War, and increasingly since the 1960s. Yet its simplicity is appealing. Many art museums have only moved slowly away from it – if at all – as their ordering principle or major 'story', even whilst acknowledging that history emerges from the contest between ideas, forces and resources, whether through co-operation or competition between parties.

This leads us to a related problem of anyone working with the past and its objects. This is how we can conceive of the 'big picture' – the overall structure – of our subject or field. This is true whether our field of study is the 'art world', or society, or 'nature'. Again, the field of concepts we possess, and our ordering of them, is key. Put another way, the figurative language we employ to construct categories and groups determines much else which will follow in terms of collecting and curating practices. How we imagine relationships between individual things or people is crucial, as is how we imagine the relationships between participants in the field of study.

Present-day historians have employed new or unorthodox individual terms from other fields to rethink how we can imagine behaviours, relations and historical processes. To take one example, Daniel E. White (2013: 3), studying Anglo-Indian relations in the colonial period has argued we can think of relations spatially, calling them "multidirectional" (underlining that despite power inequalities, there can be no unilateral actions). He also draws on literary and musical theory to say we should think of the two groups in "contrapuntal rather than unilinear terms" (as discrete but inter-dependent, with differing trajectories). And he draws on mathematics to suggest that we analyse their behaviours as "recursive" (as repeti-tively enacted, but also that the present changes the past: that sequential order must be thought about both 'forwards' and 'backwards' in time). Such notions ask us to rethink how 'history' is constructed – whose histories they are – and where they stop. They even ask to rethink the dominant European metaphor of history as 'time's arrow' flying through space in a linear direction.

Beyond the individual ideas that populate our historical, artistic, biological or sociological imagination, we need to acknowledge that since the 1960s, there have been new types of histories as well as new subjects – new *ways* of telling histories as much as new areas of exploration from oral history to 'object biography'. Some of these approaches have loose equivalents or parallels in exhibiting prac-tices. There have been exhibitions centred on single objects akin to historians' 'micro-histories'. 'Entangled' histories are ones in which places or ideas normally studied discretely are seen to be intertwined or co-dependent. For example, the claim by Spanish-speaking art historians that the modern world began with material and cultural exchanges between South America and Spain and Portugal is intrigu-ing. It challenges the familiar story that 'modernity' was forged in, and owned by the US and North–West Europe.

TRADITION VERSUS HISTORY

While acknowledging such critiques, museums need to acknowl-edge both that the 'traditional' stories still dominate the public image of our subject and that many of the social relations of dominance that produced these traditional accounts continue to persist into the pre-sent. For example, the objects that have come to be honoured with the name 'art' are still only a tiny proportion of the cultural objects produced. Almost invariably, they are those that were commissioned by and for elites. Similarly, in history museums, collections have typically been dominated by the material culture of the elites and the wealthy leading to a highly selective view of the past. In recent years there have been enormous efforts made in certain countries to try to counterbalance this inbuilt bias by collecting oral histories and targeted collecting of the under-represented in society but this can obviously only redress gaps in the relatively recent historical record.

Moreover, such attempts to redress previous imbalances or gaps in the historical record are easier said than done. It is not simple for history or art museums to construct a position or a story that is, for example, cosmopolitan and pluralistic. It is even harder to do so without becoming merely benign, celebratory or anodyne. As museum historian Andrew McClellan has recently written, a "universal[ising] humanism remains the steady establishment response to the fracturing potential of postcolonial critique. Where the new museology calls for alternative voices, mainstream art museums insist all the more vehemently on the healing, conciliatory power of a 'transcultural dialogue'" (McClellan 2008: 48). He describes museums today as often speaking "the discourse of disengaged global humanism" occupying a false ahistorical 'neutrality' in socio-political or geopolitical matters.

History museums in particular, have a special responsibility to collect artefacts that open onto wider stories and processes, as much as impress, or provide immediate stimuli. They need, somehow, to be open about disagreements both within their professional field and without, and to be clear about how power has been unequally shared. Traditionally museums have not drawn attention to more systemic inequalities or about the structural organisation of society. They have tended to focus on notable individual historical events or individuals driven by the strengths of their existing collections. Although again it is worth noting that in recent decades in several countries, this has begun to change as museums directly address issues like transatlantic slavery (the Transatlantic Slavery Museum in Liverpool, UK), the Holocaust (United States Holocaust Memorial Museum), ethnic cleansing (Kigali Genocide Memorial Centre, Rwanda), human trafficking (Museum of World Cultures, Sweden) and colonialism (National Museum of Australia).

More widely, one task for twenty-first century museums across almost every discipline is to decouple 'tradition' from academic 'history'. 'Traditions' have often been invented recently, or altered beyond recognition, whilst being *imagined* to provide a thread of continuity from past to present. Academic history examines the needs such imaginings serve. Nothing is beyond new interpretations.

Even in natural history museums, incorporating the critiques of 'anthropocentrism' over the last quarter-century – stemming from the acknowledgement that humans are not the peak of an evolutionary tree commanding over all others – presents its own challenges. Of one thing we can be sure – over the course of our forty-plus-year working lives, we can expect what is considered 'knowledge' to be challenged or even revolutionised.

We cannot cover all the debates across the historical profession here, of course, let alone in historiography but can draw attention to museum professionals' place in the intellectual landscape; that is, their dependence on the conceptual frameworks forged in other disciplines, and their co-dependence on such professions to create their discipline and its public status.

COLLECTING 'THE PRESENT' FOR THE FUTURE

Both history museums and art museums face a particular problem when collecting 'the present', however we define it. What museums collect now will be what future citizens know of us. What is not collected will not have the same status or place in history. How we lived, what we believed, and what art and culture we consumed all have to be decided upon: they cannot be taken as givens. Museums have a historical responsibility to the future, just as much as to the past. In many countries this has led to active contemporary collecting initiatives. Swedish museums, for example, led the way with the SAMDOK project which ran from 1977 to 2011 and set out to coordinate a systematic, research-based approach to collecting throughout Swedish museums. In 2011 SAMDOK ceased, but the activity continues under the auspices of COMCOL: an International Committee for Collecting, part of ICOM (the International Council of Museums) which "aims to deepen discussions, and share knowledge on the practice, theory and ethics of collecting and collections (both tangible and intangible) development" (ICOM 2015).

A more recent example of contemporary collecting can be found at the Victoria & Albert (V&A) Museum in London where the architecture and design department have developed a 'rapid response' strategy. Curator Kieran Long describes it as: "A new strand to the V&A Museum's collections policy, which can respond very quickly to events relevant to design and technology." For example, Long collected a pair of jeans sold by Primark and explained the decision in these terms:

> These jeans were made around the Plaza factory in Dhaka, Bangladesh, which collapsed in April this year, killing a thousand people. Those Primark jeans wouldn't usually enter our fashion collections. Knowing that they were made in that factory, however, gives them a particular relevance and tells us something about contemporary manufacturing and about building codes in Bangladesh, about western consumerism, about lots of issues. We thought that if we had those jeans in the museum, the day after that event, there's something very visceral about that and the object's ability to tell that story.
>
> (Etherington 2013: 7)

What is fascinating about this example is that it is an item of mass-produced, cheap, everyday clothing sold around the world. It is not 'special' in any of the senses we usually associate with objects in museums of art and design: it is not unique, hand-crafted, expensive, exclusive, timeless, or even of much 'aesthetic' interest. It is not a landmark in 'design history'. However, the jeans are able tell a story about the fashion industry, globalisation and precisely how the material world is constructed at a particular stage in the history of production and consumption. The object speaks about anonymous makers rather than celebrated artists. It talks about manufacturing conditions and, importantly, how consumers implicitly treat others and the 'invisible' relationships between them and those who make their designed possessions. It starts to illuminate the connections between countries and peoples around the world, which are normally unmentioned or unrecognised. Objects can open onto different and unexpected stories when placed in museums, at least if they are part of imaginative interpretation and display strategies, as we will see.

As this example shows in history museums, the questions of exactly whose histories come to be collected, who has a public voice and who has precedence in public space, are unavoidable, prominent and obviously political, i.e. in terms of fundamental questions such as 'who gets to speak on behalf of the community?'.

Here, we ask what the less immediately obvious, wider questions are that underpin museums' collecting activities. In this instance we might turn to philosophy for understanding. To take one example: professional philosophers such as Peter Osborne have observed that in every history – and every account of our place in the present – there is necessarily a 'politics of time' securing it (Osborne 2013). Osborne has written extensively on this topic, arguing convincingly that each of us takes a position in this 'politics' whether willingly or not. The stakes here could not be higher. It determines who gets to lay claim to ownership of the present. How we imagine our place in the flow of time determines in turn what museums are able to stand for. 'Ownership' of the present defines or redefines what culture (or society, or art) are and can be: it declares what is important to know, even what we can think about publicly, i.e. constitutes public discourse.

COLLECTING HISTORICAL ART

Collecting artefacts or artwork from our own time presents issues of what to choose from the superabundance of things in the world or artworks being made. Collecting art from the past can seem to present the opposite problem: a shortage of 'new' material to the market. As one commentator notes:

> the collections of most old museums are in effect 'closed' – that is to say the lack of available historic works of exceptional importance makes it impossible for institutions to acquire works of the kind that would dramatically change the balance and overall character of their holdings. The only field that is constantly replenished is that of contemporary art. With very few exceptions new museums are therefore focusing their activities in this area.
>
> (Schubert 2000: 91)

However, the business of attributing value to past artworks is no less complex, and the scale of changes can be surprising. The fame of the arguably two best-known Dutch Old Masters provides two contrasting examples. From 1968 to 2015, the Rembrandt Research Project systematically looked at every painting attributed or potentially attributed to that artist, often creating heated controversy. Paintings owned by museums worth millions – if their judgements were believed – became worth a mere fraction of their former value, and some new 'Rembrandts' were found. Overall, the number of 'autograph' Rembrandts in the world fell dramatically. The very idea of who Rembrandt was changed. By contrast, Vermeer is only known through around 34–35 paintings still extant of the estimated 40–60 he is thought to have made. Only half of these are signed, and only one is dated. His tiny body of work was for long relatively little-known in comparison to Rembrandt's, and barely any documentation survives. Individual artists' fortunes can change radically, in relatively short spaces of time. Equally, the relative values collectors attribute to different periods and movements continue to change.

COLLECTING CONTEMPORARY ART

The market for contemporary art has remained strong despite the global economic downturn after 2008. The investment returns for the most desirable 'blue chip' (elite status) contemporary art have been higher than almost any other asset class. The proliferation of new museums and extensions has helped cement this. Writer Terry Smith has identified a "massive, widespread, and sustained internationalization of contemporary art since the 1990s" (Smith 2013).

The very terms 'modern art' and 'contemporary art' are both contested and loaded ones. They do not just designate 'recent' and 'new'. The terms are each associated with sets of values. Moreover, recent research has rightly emphasised that throughout the twentieth-century there were 'multiple modernities'. This term refers to the idea that there has never been any monopoly on the idea of modern art or culture, nor on industrial development.

Rewriting the history of collecting institutions, rather than that of artworks, is more difficult: conventional and canonical ideas are stronger. Most traditionally, Paris and New York are the 'stars' of the story of modern art. In the years after 1945, the dominant story is that the key innovator in the field was The Museum of Modern Art, New York (usually known simply as MoMA – though notice that leaves out their choice to adopt the singular definite article in their name). Even otherwise acute critics have repeated the truism that MoMA was "*the* museum of record, whose collections [were] unrivalled in quality and scope by any other institution and whose practice influenced curators all over the world" (Schubert 2000: 91). Like most truisms this has some basis in fact, though has also become accepted by sheer repetition.

Today it is usually asserted that, irrespective of institutional weight and finances, there were throughout the twentieth century multiple interrelated 'centres' of art production. By 'centre' we mean that artists, writers, institutions and private collectors were present and usually mutually supportive; and that the activity in a city was respected by peers and believed to be of relevance to communities – 'art worlds' – far and wide. In the twenty-first century, one of the central pressures on museums collecting contemporary art is therefore to look to places whose artists that have not been 'represented' in their collections before. Since 2005, Tate Modern in London has acquired its first works by Iranian artists, and since 2000, established foundations and committees to secure works from not only North America, but Latin America, the Middle East, Africa and North Africa, and the Asia Pacific area (Tate 2012). It is an ambitious, essential and equally impossible task to scour the whole world for its prize possessions – and has echoes of colonial enterprise for some – but the fact is that what is important in art cannot be defined by two or three cities alone.

Second, the media and modes by which contemporary art is made have diversified enormously. MoMA's departmental structure in 1980, say, reflected what 'modern art' was thought to be. There were five areas of curatorial expertise and five distinct collections: painting, sculpture, drawing, film and design-and-architecture. Since then, it has been accepted that artists' ways of working are not only representational – that is, pictorial or spatial, or using media that existed in the nineteenth century. Rather they have licence to create or foster any kind of *experience,* anywhere in the world, using any method or means or materials to do so, including 'immaterial' ones.

Moreover, since the 1980s it has come to be accepted that artists inhabit what theorist Rosalind Krauss called a 'post-medium condition' (Krauss 1999). By this she means there is no privileged place for painting or sculpture. An artist can become a painter, video artist, installation artist, performance artist, or all of the above at once; their work is not necessarily defined by their mastery of skills in one medium or another. Artists can now work between media, combining them in one work, or else sequentially across projects. This places pressure on 'representative' collections supposed to be ones 'of record'. It is all but impossible to 'represent' such artists' work to the public through a single example, in contrast to the way you could own one or two paintings by (say) Piet Mondrian and fairly show his distinct contribution to the field. Instead, museums increasingly balance 'breadth' with 'depth' of representation, trying to acquire whole bodies of artists' works that are collections in themselves. In the UK, this has been exemplified by Tate and the National Museums of Scotland's joint acquisition of hundreds of works from the personal collection of the leading UK gallerist in the 1980s, Anthony d'Offay. The works are loaned as part of a scheme entitled 'Artist Rooms' to be displayed together, in rooms of their own, and seen on their own terms.

COLLECTING THE INTANGIBLE

In recent years, museums and art galleries have been confronted by the question of how to collect not the tangible, material culture with which they are so familiar but the intangible and the ephemeral, particularly where this is perceived to be threatened by the condition of contemporary globalisation. In the domain of history museums, increasable attentiveness to the importance of oral histories and personal testimony has demanded more priority be afforded to such material alongside objects. In many countries, recognition of intangible culture signals an institutional revaluing of indigenous culture, much of which may be based as much around stories, rituals, song and dance as around objects (see Chapter 1). The extent to which this shift is actually changing the nature of the museum as institution is a matter of debate.

COLLECTING THE DIGITAL

'Digital heritage' is another growth area in both museum and gallery studies practice and research. For example, curators are exploring how computer-based 'new media', 'digital art' or 'digital heritage', as they have variously been known, can be acquired by museums. Similarly, 'new media art historians' Beryl Graham and Sarah Cook argue that museum collections play a crucial role in both authorising an official account of art, in creating a history of each subculture, genre or medium, and in making things accessible to a broad public (Graham and Cook 2010). This is how the 'canon' is made. Yet, they also argue there are almost no 'new media art historians' who 'historicise' these media, or this sub-genre. It is only since 2011, for example, that Tate has officially included what it instead calls 'Net Art' in its official remit, saying that "Tate commissions Net Art for its website and also seeks to acquire works of art that use networked or non-networked digital technologies for creation, presentation and distribution, or that critique or comment on the same digital technologies" (Tate 2011).

Between 1990 and 2010 the default means to record and transmit still pictures or sounds became digital technologies. Since 2010, even cinema has become a largely digital medium too – at least in the display, if not recording of images. As above, MoMA adjusted its structure in 2006 to create a Department of Media, then renamed the Department of Media and Performance Art, that oversees "moving images, film installations, video, performance, motion – and sound-based works, and other works that represent time or duration" (MoMA 2006). Many of these media, in other words, are and will in the future be created and stored digitally – even if their histories started elsewhere.

Graham and Cook prompt us to classify new media works, which are often interactive or participatory, in terms of their 'behaviour' instead of their aesthetics. This requires a leap of imagination for collecting institutions, used to organising works by period, nation, traditional medium and technical specification. Accessioning rather than 'acquiring' works is a major problem for institutions when the technological platforms used to access them face rapid obsolescence. The question is: will digital works collected now be accessible to museums of the future?

Given that digital technologies change so rapidly, and the platforms to see works are outmoded or even become redundant equally rapidly, large-scale research projects have been set up to quantify and codify what museums can and should do in response. One conservator, Pip Laurenson, has outlined the challenges to museums of interpreting artists' intentions, continuing to preserve and operate fragile or transient technologies, and making works publically available:

> Unavoidable change does not mean that the work was designed to change. Artists and other stakeholders are at liberty to assign significance to a specific piece of display equipment, even if that object is set to become obsolete and fail. Here lies the nub of the problem: display equipment is certain to fail and become obsolete, therefore any strong link between specific display equipment and authenticity or value will mean that a degree of loss is inevitable.
>
> (Laurenson 2005)

In this sense, the lifespan of an artwork, or else the technology needed to access and show it, becomes another part of the curatorial challenge as the accepted definitions of what should be collected become more expansive.

THE LIVES OF OBJECTS

So far, this chapter has focused primarily on philosophical and conceptual issues around the practice of collecting artefacts in order to tell histories of individuals, groups and societies. However, as the quotation above indicates, we can also think about museums' contents more specifically in terms of the physical status of their objects and collections and the issues involved in acquiring and managing them.

One way to approach this is in terms of the anthropological concept of 'object biographies' developed by anthropologist Arjun Appadurai. This can be paraphrased as knowingly 'anthropomorphising' objects which means talking about them as though they were people with a 'life story' across space and time. It is a provocative way of understanding how we relate to objects, and what we invest in them. So, for example, we might think about all the different life-stages of the object from its creation, who made it, why, and where, how it was used and understood, how it was acquired by different owners, what journeys it undertook, how it entered a museum or gallery, its treatment within the institution (labelling, conserving, storage, display and interpretation), whether it was disposed or whether it lives on in perpetual display. This cultural-history approach to thinking about objects has its parallel in material culture studies which takes the objects as central to the field of enquiry and uses the insights afforded by objects to illuminate larger societal concerns.

The anthropologist Daniel Miller has argued that people create and foster relationships with others *through* objects (Miller 2010). For Miller, social relations are created precisely *through* our relations to inanimate and animate things alike – that is, through our shared involvement in making and interacting with our material world of which we are each only one part. Relatedly, if differently, the philosopher Bruno Latour asks us to dissolve our usual distinctions between human 'subject' and man-made 'object'. He emphasises that all of the things we make have an 'agency' in the world that we 'delegate' to them. Indeed he argues that objects, instead of subjects, are the key to a new way of conceiving of politics as a whole: "objects – taken as so many issues – bind all of us in ways that map out a public space profoundly different from what is usually recognised under the label of "the political" (Latour 2005: 15).

ACQUISITIONING AND ACCESSIONING

The philosophical question of what comes to be acquired by museums, what is kept and what is thrown away also leads us onto the practical, legal and ethical issues surrounding acquisition, accessioning, disposal and de-accessioning. Acquiring and accessioning objects are distinguished in a UK context amongst others. For a public museum or gallery to accession an object is to enter into a formal arrangement to preserve it 'in perpetuity', as the conventional phrase has it, that is to say, forever, so far as is humanly possible. An object 'acquired' can find a home in any one of a different number of collections: it can be in a 'study collection' for example, which does not require the same standards of care and preservation. Only objects formally 'accessioned' need be kept forever.

The process of accessioning is what distinguishes museums from all other organisations that collect similar objects. 'Accessioning' differentiates what is to be cared for forever from, for example, documentation or 'secondary' collections. In many countries, over-seeing bodies ensure that collections that are properly 'accessioned' with a view to preserving them forever in deciding who and what is awarded official museum status.

What is 'accessioned' can change even when objects are in a museum already. For example, the UK's national collection of the art of photography is now held by the V&A Museum. However, until the late twentieth century this was essentially part of the National Art Library in the same institution, and not its fine art collections. This kind of institutional detail is important because it tells us that only in the 1970s did photography become fully recognised by museums like the V&A 'as art'.

The challenge of continuing to acquire new works for collections year on year through accessions is great. The problem of funding acquisitions of artworks is perhaps most acute in the museums sector because of the strength of the private market for art, both old and new. To give two startling examples: Tate's 'core' acquisition budget from its government grant-in-aid was £1.2m in 1981–2 (when known as the Tate Gallery). In 2014–15 it was £750,000, despite massive inflation in the prices of art in the thirty years in-between. In other words, Tate's 'purchasing power' in the market has been slashed. Equally striking is that Tate acquired nearly £75m of art in 2014–15, according to its annual report (Tate 2015). We can conclude from this that despite a tiny budget for an institution of its size, many new acquisitions were made – but almost entirely through gifts and cash donations. The UK government, in that year, only supported 1% of the institution's new collecting. Extraordinarily, nearly 99% of the financial value of objects came from private sources.

DISPOSAL AND DE-ACCESSIONING

If accessioning is how objects enter permanent collections, disposal and de-accessioning is how they leave. In the UK, an Act of Parliament, the Museums and Galleries Act 1992, governs the ways in which national museums can dispose of objects which have been formally accessioned into the collection. Only in rare circumstances and if agreed by museum trustees can objects be given away or disposed of. On the other hand, the boundaries between museums' remits have been open to negotiation: Tate and the National Gallery, for example, have transferred works to each other in order to ensure that, as the chronological or geographical boundaries of their collecting policies shift slightly, their respective collections are made more coherent and representative, despite their overlapping remits (both show British painting up to 1900; Tate Modern is concerned with "international modern and contemporary art from 1900 to the present" (Tate 2011) . Tate caused controversy in 2006 when it was revealed that the organisation, out of around 1,800 nationally funded museums, was the only one not accredited with the Museums, Libraries and Archives Council (MLA). Allegedly, it did not wish to abide by guidelines that de-accessioned work should first be offered to other museums. (The MLA threatened to bar Tate from acquiring works under the Acceptance in Lieu (AIL) scheme, whereby works are given to the nation to settle inheritance tax.)

Disposals of significant works of art in European museums, for example, are relatively rare occurrences, and in the UK museums can face sanctions if they attempt to break up collections. When Bury Metropolitan Borough Council attempted to sell a valuable painting by L. S. Lowry in 2006, the chairman of the Museums Association Charles Saumarez Smith wrote:

> If the sale goes ahead, the museum will be expelled from membership of the Museums Association and will lose its accredited status with the Museums, Libraries and Archives Council. This will mean it is very unlikely to receive funding in future from bodies such as the Heritage Lottery Fund.
>
> (Culture24 2006)

Such a threat carries weight.

The Kunstmuseum Bonn attracted headlines when in 2005 it sold the former Grothe Collection to a married pair of collectors, the Ströhers, for €50m, allowing the new director, Stephan Berg, to acquire younger artists' work which may increase in value. In 2013–14, the city of Detroit's bankruptcy led to a proposed plan to sell its art collection: the national opposition mobilised to the plan demonstrates the continuing strength of the idea that a museum is a space in which artefacts are passed down from generation to generation, and should not become tradable commodities once again. This is a distinct taboo for museum professionals in many countries.

CREATING VALUE

De-accessioning and disposal are often disapproved of because the status of objects changes radically over time so no-one can really know for certain what future generations will value. One provocative account of value change is Michael Thompson's 1979 book, *Rubbish Theory: The Creation and Destruction of Value*. Thompson does not only observe that an object's value is dynamic and context-dependent, but that a capitalist cycle of fashion *requires* new revisions of old objects as well as new objects. For Thompson, the differential between commodities that are 'transient' and 'durable', and what is disposable or what a shrewd investment, depends more on the climate of opinion rather than an object's intrinsic properties. The distinction is different to that between what economists call 'capital goods' (investments which generate new production or wealth) and 'consumer goods' (disposable items) precisely because in Thompson's theory, one can effectively turn into the other.

How does this work? At the simplest level, there are what are called 'early adopters': those who lead what later become wider trends. For example, much modern art famously experienced a 'time lag' between being accepted by museums and becoming popular. We also all know that fashions have cycles: when modernism became mainstream in the 1950s in the UK, Victorian art, furniture and architecture became taboo and in many cases almost worthless – until they, in turn, became highly fashionable in the 1980s. We all know, too, that some things appreciate over time while other depreciate in value. A new car might be worth half or three-quarters of its original cost after a couple of years of use. However, 'vintage' and 'classic' cars are assets whose value rises over time. (Old cars have an anomalous status at auction: it is perfectly acceptable for much of them to be refurbished, if the chassis is original. Whereas it is expected that artworks should be are entirely 'authentic' even if restored.) If we believe Thompson, practices of 'up-cycling' and gentrification – that is, *collective* as well as individual attempts to reposition objects in the landscape of commodities – are structural features of mature competitive economies. This is because they are based on competing claims to status and therefore wealth. What Thompson and his later critics can agree on is that it is, in the last instance, the social patterns of ownership associated with classes of object, or even individual authors that ultimately determine the value they are held to have.

Thompson's observations can be married with Fred Hirsch's diagnosis that some goods are part of a 'positional' economy. The value of some objects like luxury goods and artworks is based on their exclusivity (Hirsch 1976). As economists have put it, their value is defined negatively, by the fact that most people cannot own them. Even in a world dominated by reproducible media, desirability and exclusivity or rarity are inseparable and continue to define an object's cost.

PRICELESS OBJECTS AND 'MARKET VALUE'

Such observations lead us to the relationship between cost and 'value'. This has been a subject of immense interest to political theorists, sociologists and anthropologists for more than two centuries, as well as to museum professionals. One common observation worth reiterating is that museums provide a 'reserve' currency or national bank for classes of object, by maintaining their durability. They assure buyers and sellers of art and cultural artefacts of the value and permanence of their investments. Museums, then, do not merely house exemplary individual objects. They play two crucial roles. One is underwriting the markets for cultural artefacts. The second is of ensuring that all commodities have their relative values and longevities: some merely transient and expendable, some permanent and 'priceless'. Writers have understood this as resting on what museums exclude as much as what they keep.

The values attributed to cultural artefacts have hardly remained static: as David Harvey has written,

> the growth of the art market (with its concern for authorial signature) and the strong commercialization of cultural production since around 1970 have had a lot to do with the search to find alternative means to store value under conditions where the usual money forms were deficient.
>
> (Harvey 1990: 298)

By this he means that the phenomenal rise in prices of art and other cultural artefacts has been a result of elites acting collectively – if not deliberately – as a sort of cartel. This is not only through buyers' mutual 'suspension of disbelief' in the value of their investments. These investments are given authority by museums' public endorsement of them, and their role in ensuring certain types of object are scarce (by owning many of them). For such figures as Harvey, long-term 'asset price inflation' is not an accident, but the result of a kind of public–private partnership bolstering hierarchies of value created by competitive markets.

Art and cultural artefacts have become, alongside real estate, the premier investment choice for more cultured and less risk-averse financial elites. Museums' spending power has diminished proportionately. So we might say that the shift in relative prices of artworks and cultural objects is at the direct *and* indirect expense of the public. In the European model, citizens pay for museums and their acquisitions through taxes. In the US model, taxpayers subsidise elites' tax breaks for donating cultural goods to museums and acting in the wider public good. The relationship between financial elites and most museums is, at best, a two-way street in which institution, public and benefactor benefit alike.

There are cultural mechanisms and habits of mind that allow such processes, as well as legal and governmental arrangements in the form of charity and gifting laws. Whilst admitting that art objects form a special category in Western culture, anthropologists have illuminated how high culture is one part of broader 'material culture'. Various anthropologists have analysed objects in terms of how they are acquired or consumed, and exchanged, or else are 'sacred' and therefore cannot change ownership. These are the processes by which 'things' become meaningful, and come to have a social value. Anthropologists have also implied that museums are spaces in which we all observe a set of scripted social rituals, and 'perform' our part in them, thus indicating our adherence to a shared set of beliefs. The term 'rituals' should not be thought of as simplistic: quite the opposite. Instead, it is argued that all communities have rituals and spaces to act them out – these are precisely what mark out their belief structures and allow people to learn them, and reinforce them.

REGIMES OF VALUE: EXCHANGES AND EXCLUSIONS

Perhaps most significantly for museums, Arjun Appadurai has shown there are commonalities in the ways different cultures exclude particular types of things from being exchanged. He has observed that it is the job of museums to sanctify objects, precisely by securing them for the entire community and removing them from commercial exchange thereafter. Traditionally museums do indeed preserve a small cadre of rare, elite or 'representative' objects, both in perpetuity, and on behalf of their community, whether city or nation.

Appadurai has thrown light on this process of differentiating between objects we imagine should be in a museum and those that should be kept on 'the open market'. He notes:

> Few will deny that a commodity is a thoroughly socialised thing ... the commodity phase of the social life of any thing ... [can] be defined as the situation where its exchangeability (past, present, future) for some other thing is its socially relevant feature.
>
> (Appadurai 1986: 6, 13)

All commodities are participants in what he calls "regimes of value" (ibid.: 15). Indeed events like exhibitions are time-limited "tournaments of value" specifically designed to compete between, or test acceptance of, or inspire recognition of the value of special types of artefact (ibid.: 15, 21). This requires "entire zones of activity and production that are devoted to producing objects of value that cannot be commoditized by anyone" (ibid.: 22).

"The zone of art" provides one such arena in which value is contested – an arena agreed to be at a remove from the normal rules of commercial exchange (ibid.: 22). Appadurai noted that the division between 'priceless' public property and commercial trade was akin to that between the sacred and profane realms in pre-modern Europe. Medieval European ruling elites were divided between church and state. Similarly some 'elite' objects can exert 'spiritual' powers, and others worldly, 'temporal' powers. Certain objects are luxuries speaking about their owners' wealth and status, others speak about their owners' intangible worth and 'higher' or sacred qualities.

Appadurai argues that it is precisely:

> [e]conomic exchange [that] creates value. Value is embodied in commodities that are exchanged. Focusing on the forms or functions of exchange, makes it possible to argue that what creates the link between exchange and value is politics, construed broadly. This argument ... justifies the conceit that commodities, like persons, have social lives.
>
> (Appadurai 1986, 3)

Value is then often *initially* created through the potential for exchange. It is then consecrated and made permanent by being taken outside of the social sphere of exchange – by entering a museum or gallery.

PROTECTING THE NATION'S INTEREST: EXPORTS OF CULTURAL PROPERTY

Some historical artefacts or artworks are seen of such 'national' or artistic importance that certain governments prevent them being sold to buyers in other countries. This allows museums from their own country to have a 'head start' in trying to buy them from private collectors (DCMS 2013: 12). Such objects are not always ones created by native nationals, or even in the country. In the UK in 2015 a painting by the seventeenth-century French artist Nicholas Poussin, estimated to be worth £14m, was placed under 'export deferral'. In the UK there are three criteria used to judge whether the 'national interest' can override the free market. These are the so-called 'Waverley Criteria':

(a) Is it so closely connected with our history and national life that its departure would be a misfortune?
(b) Is it of outstanding aesthetic importance?
(c) Is it of outstanding significance for the study of some particular branch of art, learning or history?

(DCMS 2013: 12)

While the export deferral is in place, the sellers' rights are temporarily suspended. The adjudicating committee takes advice from museum professionals as to whether action is required "to avoid national misfortune" (DCMS 2013). The process is parallel to the 'listing' of buildings as it is known in the UK (see also Chapter 1). This is a system of heritage management by which some governments ensure that private citizens cannot alter or destroy buildings even if they own them outright. Buildings can be listed if they are deemed to be of architectural significance, of special significance to their place. Sometimes they can also be listed for their historical significance – that is, the buildings are fundamental to a community or nation's shared social history. In both instances, the law rests on the idea that there is a shared 'heritage' that it would be wrong to remove, amend or allow to leave the community.

MANAGING AND CARING FOR COLLECTIONS

While national agencies are responsible for the oversight of a community's material heritage, individual institutions have the ongoing responsibilities of caring for artefacts, normally held in collections. The conservation, preservation and documentation of collections is, as we have established, of paramount importance to almost all museums. The long-term consequences, complications and costs of maintaining any cultural property, art works amongst them, should not be underestimated. Tate estimates that the cost of acquisition is only about half the total outlay required when accessioning a work. The remainder is for the work's storage and care.

Across the last two to three generations, the expected standards of temperature, humidity, security and pest control in both display and store areas have been transformed. With these standards and rising fuel costs, the running costs of maintaining both display and storage areas in completely stable environmental conditions – twenty-four hours a day, 365 days a year – have become considerable. Some critics argue that such practice is environmentally unsustainable and therefore may have to be curbed. The recently rebuilt Whitworth Art Gallery in Manchester, UK, spent £15m on a new building without a full artificial cooling system, preferring natural ventilation and more sustainable means of controlling temperature and humidity. This is a new development for museums and galleries. As the architecture critic Rowan Moore has written, there is a national

British Standard – BS5454 – that specifies the design requirements for buildings used for "the storage and exhibition of archival documents" (quoted in Moore 2015). The Whitworth has deliberately not met that standard through the usual means for a reason other than to be eco-friendly. It is in recognition that museums in less wealthy countries cannot borrow objects from UK museums, and therefore are effectively excluded from the global trade in exhibits.

Who looks after objects? Professional conservators often specialise in certain types of media. However, there are some basic principles at stake both in understanding artefacts' material constitution in time, and shared received wisdom about certain courses of action. Firstly, almost no organic object of any kind remains identical over any long stretch of time. As the art historian Boris Groys (2009) has written, the mission of the museum is in effect to 'defy' time: to pretend that objects can stay the same forever. Conservators know that they cannot. Accordingly, their job is to either minimise, reverse, or redirect material changes, or to accept them while keeping an object in a stable and exhibitable state.

CONSERVATION, PRESERVATION OR RESTORATION?

To begin with: change is not always deterioration. In social history and natural history museums, the accumulated history of changes an artefact has been subject to is often the source of its value and interest. Even in art museums, there is debate as to whether returning historic objects to the state we imagine they were created in is worthwhile or desirable. For example, a high proportion of classical and medieval sculptures were originally painted. These include those on the facades of most European cathedrals. It is not current practice to 'restore' such facades to their 'original' appearance in the eleventh century by repainting them.

By contrast, Michelangelo's Sistine Chapel in the Vatican was 'restored' to what are believed to be the colours chosen by the artist in the sixteenth century, and which are vivid, bright and bold. Their new appearance is dramatically different to the low-toned, smoke-dulled colours seen throughout the twentieth century. To some, the work's subtle character had been lost.

In a more extreme example, Italy's former leader Silvio Berlusconi captured media attention for authorising replacement body parts, a hand and a penis, to be added to antique statues loaned to his office. The architect responsible, Mario Catalano, was reported as saying that:

> There are two philosophies of restoration. One is just to clean the work and leave it as it is. The other involves making the work whole again, without damaging it, to provide an image of the work as it was originally conceived.
>
> (Hooper 2010)

Catalano's remark illustrates one difference between 'restoration' and 'conservation'. 'Restoring' works is rarer, because it is often difficult to know what objects 'really' looked like, and because interventions can be irreversible, anachronistic, or later proven to be inappropriate. Conservators face a series of decisions about what they should attempt to undertake. In most instances, the fundamental goal is to arrest or prevent any inessential change, as far as possible. Less frequently it is to intervene, and actively restore or alter the character of an object. To what point in its lifespan should you 'restore' an object? To the moment of its inception, or at an 'ideal' point when it was most revered?

To summarise: 'conservation', 'preservation' and 'restoration' should be seen as distinct and separate concepts, each having quite distinct activities and courses of action associated with them. In each instance, scientific research and close, painstaking observation underpins any understanding of how materials change in time and how any treatment may affect them. There are numerous sources that professionals consult for reference and several postgraduate courses in conservation. John Thompson's *Manual of Curatorship: a Guide to Museum Practice* (1992) is one such source. There have been in-depth studies of almost every aspect of museums' technologies and conditions. These include lighting and its different sources, measured in intensity (by lux), by colour temperature (measured in kelvins) and crucially, whether ultra-violet parts of the light spectrum hit objects. In the UK, the Museums Association, through its journal *Museum Practice* (in print and online) monitors debates about the virtues of such new technologies as energy-saving LED lights. Each part of the field is so specialised that there are experts in every sub-sector in larger countries, whose services to museums seldom come cheap. Their costs are a reminder that the conservation of cultural heritage is a vital service to the whole community, at best, and one under-pinned by a code of ethics as much as by technological advances. Curatorship and conservation are both forms of 'stewardship'. Both sets of professions aim to ensure that the objects in their care can be appreciated by the greatest numbers now, and in the future.

CONCLUSION

Objects and collections remain a defining characteristic of muse-ums and galleries, despite the many ways in which these institutions have changed in recent years. As we have argued, societies from all around the world have invested these material traces of the past with extraordinary importance and status and continue to do so. However, the meanings and values which societies, communities, experts and individual visitors may attach to these objects are far from static or singular. Perspectives change as new interpretations are offered leading to a re-evaluation and revaluing of artworks and artefacts. Historic objects once hidden away may take on a new resonance and move centre stage in international politics because of their significance for contemporary politics. Looking after objects and collections remains a central function of the work of muse-ums and galleries today, as it has always been with all the attendant resourcing implications for storage, conservation and collections management. In recent years, digital objects and intangible herit-age have presented new challenges in terms of how museums and galleries collect, manage and interpret their collections. New tech-nologies, like 3-D printing, are offering new possibilities for creat-ing handling collections and replicas of certain kinds of artefacts, although it seems that the original object continues – for now at least – to be prized for its uniqueness. Looking forward, the crucial question is what should and can museums and galleries hope to col-lect and why? What picture of our contemporary societies will we leave to our children and grandchildren's generations? What will our descendants wish that we had collected for them to see and know about us? Given the proliferation of material objects in today's mass-produced, consumer society, the ability to make digital records of everything, and the environmental and financial costs of looking after it all, the challenge for museums and galleries to decide what and why to collect becomes ever more pressing. Whatever the challenges, it is a question that must be answered because the remains of our present will become tomorrow's past.

REFERENCES

Appadurai, A. (1986) 'Introduction: Commodities and the politics of value', in A. Appadurai (ed.) *The Social Life of Things: Commodities in Cultural Perspective*. Cambridge: Cambridge University Press.

Falk, J. and L. Dierking (2016) *The Museum Experience*. London and New York: Routledge (first edition 1992).

Graham, B. and S. Cook (2010) *Rethinking Curating*. Cambridge, MA: MIT Press.

Harvey, D. (1990) 'Time–space compression and the post-modern condition', in *The Condition of Postmodernity*. Oxford and Cambridge, MA: Basil Blackwell.

Hirsch, F. (1976) *The Social Limits to Growth*. Cambridge, MA: Harvard University Press. (New edition 1995, London: Routledge and Kegan Paul.)

Knell, S. (2004) *Museums and the Future of Collecting*. Farnham: Ashgate.

Krauss, R. (1999) *A Voyage on the North Sea: Art in the Age of the Post-Medium Condition*. London: Thames & Hudson.

Latour, B. (2005) 'From Realpolitik to Dingpolitik or how to make things public', in B. Latour and P. Weibel (eds) *Making Things Public: Atmospheres of Democracy*. Karlsruhe: ZKM Centre for Art and Media.

McClellan, A. (2008) *The Art Museum from Boullée to Bilbao*. Berkeley, CA: University of California Press.

Miller, D. (2010) *Stuff*. Cambridge: Polity Press.

Osborne, P. (2013) *Anywhere or Not at All: Philosophy of Contemporary Art*. London: Verso.

Schubert, K. (2000) *The Curator's Egg*. London: One-Off Press.

Thompson, M. (1979) *Rubbish Theory: The Creation and Destruction of Value*. Oxford: Oxford University Press.

Thompson, J.M.A. (ed.) (1992) *Manual of Curatorship: A Guide to Museum Practice*. Oxford and Boston: Butterworth-Heinemann.

White, D.E. (2013) *From Little London to Little Bengal: Religion, Print and Modernity in Early British India*. Baltimore, MD: John Hopkins University Press.

WEBSITES

bmorenews (2016) 'National Museum of African American History and Culture: Dedication and Grand Opening Saturday, September 24 2016'. 18 June. URL: http://www.bmorenews.com/home/2016/06/18/national-museum-of-african-american-history-and-culture-dedication-and-grand-opening-when-saturday-september-24–2016/?page_number_0=15

Culture24 (2006) '22.09.2006 – Bury Museum could lose museum status after Lowry sale says MA chief', in News In Brief: Week Ending 24 September. URL: http://www.culture24.org.uk/history-and-heritage/art40533

Department for Culture, Media and Sport (DCMS) (2013) *Export of Objects of Cultural Interest 2012/13*. URL: http://www.artscouncil.org.uk/advice-and-guidance/browse-advice-and-guidance/export-objects-cultural-interest-report-201213

Etherington, R. (2013) 'V&A acquires Katy Perry false eyelashes as part of new "rapid response" collecting strategy', *Dezeen*, 18 December. URL: https://www.dezeen.com/2013/12/18/rapid-response-collecting-victoria-and-albert-museum-kieran-long/

Givernet Organisation (2016) 'Giverny Museum of Impressionisms'. URL: http://giverny.org/museums/impressionism/presentation/

Groys, B. (2009) 'Comrades of Time', *e-Flux* #11, December. URL: http://www.e-flux.com/journal/11/61345/comrades-of-time/

Hooper, J. (2010) 'New penis for statue in Silvio Berlusconi's office', *The Guardian*, 18 November. URL: https://www.theguardian.com/world/2010/nov/18/fake-penis-statue-silvio-berlusconi-residence

International Council of Museums (ICOM) (2015) 'COMCOL: ICOM International Committee for Collecting'. URL: http://network.icom.museum/comcol/

Laurenson, P. (2005) 'The management of display equipment in time-based media installations'. *Tate Papers*, Tate website. URL: http://www.tate.org.uk/download/file/fid/7344.

Moore, R. (2015) 'Whitworth Art Gallery redesign is a breath of fresh air'. *The Observer*, 1 February. URL: https://www.theguardian.com/artanddesign/2015/feb/01/whitworth-gallery-manchester-muma-redesign

Museum of Modern Art, New York (2006) 'Explore the collection: Media and performance art'. URL: http://www.moma.org/explore/collection/media

Smith, T. (2013) 'Proposal for a museum: "You can be a museum, or contemporary…"', *San Francisco Museum of Modern Art Open Space*. URL: http://blog.sfmoma.org/2013/02/proposal-for-a-museum-terry-smith-you-can-be-a-museum-or-contemporary/

Tate (2011) 'Tate acquisition and disposal policy'. URL: http://www.tate.org.uk/download/file/fid/11111

Tate (2012) 'Acquisitions'. URL: http://www.tate.org.uk/about/our-work/collection/acquisitions

Te Papa Tongarewa Museum of New Zealand (2015) 'Our history'. URL: https://www.tepapa.govt.nz/about/what-we-do/our-history

FURTHER READING

Dudley, S., A.J. Barnes, J. Binne, J. Petrov and J. Walklate (eds) (2012) *Narrating Objects, Collecting Stories: Essays in Honour of Professor Susan M Pearce*. London and New York: Routledge.

Graham, B. and S. Cook (2010) *Rethinking Curating*. Cambridge, MA: MIT Press.

Knell, S. (ed.) (2016) *Museums and the Future of Collecting*. London and New York: Routledge.

Obrist, H.U. (2008) *A Brief History of Curating*. Zurich and Paris: JRP/Ringier & Les Presses Du Reel.

O'Neill, P. (2012) *The Culture of Curating and the Curating of Culture(s)*. Cambridge, MA: MIT.

Pearce, S. *et al.* (eds) (2016) *The Collector's Voice: Critical Readings in the Practice of Collecting*, Vols 1–4. London and New York: Routledge.

Smith, T. (2015). *Talking Contemporary Curating*. New York: Independent Curators Inc.

3

VISITORS AND AUDIENCES

WHO ARE MUSEUMS AND GALLERIES FOR?

As we have suggested, the answer to this question might be assumed to be obvious: 'everyone'. Yet as we have already seen, there have been formal barriers to visiting in the past, and in practice there are still marked differentials between who visits today, even where museums are free-entry. In the early years of public museums and galleries in the UK, entry was sometimes restricted to visitors who had a letter of invitation and adhered to the correct dress-code (see introduction). We might feel that these kinds of restrictive or elitist attitudes are long gone in today's public museums and galleries, and that museums welcome all people irrespective of age, gender, ethnicity or class. It is true that on the whole, there are few formal restrictions on admission in most countries. However, this does not mean that everyone goes to museums and galleries or feels that they are necessarily 'for them'. In fact, there are clear and repeated patterns in the profiles of visitors and non-visitors across many countries. It is easy to demonstrate beyond doubt that there are factors affecting why some people engage with museums and galleries and others do not, but the precise nature of the patterns, and their explanations, have been hotly debated. In this chapter we explore why this is the case, how museums and galleries have tried to respond to such issues, and the wider implications of these patterns.

WHO VISITS MUSEUMS AND GALLERIES? UNDERSTANDING VISITOR PROFILES AND GLOBAL TRENDS

There is an enormous amount of data on this topic internationally. 'Visitor studies' is a research area in its own right. It must also be remembered that visitors can now engage with museums both in person and online, and that museums assess both types of 'visit', even if not always equally. The broadest possible outlines of the data show that what are called 'traditional' visitors to museums and galleries in many parts of the world, for example, Western and Northern Europe, North-America and Australasia, are characteristically white, middle-aged adults, educated, relatively comfortable in financial terms, in employment, and in 'white collar' work. Time and again, surveys show that there are strong links between these socio-economic attributes and museum and gallery visiting. So what are they precisely, and how do we identify them or suggest causes?

It is possible to correlate the level of education with people's likeliness to visit: in fact this has long been identified as the single strongest 'correlate'. This is not to say that education *causes* visiting. Things are not so simple. There is no straightforward equation of cause and effect between 'being educated' and being 'a museum visitor'. It is rather more likely that a good proportion of people who are well-educated feel it is their 'role' to undertake such kinds of social activity in their leisure time rather than others and that they live in places where they are able to do so.

We all inhabit social circles in which some hobbies or leisure activities are positively approved of, others disapproved, and others considered inessential or we never think of doing them. We also know that certain activities require prior knowledge or 'practice' to be undertaken comfortably or 'properly', as it will be broadly understood within our own social peer groups. Broadly speaking, the research tells us that the higher people's educational attainment, the more likely they are to have been introduced to, and be comfortable in, museums and galleries as children. Those who frequently visit museums and galleries will also tend to socialise with, and know, other people who also feel that these places offer good ways to spend their leisure time, or that it is a social prerequisite to know about them. Those with PhDs are more likely to visit than graduates, who are more likely to visit than those who left school at 18, who are more likely to visit than those who left at 16.

Those who visit art galleries are even more likely to be highly qualified than those who visit museums, though this is, of course, to generalise from overall figures. "In the USA, among adults who visit an art gallery or art museum at least once in 12 months, 80 per cent have some college education, with 52 per cent of those with graduate degrees visiting" (NEA 2009 cited in Black 2012: 23). Black indicates a similar pattern in Canada and Australia where a study at the Australian Museum in Sydney "suggests 50 per cent of their audience have a university education or above" (AMARC 2003 cited in Black 2012: 23). Davison and Sibley (2011) reports a similar pattern in New Zealand. When a phenomenon is truly international like this, it requires investigation.

The following commentary on visitor profiles in Denmark also reinforces this picture, even though a 2011 study found that visiting is still more common overall in Scandinavia and the Netherlands than other parts of Europe (Brook 2011: 4):

> 26% of museum visits by people who live in Denmark are made by people with the highest education who make up only 7% of the population. 59% of visits to museums are made by people in the two highest educational brackets who compose only 21% of the population. Only 15% of museum visits are made by people with vocational training who make up 33% of the population, and only 17% of the visits are made by the 42% who have the lowest levels of education.
>
> (Sandahl, n.d.: 175)

A person's highest educational qualification is regularly found to be the single most important *predictor* of whether they will regularly visit museums and galleries (Brook *et al.* 2008). It is far from the only factor, but it is entangled with many others such as class, status, geography, as well as ethnicity and age in different ways. It is also itself correlated to other factors, such as wealth, professional identity, and geography. Put another way, when we breakdown the proportion of people who engage with the arts in England (not museums) by the local area they live in, we can see a stark hierarchy. Let us take London as an example. The single most expensive part of London, the Royal Borough of Kensington and Chelsea, has the highest proportion of people who make use of free and state-subsidised arts activities. The poorer parts have a lowest uptake, as we will see.

UNDERSTANDING THE STATISTICS: AN EXAMPLE

Statistics can be read in several ways. Let us look at four research reports from within one organisation, Arts Council England, to see how they offer quite contradictory conclusions. Their *Active Lives Survey* of 2009 "measured adult engagement with arts and culture in each local authority area in England", taking 'arts and culture' in its broadest sense (Arts Council England 2009). In that research, the very lowest level of uptake nationally of all subsidised cultural activities is in London: 29% of all adults, in Newham, East London. The highest is 65%, only a few miles away, in Kensington and Chelsea. If we look at another report, their 2011 *Audience Insight Survey*, we find that only 7% of all adults in England are "highly engaged". Only 3% are positively engaged with new rather than traditional art forms (Arts Council England 2011). Over a quarter of people do not participate in any cultural activity (as defined by the survey) or attend any institution. There might be two obvious answers to this. One is 'you can't force people to like museums: everyone has different tastes'. The other is 'not everyone lives in or near big cities where the most money is spent on museums and galleries'. The first is about motive, the second is about means. We might think it obvious that the more opportunities there are to visit cultural venues the higher the take-up. This is very broadly true, but people living in east London are (roughly) as near to many big museums as people in richer west London. So 'motivation' is a major factor. The effects of location and geography have been focussed upon recently because visitor studies had, in part, previously tended to prioritise individuals' demographic factors such as their socio-economic position and their motivations (Brook 2011).

The *Taking Part Survey* of 2014 (see Box 3.1) has various other factors to consider. Gender is not correlated to likeliness to visit overall, though ethnicity and age are to some extent.

BOX 3.1

QUESTION: DURING THE PAST 12 MONTHS, HAVE YOU VISITED A MUSEUM OR GALLERY?

Year	Yes
2014/15	52%
2005/06	42.3%

Age	16–24	25–44	45–64	65–74	75+
2015/16	47%	53%	56%	56%	34%

Year	White	Black or ethnic minority
2014/15	52%	48%

Year	Upper socio-economic group	Lower socio-economic group
2014/15	60%	38%

Note: The figures here indicate percentages of each category.

We might think this paints a fairly positive picture – though it only asks people about one visit in any year. However, if we ask how many *regularly* spend their leisure time on museums and galleries when averaged out from the whole country it is at most 22% (Morris Hargreaves McIntyre 2006: 11). With regard to just the arts (not museums) a 2008 report claims "84 per cent of the population fall into either the 'Little if anything' or the 'Now and then' groups, attending arts activities occasionally at most"

(Bunting *et al.* 2008: 7). So far, so confusing, perhaps but we can draw some conclusions.

First, some of these findings broadly tally with those in the US. According to the National Endowment for the Arts Survey of Public Participation in the Arts 2012: "US Museum-going saw a decline: 21 percent of adults (or 47 million) visited an art museum or gallery in 2012, [even if] down from 23 percent in 2008" (NEA 2012). New initiatives to remove charging for entry in the US may well have affected these figures since this study, though so far only a small number of places are providing free entry for the first time in their history.

Second, a recent study (Brook 2011) looking at cultural engagement across European countries has also tentatively proposed that there is a correlation between levels of government spending on culture and the number of people engaged. This much might seem obvious but it is worth reiterating given that levels of spending have been (and remain) under threat across most of Europe after the financial crisis of 2008–10.

Third, as we suggested, a key predictor of whether people will visit museums and galleries is both whether they were taken as a child and whether this early experience was positive. The importance of visiting as a child points to a fourth key feature of typical audiences to museums and galleries: the majority of such audiences today in many countries are family groups, although there are differentials between museums and galleries. In terms of family audiences, Black observes that they typically represent: "40 per cent to 55% of total visitor numbers" and that "for most of our users, a visit to a museum represents an occasional leisure-led event" (Black 2012: 18).

This ties to the fact that visiting habits are also influenced not just by age but by the 'stage' of your life. In other words your tendency to visit may well change over your lifetime. One UK study reported that:

Young adults (aged 15–24) with no children have the lowest average visit frequency, making 2.9 visits per annum. This age group is the most under-represented in museum and gallery visitors. Adults aged 55–64 who typically may have more leisure time because their children have grown-up or the adults are now retired visit most often, averaging just under 4 visits per year.

(Morris Hargreaves McIntyre 2006: 20)

DOES IT MAKE A DIFFERENCE IF MUSEUMS ARE FREE OR CHARGE?

When free admission was re-introduced in the UK's national museums and galleries in 2001, visitor numbers to those national museums and galleries which previously charged an entry fee increased significantly: by 128% at some sites between 2001 and 2009. The overall percentage of UK adults visiting museums and galleries has also increased, albeit by a much smaller degree. However, commentators have noted the *overall demographic profile* of museum and gallery visitors has tended to stay broadly the same. In other words, the introduction of free admission to national museums in the UK has meant, by and large, that more of the same kinds of people visit, rather than that there has been a massive broadening of types of visitors (MA 2010). These kinds of generalised national trends can help us see 'the big picture' but it is crucial to recognise that there are often enormous variations between different institutions. For example, the same report noted that "from 2007 to 2008 in England, although 57% of museums experienced an increased number of visitors, 35% experienced a decrease" (MA 2010).

Whilst we have talked about *predictors* and *correlations*, we have to make several qualifications. Not every educated person spends every weekend in a museum. The work of academic sociologists including Tak Wing Chan and John Goldthorpe is useful here. In a report for Arts Council England, Chan and a team of researchers systematically cross-compared multiple attributes against each other to see how they inter-relate. Overall, their findings echo our conclusion that

> The importance of social status in particular suggests that arts attendance is driven by some concept of identity – who we think we are, the type of people we perceive as our social status equals and the kind of lifestyle we deem appropriate ...
>
> (Bunting *et al.* 2008: 7–8)

Their conclusions, whilst drawn on European research generally, but here about England specifically, are worth repeating:

Two of the most important factors in determining whether somebody attends arts activities are education and social status .... Gender, ethnicity, age, region, having young children and health are also important factors. When all other factors are held constant women are more likely to attend the arts than men, older people more likely than younger people, white people more likely than Black or Asian people, Londoners more likely than those who live in other regions, people without children more likely than parents of young children.

(Bunting *et al.* 2008: 7)

In other words, education and what the authors call 'status' outweigh every other factor, including income. For them, 'class' and 'status' are different (Chan and Goldthorpe 2007). 'Status' is ultimately determined by 'who you know' and who you aspire to be. So, patterns of arts attendance and museum visiting are more complicated than the simple class-based picture presented by sociologists in the 1960s and 1970s. Rather, the researchers argue that

there does not appear to be any evidence of a cultural elite that engage with 'high art' rather than popular culture: the groups that are most active in the more niche arts ... are also the most frequent attenders of those activities that might be classed as popular culture.

(Bunting *et al.* 2008: 8)

Of course there remain important variations across the sector. Firstly, there are distinctions between different kinds of institutions (science centres versus galleries, say). Secondly, there are variations relating to geographical location, and the numbers and types of tourists that visit a city.

For example, in 2014–15, Tyne and Wear Archives and Museums in the North-East of England had only 5% of visitors from overseas, and 78% of visitors were 'local', i.e. live in the same region. Nearly two-thirds of all the visitors to the British Museum in London in the same year were from overseas (4.3m of 6.7m: 64%).

The economy of some museums can therefore be determined by international tourism or its absence. Do entrance costs deter visitors? The answer depends on whether we are talking about local visitors and tourists, and between one-off visitors or regular repeat visitors. This makes sense. If you have spent a large sum to go on holiday, an extra amount to go to a great museum is trivial as a proportion of that holiday. People simply see it as one small extra expense, and would not turn down the opportunity to visit (Been *et al.* cited in Black 2005: 19). By contrast, locals tend to view paying in isolation and in relation to what economists call an 'anchor price' of what they expect those individual things to cost. Given tourists' willingness to pay for museum and gallery visits, it is somewhat ironic in the UK that the policy of free admission applies to everyone. Tourism is of such value to many cities, and museums a central attraction, that their decisions have important effects (see Chapter 4 for further discussion). We might say that these museums are akin to the 'stars' in the Hollywood 'star system': a tiny proportion who command disproportionate resources and attention. It is worth reiterating that the majority of visits in total in many countries are 'local' ones, made by family audiences in their leisure time within their own region (Black 2012: 22–23). The time of travel is crucial: most visits are to institutions in under an hour or an hour and a half's drive away.

WHY DO PEOPLE VISIT? UNDERSTANDING VISITOR MOTIVATIONS

Having established who visits, we can ask why people visit museums and galleries. Lynda Kelly, head of the Australian Museum Research Unit, summarises why people choose to visit museums as follows (2009):

- as a worthwhile leisure activity;
- to be with, or do something as, a family or other social group;
- to be challenged;
- to actively participate in new experiences;
- for personal satisfaction and enhancing self-esteem;
- for fun and entertainment; and
- for education and learning.

Kelly's summary is consistent with research findings into visitor motivations in European, North American and Antipodean museums and art galleries (Black 2005; Davison and Sibley 2011).

Figure 3.1 Visitors at the Great North Museum: Hancock, Newcastle University.
© Colin Davison/Tyne and Wear Archives and Museums.

Interestingly, the precise order in which people give these reasons varies from group to group. Frequent visitors rank their reasons for visiting differently to occasional ones. It also varies according to nation, and to the kind of museum. For example, a three-year long, European-wide study of visitors to national museums found that in countries like Sweden or the UK 'entertainment' and 'pleasure' were ranked most highly. In countries "with more conservative educational agendas" visitors cited their own educational motivations most highly of all (Bounia *et al.* 2012). National museums are specifically expected to tell the story of nation's history authoritatively: finding out about this story is a key motivation for nationals as identification with it, or dis-identification, has such high stakes for both self-image and social position (ibid.). Visitor motivations will clearly differ in such a context.

Citing 'education' as a motivation for visiting remains significant in many countries because it is an expectation for many or most schools to take children and young people to them as part of their formal education. The links between the formal education system, and the 'informal' learning of self-directed visitors undertaken by families, have been studied closely. How closely aligned institutions are to agendas set by the formal education sector is often both determined by existing audiences, and the desire to ensure children visit because this activity is tied to governmental funding. In some cases, curatorial staff will design exhibitions specifically around key topics which they know are taught in schools because this is more likely to regularly attract school visits.

As indicated above, in European countries museum and art gallery visiting is often a family activity (Black 2005). For museums, it is essential to understand their visitors in terms of their leisure activities, and in terms of how they plan a 'family day out' and choose one destination over another. Minor differences can impact on such decisions. The key point is that the motivation to visit hinges both on the practical needs of the group, and the perceived 'fit' between their self-image, their social group, the museum's projected image and existing visitors, and what people want from their leisure time. Can the museum satisfy those needs or not?

Some scholars see museum or gallery visiting as a social activity or leisure pursuit above all else, comparable to, say, shopping and indeed competing for people's time with it (Savage *et al.,* 2005). Even in those contexts where public museums and galleries receive public subsidy, many have been repositioned by governments, and by directors, as part of the leisure and tourism sector. This shift presents museums with potential for expansion and higher income streams, especially when public subsidy is decreasing (Foley and McPherson 2000). The incomes generated from merchandising, shops and cafes can be substantial in larger cities and where tourists are plentiful. However, thinking about museums and galleries primarily as leisure attractions is not without its drawbacks. The perception that museums and galleries are, at root, part of the leisure and tourism industry rather than places for research and scholarship has implications for programming because of the emphasis it places on the need to attract numbers, and specifically repeat visitors. Viewed in this way, 'permanent' displays can seem a problem. Research has consistently identified that people do not go back to museums because they imagine 'nothing has changed' so they believe there is no incentive to go again.

This finding can be connected to the transformation of 'permanent' collection displays; to the growth in 'blockbuster' exhibitions; and to the rise of attention now given to programming events more broadly, as well as the attempt to 'incentivise' visits by creating a sense of an 'event' around every type of activity. Davison and Sibley (2011) argue that visitors are particularly motivated by the idea of time-limited availability. In other words, if someone believes that this is their only chance to see a particular exhibition, it prompts people to act. The high demand for high-profile, one-off blockbuster exhibitions described in the introduction to this book is evidence of this.

It is an obvious point, but it is clear that visitors' motivations and their perceptions of museums and galleries are also strongly affected by their relation to the 'public sphere', and to government, therefore. In many countries 'culture' is believed to have a high degree of autonomy, although no museum is completely free from state regulation and tax regimes. This is not always the case. In Romania, for example, the National History Museum was opened in 1972 to glorify and validate the rule of the dictator, President Nicolae Ceausescu and Comrade Elena Ceausescu, as Light notes:

> Following Ceausescu's overthrow, the National History Museum (in common with all other museums in the country) immediately closed the galleries which dealt with Ceausescu and the communist period. The museum [now] currently receives around 22,000 visitors a year, most of whom are from outside Romania.
>
> (Light 2000: 154)

AUDIENCE SEGMENTATION

As the above discussion makes clear, an understanding of *why* people visit museums and art galleries is inseparable from research into *who* visits. For many years organisations have approached this through the technique of 'segmentation'. This is a technique first developed in consumer and political research and involves various ways of classifying people. The question is which method will best identify both who does and does not visit and why. The challenge is to create the closest and most convincing correlation between visitation patterns and wider demographic factors. The essence of segmentation is to profile people by social type, by analysing their demographic characteristics and motivations. This profiling aims to capture a sense of how museum visiting does, or does not, fit into an individual's leisure habits and lifestyle.

The specific categories employed within segmentation approaches vary widely but the different typologies identified in various Arts Council England reports (Box 3.2) give a good sense of how it works. These three examples of categorisation are all based around the idea of different 'social types and associated lifestyles'. The first has thirteen types and the second has ten; the third merely identifies levels of engagement rather than being a proper 'segmentation'. All three are intended to identify the existing degree of engagement from highest to lowest and the percentages refer to the general adult population in England.

BOX 3.2

EXAMPLE 1

'Metroculturals'	Prosperous, liberal, urbanites interested in a very wide cultural spectrum	5%
'Commuterland culture buffs'	Affluent and professional consumers of culture	11%
'Experience seekers'	Highly active, diverse, social and ambitious, engaging with arts on a regular basis	8%
'Dormitory dependables'	From suburban and small towns with an interest in heritage activities and mainstream arts	15%
'Trips and treats'	They enjoy mainstream arts and popular culture influenced by children, family and friends	16%
'Home and heritage'	From rural areas and small towns, engaging in daytime activities and historic events	10%

'Up our street'	Modest in habits and means, occasional engagement in popular arts, entertainment and museums	9%
'Facebook families'	Younger suburban and semi-urban. They enjoy live music, eating out and popular entertainment such as pantomime	12%
'Kaleidoscope creativity'	Mix of backgrounds and ages. Occasional visitors or participants, particularly community-based events and festivals	9%
'Heydays'	Older, they are often limited by mobility to engage with arts and cultural events. They participate in arts and craft making	6%

Arts Council England/The Audience Agency (2016).

EXAMPLE 2

Highly engaged	'Urban arts eclectic'	3%
Highly engaged	'Traditional culture vultures'	4%
Some engagement (attend and may also participate)	'Fun, fashion and friends'	16%
Some engagement	'Bedroom DJs'	2%
Some engagement	'Mature explorers'	11%
Some engagement	'Mid-life hobbyists'	4%
Some engagement	'Retired arts and crafts'	4%
Some engagement	'Dinner and a show'	20%
Some engagement	'Family and community focused'	9%
Not currently engaged	'Time-poor dreamers'	4%
Not currently engaged	'Older and home-bound'	11%
Not currently engaged	'A quiet pint with the match'	9%
Not currently engaged	'Limited means, nothing fancy'	3%

Arts Council England (2011: 6).

(Continued)

(Continued)

EXAMPLE 3

'Voracious'	4%
'Enthusiastic'	12%
'Now and then'	27%
'Little if anything'	57%

Arts Council England (Bunting et al. 2008: 8).

An alternative approach is adopted by the UK based consultancy firm, Morris Hargreaves McIntyre, who have carried out extensive segmentation research in the UK to develop eight types based on *different motivations* rather than *social types*. They label these motivations: "Enrichment, entertainment, expression, perspective, stimulation, affirmation, release and essence" (Morris Hargreaves McIntyre 2010: 5–6). Do you identify yourself, or your immediate social group in any of these categories around types, lifestyles or motivations?

There is no universal consensus about the process of segmentation, and indeed marketing and visitor studies experts disagree about which kinds of segmentation and which kinds of correlation are useful for museums, even though it has been adopted as common practice for many years. Some museum studies scholars (Dawson and Jensen 2011) are sceptical of what segmentation can achieve. They argue that it fails to capture the degree to which people's attitudes and motivations are 'situational', and dependent on context. They would argue there is a difference between discovering patterns of behaviour from samples of visitors and 'reading in' too much to that data. It is also the case that motivations and behaviours will vary whether a visitor is alone or with family (Falk 2009) so that the same individual might adopt different visiting habits towards one museum against another. We also know people's attitudes towards their spending habits differ at home from when travelling, as discussed above. So the same individual may hold one set of values towards visiting museums in their home town and another set when they are visiting museums while on holiday.

Notwithstanding these arguments, segmentation is the central method employed by museums and galleries to understand their audiences, communities and visitors. The only real alternative is to undertake in-depth qualitative research methods which are both time-intensive and resource-intensive. These are not always able to be used to provide the kind of statistical data required by funding bodies and government agencies to prove who is reached by museums.

WHAT IS THE DIFFERENCE BETWEEN AUDIENCES, VISITORS AND COMMUNITIES?

We see this as a simple but important distinction to keep in mind. Visitors are those people who are *already* coming to the museum or gallery. Audiences are the wider *potential* range of people who could visit but may or may not yet. Museums and galleries, as we will see below, often identify key audiences that they wish to develop or with whom they consider they already have a good relationship, for example, a 'family audience'. We use the term 'community' to mean the group which the museum or gallery – as an institution – feels it has an obligation towards either to represent or to engage more actively. Typically these are the people who live within a particular radius of the institution and would therefore be considered its local community and its most likely pool of visitors (actual or potential). As should be clear by now, what proportion of the potential audience are already actual visitors will depend significantly on the educational and socio-economic profile of the local population, among other factors like the museum or gallery's reputation or how well it is marketed. This can be complicated when the demographic profile of the locality changes over time. In other words, the museum or gallery may be called upon to reinvent itself at different points in its history to keep pace with the changing nature of its local communities.

Alternatively, the 'community' may not necessarily be geographically defined, but still considered important to the museum because of their relationship with a particular aspect of the institution's collections or remit. For example, if a museum has a collection of model ships that are of special importance to a group of experts in maritime history, they might be considered one of its important community groups wherever they live. They may also be seen as amongst its key stakeholders (those with a stake in the future of the institution). Funding again plays a role in determining how a museum or gallery will think about its audience, community and visitors. If a museum or gallery is mainly funded by local taxpayers through public subsidy, as is often the case in Europe, there is a particular responsibility for the institution to acknowledge that. In practice this means being attentive to the demographic make-up of its audiences, communities and visitors, and particular needs or concerns of key groups. In this kind of case 'community interests' are typically seen to be represented by locally elected political representatives, or community spokespersons.

UNDERSTANDING NON-VISITORS' MOTIVATIONS

The *Taking Part* survey of 2015/16 found that in the previous year 52% of adults in the UK had visited a museum or gallery (DCMS 2016). This non-visiting statistic (48%) represents an improvement since 2005/06 when 42.3% visited and 57.7% did not. Notwithstanding these improvements, non-visiting remains a crucial issue in museum and gallery studies and in the sector as a whole. The *Taking Part* survey team has, like many other organisations, attempted to understand why people don't visit. In part, the way in which questions in these kinds of studies are asked determines the kinds of answers given. *Taking Part* reported that when people were asked spontaneously to say what stops them from attending museums or galleries, they frequently received 'generic' responses like 'lack of time'. However, when the researchers probed more deeply, it became evident that there were what they called deep-rooted "cultural, social and psychological factors" at stake (DCMS 2011). Some of these factors include a fear of feeling out of place, anxiety about not knowing the required social etiquette, fear of feeling intellectually inadequate, not knowing how to behave, or not belonging to social networks where others place value on museums and galleries. These factors echo Goldthorpe's observations as mentioned above and they underscore the old adage that 'we are the company that we keep'.

UNDERSTANDING ACCESS, AND BARRIERS TO ACCESS

These efforts to understand what might prevent people from visiting museums and galleries have led to a whole area of museum studies research around 'barriers to access'. Museum studies researchers, Dodd and Sandell (1998) have identified several forms of access, and barriers:

1 Physical access
2 Sensory access
3 Intellectual access
4 Financial access
5 Emotional/attitudinal access
6 Cultural access.

This approach has been very influential in informing museum and gallery practice and policy in the UK context. For example, the Cambridge Museum of Archaeology and Anthropology explicitly draws on this scheme in their 2014 Access Policy Statement. Such policies are standard practice in the UK and they explain the purpose of their policy as follows: "This policy guides MAA's approach to providing access to its collections and associated information. We define access as something that is enabled when physical, sensory, intellectual, cultural, emotional and financial barriers are removed, reduced, or overcome" (University of Cambridge 2014).

They interpret the categories as follows:

In order to eliminate barriers to access we will consider the following forms of accessibility:

Physical:	to enable people with physical disabilities to reach and appreciate every part of the museum. This includes the needs of the elderly and of people caring for young children. Where physical access poses severe problems, alternative arrangements will be made to provide some experience of that part of the collection or service for visitors.
Sensory:	to enable those with impaired vision or hearing to enjoy and appreciate the museum's building, exhibitions and collections.
Intellectual:	to enable people with learning disabilities to engage with and enjoy the museum and its collections. We also recognise that people have different preferred modes of learning and will provide interpretation to suit a range of learning styles.
Cultural:	to enable those for whom English is not a first language, or whose knowledge of English history and culture may be limited.
Emotional and attitudinal:	to ensure that the museum environment and workforce are welcoming to all types of visitors.
Financial:	admission to MAA is free.

(University of Cambridge 2014)

The need for 'physical access' is to ensure that all visitors (able-bodied and those with physical disabilities) can actually enter and negotiate buildings or sites on equal terms and with equal ease. (Access to museum websites also needs to be taken into account.) Physical access can be a problem where a building is a historic property that cannot be readily amended but the institution needs to show it has endeavoured to find ways around this problem. 'Sensory' access is also about whether museum or gallery collections, spaces and interpretation are available to visitors with disabilities, for example, sight or hearing. Much work has been done in recent years around alternative methods for making collections accessible, for example creating opportunities to touch objects for those with sight impairments or to provide audio descriptions for those with hearing impairments.

'Intellectual' access refers to the level of knowledge required to understand and engage with the content and interpretation of museums and galleries. In the past, the interpretation of many museums and galleries was pitched at a level which would have been much higher in educational terms than the average member of the public, measured by reading age. Again, in some countries, efforts have been made to recognise that people come with differing amounts of knowledge about a given topic, and about visiting. In addition, many museums and galleries (as above) have adopted the idea of 'learning styles' in order to cater for visitors' preferred manner of accessing information (e.g. through touch, audio or text), although we must point out that this idea has been subject to significant recent critique in related fields (see Coffield 2013).

'Financial' access is about recognising that for some groups on a low income the cost of admission could be a deterrent, particularly when the overall cost of the visit is factored in. For example, there is a balance to be struck between a museum's cafe or paid-for activities making profits to subsidise the organisation, and making visits prohibitive for lower-income groups. This last point is much debated because research into visitor motivations has shown that cost is not necessarily the main barrier to visiting. This has been proven when admissions charges have been removed, as in the UK (in 2001) and certain US institutions recently. As indicated above, one conclusion to be drawn from this is that there are other more deep-rooted reasons as to why certain demographic groups feel that museums and galleries are not, or even never will be for them.

Returning to Dodd and Sandell's terminology, it is important to note they highlight that barriers are often about 'emotional and attitudinal' access. This is obviously more difficult to address. Many people see institutions as precisely that: 'institutional' or associated with authority they reject, or associated with other types of people, or simply boring or irrelevant. In the particular case of art galleries, there is plentiful research that when meaning is not immediately self-evident, people feel either they, or the object, must be 'deficient' for it to fail to signify. The only logical responses are that either they cannot see what they are meant to and must be ignorant of something others can see, or else the artwork itself is fraudulent or a failure as an artwork meant to communicate something.

'Cultural' barriers are closely related to attitudinal and emotional but may have a specific inflection; for example, the association of particular museums with a history of empire may be directly off-putting to potential visitors from ethnic groups with a particular historical experience of colonialism. If a museum holds a collection of historic materials which depicts certain ethnic or religious groups in what would now be seen as racist and derogatory terms, this might well be judged as offensive. This raises thorny ethical and philosophical questions. Should a museum or gallery in that situation remove such materials from display to avoid offence to current audiences or should they leave them on display with new interpretation precisely to warn contemporary visitors about the history of racism and past persecution of certain groups? If they remove them there is the risk that we might forget such histories ever happened and not appreciate what those groups suffered. If we leave them on display there is the risk of somehow appearing to give recognition and space to ideas that contemporary society would find unacceptable. What is offensive to one community may not be offensive to another. Access policies run into similar ethical conundrums in terms of 'restricted knowledge' which is knowledge held as sacred, secret or private to a particular group. In this instance, a community may argue that artefacts related to such knowledge are not for public sharing and that it is not the museum's right to break their conventions of confidentiality. At the Cambridge Museum of Archaeology and Anthropology they deal with this as follows: "Access may be restricted in cases where the cultural sensitivity of the material in question means that providing access would contravene the expressed opinions of stakeholder communities" (University of Cambridge 2014).

Access to information and to decision-making processes are identified more generally as significant barriers. In the first instance, potential visitors may simply not know about the museums or galleries even when they are free because they do not move in the kinds of networks where this information circulates. This is an issue which closely relates to marketing and how institutions think about the potential audiences they may be able to reach through different media channels. Access to decision-making refers to the idea that for many people visiting a museum or a gallery may seem like a passive activity and their sense of what happens behind the scenes is very unclear. The argument here is that this, in some cases, may result in a sense that the museums have no relationship with entire *communities* rather than individual visitors. This is an area where much work has been undertaken in recent years in many countries under the heading of 'community engagement'. All of the above barriers can be seen to be interrelated, overlapping, or mutually compounding; isolating them can be difficult.

The *Taking Part* report confirms many of these same factors but organises them according to three main headings: *intra-personal, inter-personal and external factors*. These distinctions are very useful in clarifying how people are aligned, and on what grounds. *Intra-personal* factors are identified as:

> The attitudes, beliefs, knowledge and skills that every individual builds from their environment, culture, and past experiences pre-dispose people to participate or avoid participation. These factors determine whether a person will want to experiment with a new activity or event, and whether they are likely to persevere with something they have already tried out.
>
> (Arts Council England 2011: 13)

Inter-personal factors are seen as:

> Approval from one's wider community, and from family and/or friends, can be an implicit motivating force for engaging in an activity or event; on the other hand, when others in a person's social network disapprove or show a lack of interest or familiarity in a type of activity or event, a person is less likely to develop an interest or desire to take it up.
>
> (Ibid.: 14)

We might describe this as forms of peer pressure, though we note that the anticipation of reactions is as important as real ones. *External factors* are outlined as being:

> whether individuals feel that the physical environment is accessible both internally in terms of lifts but also externally in terms of transportation and time (e.g. how far away it is) and welcoming. The perceived quality of the provision is a factor here as is availability of information about what is on offer.
>
> (Ibid.: 14)

What is striking about this analysis is that it highlights the extent to which people base their decisions to visit on a cost–benefit analysis of sorts, and what they imagine it would provide: what opportunities there are for enjoyment, social approval or validation, and what threats to one's identity or investments are at stake.

This is also where changes in people's life-stages are important, as identified above. It may be that when individuals become parents or grandparents that they become motivated to visit museums or galleries again, after a period of feeling it was not worthwhile. As we have seen earlier, broadly speaking, family groups account for the majority of visits. One study, in particular, argued that parents do precisely visit museums in order to perform 'good parenting' behaviours to themselves, to their children and to their peers (Savage *et al.* 2005). Many of these issues around access and barriers were described or anticipated by the French sociologist, Pierre Bourdieu.

BOURDIEU'S THEORY OF CULTURAL CAPITAL

Pierre Bourdieu (1984; Bourdieu *et al.* 1991) is one of the few figures to have genuinely transformed the way we can see museums and galleries. Very broadly, he proposed that in modern, competitive societies, status hierarchies govern who we are and are able to be. We all know that the best-known form of 'capital' – money – allows us to do certain things and not others. With certain amounts of money we can be certain types of people, living in particular places and by doing certain things, we can become a certain type of person. Bourdieu argued that in 'capitalist' societies, all other forms of status could be measured using the same term – so that we all have different types and quantities of what he called 'social capital' and 'cultural capital'. Very broadly, 'cultural capital' refers to the amount of knowledge and skills people have in regard to what Bourdieu called 'legitimate culture': that given 'official' recognition by elites and accepted as the culture of people of 'distinction'. The forms of capital can be converted into one another when needed: we can try to buy social advantages by living and working amongst certain types of people rather than others, and can buy access to information and knowledge, even if education itself requires more than money.

Bourdieu argued that we build our stocks of 'cultural capital' in several ways. We acquire it through the schooling we receive in the formal education system by what we are taught, where, and by whom. Schools work to differentiate us: in Bourdieu's scheme, they act as a sorting machine for providing society with different people to undertake different professional and social roles. Crucially, each role we play reinforces the others. Through extensive empirical research into Europeans' leisure activities, tastes and preferences, Bourdieu established that society does indeed classify people into groups whether we admit it or not, and that people's income, social position and 'tastes' mostly align. Our 'choices' are not quite as personal, as random or as unpredictable as any of us would like to imagine. He established beyond any reasonable doubt that participation in the arts, and museum visiting, is a matter of possessing 'cultural capital' and is correlated to, if not directly caused, by identification with or membership of one status group or another. Later sociologists, including John Goldthorpe and Tak Wing Chan, broadly concur with this as we have discussed above.

At another level, it relates to national issues, for example, whether a country has a national curriculum which is broadly standardised. Underpinning that national curriculum will be broader cultural perceptions about what is 'valid' *as* culture and as knowledge. This 'official' knowledge is known as 'the canon'. The canon is the body of knowledge of a particular field, profession or community, which is given privileged status as its authorised account, or as the sole account. Bourdieu's work suggests that 'knowledge' and 'culture' always advance some people's interests, and not others. How education can be a political and ideological battleground is, of course, an enormous issue.

Bourdieu's central contribution, however, was to emphasise that 'cultural capital' is not *only* accumulated through formal education. He argued that the individual also receives their knowledge of cultural forms, such as art, at home and from their family. Our position in society is in large part created by what he called our "habitus": the nature of our upbringing and the type of education we receive. Parents with high levels of cultural capital will pass this on, precisely by taking their children to art galleries, by teaching them about art, or simply by owning books about art in their houses, which normalises that interest.

Individuals learn not just about the canon as a set of works, but about museums and galleries as *social* institutions to which they own the intellectual 'keys'. Bourdieu's more contentious point is not that knowledge is acquired through socialisation, but that knowledge as it stands is socially *divisive*. His argument is that in creating distinctions – status differentials – the arts in particular are not socially neutral, but serve particular interests, at least in their current forms.

Whether or not individual artists believe his argument, Bourdieu would argue that 'the arts' and the sector of 'official culture' act both as a shield to defend the existing social hierarchy, and as a weapon that classifies some as 'superior' and others 'inferior'. If we accept even part of this thesis, several questions follow. Can we avoid this? Can a system be changed 'from the inside'? Are European museums and galleries intrinsically socially divisive? Are non-Western institutions different? Have things changed since Bourdieu formulated these ideas?

Bourdieu began writing in the 1960s, and carried out his research in France. His definitions of culture at that time were based on a view of a clear distinction and hierarchy between 'high' culture and popular culture. Much more recent analyses like Goldthorpe and Chan's have either blurred these categories, or shown that elites command knowledge of *both* areas and have expanded their 'cultural capital' across all fields where status is at stake. They have written extensively about this: the 'omnivore' hypothesis is the idea that higher status groups can access *both* 'high' and 'popular' forms with equal ease, as though culturally multilingual, in the way that lower status ones cannot. This has become one of the main arguments in visitor studies.

Some sociologists may qualify his main argument but the power of Bourdieu's argument remains undeniable. Evidence bears out that our 'disposition' to gallery-going in particular and museum attendance more widely, is created or at least reinforced by particular types of education and socialisation. They are habits that are both acquired by them being thoroughly social activities, through a long process of acculturation. It also cannot be denied that 'high' culture retains a special status nearly fifty years after Bourdieu began his work even if it is no longer class-specific in its take-up. In many countries, the fine arts are still given state subsidy or tax breaks, while pop music and computer games rarely are. Only the former are 'legitimate culture' in Bourdieu's terms, supported by governments and collected as investment-class assets by elites. Artists themselves have complicated some of these distinctions since Bourdieu began his career – but the distinction holds, as do many of the patterns of visitor demographics. We will return to the implications of these issues at the end of this chapter. At the same time, it must be stressed that many museums and galleries have transformed themselves into much more welcoming and more accessible places than ever before. Despite these advances, one barrier remains particularly challenging to overcome: ethnicity.

ARE MUSEUMS AND GALLERIES 'WHITE SPACES'?

In 2015, the Whitney Museum of Art in New York reopened in a new building. The guest of honour at that opening ceremony was Michelle Obama, the first lady of the United States of America and the first and only African-American first lady in American history to date. In her speech, she said:

> [T]here are so many kids in this country who look at places like museums and concert halls and other cultural centers and they think to themselves, well, that's not a place for me, for someone who looks like me, for someone who comes from my neighborhood ... I know that feeling of not belonging in a place like this ... I know how that feeling limits the horizons of far too many of our young people.

Michelle Obama's comment reflect repeated calls in recent years for US museums and art galleries in particular, but European ones as well, to recognise that the profile of their visitors is skewed, not only in relation to socio-economic and educational factors, but in relation specifically to race and ethnicity. The American Association of Museums (AAM) has clearly identified the same issue, noting that disparities of access have become wider, not narrower, over time:

> [W]hite Americans were over-represented among adult art museum visitors in 2008 (78.9 percent of visitors, while just 68.7 percent of the U.S. population) while Hispanics and African Americans were significantly

underrepresented . . . . Between 1992 and 2008, the gap between the percentage of white and non-white Americans who visit art museums also grew steadily

(Farrell and Medvedeva 2010: 12)

Similar discussions are evident in European countries such as the UK. While the statistics tell a clear story, there are multiple intersecting reasons. In the US, for example, the history of racial segregation and exclusion of Black people from public spaces has a long legacy because it has resulted in lower level of museum-going tradition among African-American families compared with their white American counterparts (Falk 1995 cited in Farrell and Medvedeva 2010: 12). Despite some variables, in this study African-Americans reported a generalised perception that museums were not 'for them' and it was identified that they were much less likely to have been taken as a child or, as adults, to be socialising with others where it was a common and valued leisure pursuit. If Bourdieu is right about the extent to which children's early socialisation forms their lifelong attitudes towards cultural consumption, this means that wholesale structural change in this regard may only be achieved generationally, rather than over a rapid timescale.

A significant disincentive for some ethnic groups also relates to the history of European colonialism and its legacies, which can still be seen in many museums. As already discussed, many European museums routinely collected cultural property and human remains from indigenous people in territories that became European colonies. It is unarguable therefore that from the nineteenth century, even if very broadly speaking, European museums were part of a coherent worldview in which 'races' were hierarchically ordered in terms of their degree or stage of supposed 'civilisation' and culture. These attitudes were overturned by political change in some countries through the winning back of independence for those former colonial countries in the latter part of the twentieth century, although some would say that the decolonisation of museums has still not fully happened in all places.

Where change has been slower is in those countries where indigenous or former colonial peoples are ethnic minorities with limited access to the kind of power required to effect widespread institutional change in the public sphere. We might take as examples first-nations people in North America, or aboriginal peoples in

Australia. In these contexts, people from so-called 'minority ethnic groups' continue to report a residual sense that the culture on display is not *their* culture; or that they are under-represented in the types of histories told. There is undoubtedly validity to these points. Few European powers, for example, have public museums which provide full or candid accounts of their colonial histories and empires. These histories are crucial to understanding contemporary, multicultural European society. Yet they are seldom explicitly told or acknowledged, let alone understood even though evidence of them is present in almost all museum collections.

VISITING PATTERNS IN RELATIONSHIP TO STAFF DEMOGRAPHICS

Another way in which museums and art galleries are reportedly perceived as 'white spaces', and unwelcoming to audiences of other ethnicities relates to the demographic of their staff (Farrell and Medvedeva 2010). In recent years, studies have shown that the most staff of North American and European museums and galleries are not only largely but overwhelmingly white, middle-class, middle-aged and born into higher status social groups. Concern over this within the sector gave rise to almost a decade of positive action initiatives from around 2000 in the UK administered by the Museums Association and the Arts Council of England with the aim of increasing the numbers of black and minority ethnic staff in museums and public art galleries. Information over the nature of these schemes and their successes and shortcomings can be found on the websites of these organisations and within professional magazines. Whilst the arguments around affirmative action have moved on in certain respects, most European countries and North America are a long way from reaching a point where it will never be needed.

INCLUSION INITIATIVES AND POLICY AGENDAS

Concerns over visitor demographics have also led to policy initiatives intended to target specific 'hard-to-reach' audience groups. These initiatives have originated both with funding bodies and governmental priorities, and from within the sector. Between 1997 and 2010 the UK government took the view that what they termed 'social exclusion' was an underlying problem in many aspects of British society, and affected health, crime, unemployment and education. All government departments were required to consider how they could contribute to tackling the causes of the marginalisation or 'exclusion' of particular demographic categories. With their visitor demographics weighted towards those with more wealth, education and cultural capital, state-subsidised museums and art galleries were subject to such policies. At the same time, some art galleries and museum professionals – for example, those with a commitment to social history, community history or equality generally – were already making the same case from within the sector. The result was a period where governmental funding flowed towards initiatives oriented at tackling inequality, as experienced through 'exclusion' from public culture and its institutions. Emphases have changed recently and funding has been rerouted to some extent, although equality legislation in EU states remains committed to such principles.

AUDIENCE DEVELOPMENT

Within the sector and much academic literature, the political and ethical desire to contribute to broadening museum and gallery audiences is a long-term project. New thinking about the representation of gay, lesbian and transgender people in museums and galleries is creating alternative forms of engagement. For example, the Van Abbemuseum in Eindhoven's project of 'Queering the Collection' continues its commitment to radical ideas by "contributing to the visibility of the LGBTQ heritage in the arts" but goes well beyond merely acquiring work by gay artists. Instead, this commitment is being realised across the entire institutional apparatus: programming, collecting and publishing (Van Abbemuseum 2016). Even the museum's visitor facilities have been changed accordingly:

> People who do not have such an obvious identity feel victimized, classified in boxes [in gendered toilets], and feel that others tell them which toilet is for them and which is not. The Van Abbe would like to avoid these unfortunate confrontations by introducing gender-neutral toilets.
>
> (Ibid.)

This reaching out and considering the viewpoints of 'new' or 'hard to reach' groups is described as audience development.

'Audience development' refers to work specifically undertaken across all areas of the organisation to develop existing audiences or build relationships with potential new ones. Typically, audience development is concerned with more than simply increasing numbers, although this may be one goal. Usually, the intention is to broaden the range of visitors and, in some cases, it is to diversify them in terms of specific categories, often relating to identity or socio-economic groups. Audience development can take many forms, and as we have seen, can be addressed across all aspects of the organisation's activities including ones that would never previously have been addressed or thought about in terms of access and development. The longer the duration of initiatives, the greater the institutional commitment and buy-in from the top management, and the more concentrated they are, the greater the likelihood of impact.

BUILDING NEW AUDIENCES THROUGH COMMUNITY ENGAGEMENT

These efforts to broaden audiences and target those who have not attended previously are also undertaken through a whole range of community engagement work and outreach activities. Many museums and art galleries have a long tradition of community engagement work, particularly where the largest community demographics are not that of typical museum visitors elsewhere. This work has been motivated by a belief on the part of museum and gallery professionals that their institutions have a responsibility to engage with the communities who surround them and whom they claim to represent. In many cases, there is also a recognition of the political dimensions of this responsibility and how inequality in terms of access to cultural resources links to, and can reinforce, inequalities in other aspects of society.

In recent years, questions of community engagement have become debated intensely. In much of Europe, the imperatives to increase access have become sharper as public funding has been reduced and the justification of resources has become harder. In some cases activities are a response to the new museological ideas discussed above and to the growing recognition of the fact that visitor demographics are simply not representative of the entire population in almost any country.

A key driver for community engagement in some countries is to recognise and redress the political imbalances around the representation of minority or marginalised groups, as we outlined. In such contexts it is recognised that a specific community group or individuals do possess a specific body of knowledge, and type of experience which gives them the authority to speak about a given topic. Michael Frisch helpfully identifies this as the authority which "is grounded in culture and experience rather than [necessarily in] academic expertise" (Frisch 1990: xxii; see also Hutchinson 2013: 145).

A striking example of this is the involvement of the Native American people in the creation of displays about their own cultures in the National Museum of the American Indian in Washington, USA (Figure 3.2).

Figure 3.2 Exterior view of the National Museum of the American Indian, Washington, DC.

© Rhiannon Mason.

This museum was first planned in 1980 and finally opened in 2004 with a ceremony which included a six-day "First Americans festival and a Native Nations Procession" (NMAI 2005). The NMAI describes itself on its website as being

> steadfastly committed to bringing Native voices to what the museum writes and presents, whether on-site at one of the three NMAI venues, through the museum's publications, or via the Internet. The NMAI is also dedicated to acting as a resource for the hemisphere's Native communities and to serving the greater public as an honest and thoughtful conduit to Native cultures – present and past – in all their richness, depth, and diversity.
>
> (NMAI 2005)

In this museum, the interpretation is largely delivered through contributions from individual tribe members who are identified as community curators, by name and tribe, and given full recognition as experts on their own cultures and histories.

Example text from a label at NMAI:

> "Today we, the younger generation, seem to lack knowledge about the importance of the drum. We have become ignorant about the care and respect for it."

> Marie Meade, known as Cupluar in Yup'ik, is 55 years old. An interpreter and translator, she teaches the Yup'ik language at the University of Alaska, Anchorage. She studies Yup'ik collections in museums throughout the world, and brings the knowledge home to the Yup'ik people.

In some cases, as shown here, those individuals are also spokespeople, academics, and experts in the scholarly sense. These people embody both forms of Frisch's expertise. This museum is undoubtedly one of the most powerful examples of how community knowledge has become accepted as a valid and valuable form of 'expertise' in its own right. In this respect, this museum represents a high-point of community involvement and ownership.

MODELS OF 'COMMUNITY ENGAGEMENT'

Various scholars and curators have created typologies of the models of 'community engagement' practised by museums and art galleries.

We should begin by saying that neither the term 'community' nor 'engagement' has a universally agreed definition. However, author and curator Nina Simon categorises them as follows:

- In *contributory* projects, visitors are solicited to provide limited and specified objects, actions, or ideas to an institutionally controlled process. Comment boards and story-sharing kiosks are both common platforms for contributory activities.
- In *collaborative* projects, visitors are invited to serve as active partners in the creation of institutional projects that are originated and ultimately controlled by the institution.
- In *co-creative* projects, community members work together with institutional staff members from the beginning to define the project's goals and to generate the program or exhibit based on community interests. The staff partners with visitors to co-produce exhibits and programs based on community members' interests and the institution's collections.
- *Hosted* projects are ones in which the institution turns over a portion of its facilities and/or resources to present programs developed and implemented by public groups or casual visitors. This happens in both scientific and cultural institutions. Institutions share space and/or tools with community groups with a wide range of interests, from amateur astronomers to knitters. Online, programmers may use cultural object registries or scientific data as the basis for their own research or products. Game enthusiasts may use the grounds of an institution as a giant game board for imaginative play. Hosted projects allow participants to use institutions to satisfy their own needs with minimal institutional involvement.

(Simon 2010: n.p., authors' italics)

Like Simon, many commentators agree that there are significant differences between the types of community engagement and participatory work that are possible. There are ideological differences about what *type* of relationship an institution can have with groups, and about what are the ideal process and outcomes, not merely what *degrees* of engagement are possible. 'Higher' degrees of involvement do not intrinsically or necessarily mean better outcomes for either groups involved, other visitors, or institutions.

A common question raised by this kind of work is should 'the community' be read as representatives of existing visitors, or should representatives of particular demographic groups be involved in every kind of decision making at the highest level? Where does that leave museums' expertise? To recap: the point as Simon stresses is that we should not think of engagement in a hierarchical way, where contribution is automatically viewed as less valuable than co-creation. Each project and museum or art gallery needs to identify not only the partnership desired, but a distinct way of relating to people that is appropriate for the goals of that institution and for its relevant communities. This is seldom easy, and it is hardly possible to please everybody at the same time, if at all.

At the same time, it should be acknowledged that certain types of community projects have received criticism precisely for their lack of real 'engagement'; they have been called "participation-lite" (Lynch 2010). The criticism here is that such work either does not, or cannot go far enough and is 'tokenistic', however sincere the intentions. Lynch raises a real question: does the institution itself remain fundamentally unchanged? Simon believes that "the differences among participatory project types are highly correlated with the amount of ownership, control of process, and creative output given [both] to institutional staff members and visitors" (Simon 2010: 1).

A critical issue here is how we understand the core concept of 'community'. In recent years, museums and galleries have been strongly encouraged by academics and funders to engage with their communities, and this has been a powerful rallying cry to make these institutions think about their role in society and barriers to access for their audiences. Yet, the very term has been criticised in academic literature as an idealistic one, as falsely unifying people into a simple category. Used uncritically, the term 'community' can run the risk of suggesting that diverse people are a homogenous group which can be given voice by simply providing access to the museum as a public space. As a mere synonym for 'the general public' or 'audience' it is a weak term: we avoid using it in that sense. These terms are not the same, and require great care (Watson 2007).

It is important therefore when working with community groups to think carefully about the criteria for deciding who constitutes a community. Are they self-defining or being defined by other parties, like governmental agencies? Do they respect other communities and ethical principles like human rights and equality? It is essential to establish a clear, ethical and institutionally agreed set of principles for deciding how to judge different groups' claims to being a legitimate community. For example, far-right political leaders often claim to 'represent' an oppressed 'community' but their claim is not one that would be usually recognised or acceptable to the broader public and most museum and gallery professionals.

'Community leaders' can be self-appointed, or not fully represent a diversity of views even within one group. Have they been formally nominated by a group? How did these individuals achieve their position of visibility or 'representativeness'? These issues matter because authority and legitimacy are closely tied together just as much for community groups as they are for museums. Another important consideration when thinking about community involvement in museums is that individual 'communities' may well not necessarily share, or even adhere to, the museum's broad remit to represent the 'public' more widely. There can be both inter-group and intra-group conflicts that museums need to be aware of and indeed careful of. In zones of explicit conflict or with contested histories this can be challenging, if not an ultimately insoluble problem. In some situations, different community groups simply may not want to share the same public spaces.

The Polish artist Artur Zmijewski created an artwork called *Them* that vividly dramatises this problem. It was first shown at the world's largest art exhibition, *Documenta*, in Kassel in Germany in 2007. *Them* illustrates the problems of representation that museums face in modern democracies. The artist asked members of four groups of irreconcilably different views namely leftists, Jewish liberals, nationalists and Catholics to each paint a large canvas with symbols of their beliefs. The results were four 'world-pictures' illustrating different 'world-views' in the most literal sense. The twist in the tale was that Zmijewski then asked each group to swop their pictures three times, and amend each other's so they fitted their beliefs as well as the originators'. Inevitably, the pictures couldn't be all things to all people. After hours of argument and difficult compromises, the project ended when one group set fire to another's work. As the political theorist Chantal Mouffe (1992) argues, 'politics' is about disagreements, and not all arguments can be resolved. Not all conflicts can find happy solutions. The question this raises is whether such conflictual situations should be avoided or addressed, even if the process results in argument or worse. On a positive note, many museums have clearly decided that the answer to the question is yes and are already engaging passionately with communities from different backgrounds in order to broker cross-cultural, or intercultural understanding and dialogue.

IF COMMUNITIES CAN TELL THEIR OWN HISTORIES DO WE STILL NEED CURATORS?

The answer here is perhaps obvious, but there are serious questions at stake. Underpinning these debates are issues about the roles museum and gallery professionals play, and a principle of 'delegated authority'. This applies in democratic party-politics: we elect people to make decisions on our behalf, as our elected 'representatives'. Government cannot be conducted by having referendums about every issue: we need experts to act on our collective behalf on a day-to-day basis. Culture and other parts of the public sector work in parallel ways to some degree. To use the correct language, objects are held 'in trust' by museums on behalf of the public: people's trust is placed in museum professionals.

However, Viv Golding argues that it is possible to go beyond "narrow, dualistic conceptions of curatorial practice versus community" (Golding and Modest 2013: 1). Frisch similarly argues that we need to think in terms of a "shared and sharable authority" by valuing what both parties can bring to a museum or gallery. If we accept this premise, how are actual displays constructed? How would or could such an idea work in practice? (Hutchinson 2013; Mason et al. 2013). We argue that curators play a critical role in taking an overview, mediating between perspectives of different groups, adjudicating in conflicts, keeping a consistent position and contributing their understanding of how to transform individual experiences into engaging and accessible displays.

IS WORKING DIGITALLY ONE ANSWER?

Much of what we have been talking about above revolves around the question of how museums and galleries might share more of the process, authority and responsibility for how societies come to represent their multiple pasts. The 'sharing' of authority has been thought of as something that digital and social media can help achieve. This requires some caution. No forms of communication, representation and technology are universal, and all have implicit exclusions, digital media included. Notwithstanding this, we can say that access to information, the ability to participate in public discussions, and the circulation of images of objects *in reproduction* have been transformed by digital working, especially in larger museums. Moreover, many projects and artworks have been created for online platforms specifically for, or by, museums. As the former Tate Director Nicholas Serota notes, this allows entirely different forms of access, and different forms of art to be created:

Tate ... develop[ed] a form of commission that occupies a completely new space: the virtual. Since 2012, Tate has been commissioning performance works under the rubric Performance Room, presented through live web broadcast with no audience present but with thousands viewing across the world in real time. These are the first performance works commissioned by a museum purely for the online space.

(Serota 2016)

Serota also believes that

changes in society [include] a willingness to challenge, to exchange views and to be a participant through social media and digital platforms. How should we as curators react to this appetite for new forms of exhibition and for debate, discussion and dialogue? Can we respond without abandoning the commitment to traditional curatorial endeavour and scholarship? . . . Open exchange is different from formal instruction in which experts debate with their peers and pass on accumulated knowledge to the next generation. It is closer to the spirit of shared ownership and experience implicit in the term "commonwealth", an idea that has particular significance for museums at this moment .... We have to recognise that knowledge about the collections is not confined to the experts who work in the institution .... We might also appeal for expertise – the research equivalent of crowdfunding.

(Ibid.)

Tate, for example, invited people to contribute their knowledge of places to a project called 'Art Maps', which are about rethinking the geography of the 'art world' beyond the West. Their collection has nearly 70,000 artworks online in varying degrees of detail (copyright permissions are not always easy to secure). So far, around one-third of these have been tagged to a particular geographic location. Tate invites people to provide more detailed and supplementary information to enhance the information associated with each artwork based on their own local knowledge.

In the US, history exhibitions are also being developed through types of crowdsourcing. In New York, for example, the 9/11 Memorial Museum hosts an online archive of individuals' photographs of tribute and commemorative sites. It is described by the museum as follows: "Make History is a *collective telling* of the events of 9/11 through the eyes of those who experienced it, both at the attack sites and around the world" (National September 11 Memorial & Museum 2016). What differentiates this kind of project from simply a project based around people's memories and oral histories is that the medium and the message are as one; an event experienced collectively is narrated collectively through "collective telling" (National September 11 Memorial & Museum 2016).

CONCLUSIONS

This chapter has looked at the issue of who visits, who doesn't visit, and all the many reasons underpinning these patterns and choices.

We have also explored the different ways that museums and galleries think about, and interact with their visitors, communities and audiences. One of the really challenging issues in this area of museum studies is how these demographic patterns of visiting and non-visiting are interpreted and feed into matters of cultural policy and public funding. It is clear that visitor profiles in many parts of the world are heavily skewed towards the more affluent and well-educated in society. As a result, there has been a tendency by those against public subsidy for the arts and culture to seize on this information as justification for cutting back public funding. Their argument is that it is unfair to ask everyone to subsidise public culture if the evidence shows that only a selected proportion of the population enjoy and benefit from it. Moreover, they argue, if the people who do visit museums and galleries most regularly are already those who tend to be wealthier then they could afford to pay for it themselves as they do with other leisure pursuits like going to the theatre.

There are undoubtedly serious questions here. In our view it is certainly fair to ask museums and galleries to try their hardest to reach out to those who might not think that these institutions offer something for them; many are already doing great work in this regard but more could be done. However, we would definitely not agree that the skewed profile should simply lead to a withdrawal of public funding. Museums and art galleries are amongst the few open-access public spaces in cities where people do not have to engage in a financial transaction to be able to participate. In our ever increasing consumerist and marketised societies, we believe it is essential to retain some public spaces which are not simply about shopping.

Moreover, as we have been arguing, museums and galleries are spaces which hold the material evidence of our shared past, both good and bad. In many countries, this means that museums and galleries are the primary places where the histories of nations, communities, and groups are put on display for all to see, agree or disagree. All members of society have the right to know about these matters and have access to these spaces.

We have also seen how restricted access to certain forms of culture is connected to a host of other inequalities and can reinforce a sense of being excluded from certain networks or groups. Think back to the comments from Michelle Obama discussed earlier. If we accept that museums and galleries are just for those who can pay or who already feel comfortable within them, then the gaps between those on 'the inside' who know about certain forms of culture, and those on 'the outside' who don't will become wider with all the associated consequences for other areas of life.

So, rather than seeing the skewed visitor profile as a reason to discount museums and galleries as public spaces, we argue that this is precisely why we need to keep paying attention to these matters and thinking about how to redress them. For us, museums and galleries remain vital spaces of civic and public culture. The task is to continue to challenge perceptions that they only serve the few and to take action to change the status quo. To return to where we began this chapter, our answer to the opening question, 'who are museums and galleries for' *is* 'everyone'.

REFERENCES

Black, G. (2005) *The Engaging Museum: Developing Museums for Visitor Involvement*. London and Oxford: Routledge.

Black, G. (2012) *Transforming Museums in the Twenty-First Century*. London and Oxford: Routledge.

Bourdieu, P. (1984) *Distinction: A Social Critique of the Judgement of Taste*. London: Routledge and Kegan Paul.

Bourdieu, P., A. Darbel, with D. Schnapper (1991) *The Love of Art: European Art Museums and Their Publics*. Cambridge: Polity Press.

Brook, O. (2011) *International Comparisons of Public Engagement in Culture and Sport*. DCMS and ESRC. London: Department for Culture, Media and Sport.

Brook, O., P. Boyle and R. Flowerdew (2008) *Demographic Indicators of Cultural Consumption*. Research Findings: Understanding Population Trends and Processes. October. UPTAP. ESRC (www.uptap.net).

Chan, T.W. and J. Goldthorpe (2007) 'Class and status: The conceptual distinction and its empirical relevance'. *American Sociological Review*, 72(August): 512–532.

Davison, L. and P. Sibley (2011) 'Audiences at the "new" museum: Visitor commitment, diversity and leisure at the Museum of New Zealand Te Papa Tongarewa'. *Visitor Studies*, 14(2): 176–194.

Dawson, E. and E. Jensen (2011) 'Towards a contextual turn in visitor studies: Evaluating visitor segmentation and identity-related motivations towards a contextual turn in visitor studies: evaluating visitor segmentation and identity-related motivations'. *Visitor Studies*, 14(2): 127–140.

DCMS (2011) *Taking Part: The National Survey of Culture, Leisure and Sport. 2010/11 Statistical Release.* London: Department for Culture, Media and Sport.

DCMS (2016) *National Statistics: Taking Part 2015/2016 Quarter 4: Adult Statistical Release: Key Findings.* London: Department for Culture, Media and Sport.

Dodd, J. and R. Sandell (1998) *Building Bridges: Guidance for Museums and Galleries on Developing New Audiences.* London: Museums and Galleries Commission.

Falk, J. (2009) *Identity and the Museum Visitor Experience.* Walnut Creek, CA: Left Coast Press.

Foley, F. and G. McPherson (2000) 'Museums as leisure', *International Journal of Heritage Studies*, 6(2): 161–174.

Frisch, M. (1990) *A Shared Authority: Essays on the Craft and Meaning of Oral and Public History.* Albany, NY: State University of New York Press.

Golding, V. and W. Modest (eds) (2013) *Museums and Communities: Curators, Collections and Collaboration.* London: Bloomsbury Academic.

Hutchison, M. (2013) '"Shared authority": Collaboration, curatorial voice, and exhibition design in Canberra, Australia', in V. Golding and W. Modest (eds), *Museums and Communities: Curators, Collections and Collaboration.* London: Bloomsbury Academic, 143–162.

Light, D. (2000) 'An unwanted past: Contemporary tourism and the heritage of communism in Romania'. *International Journal of Heritage Studies*, 6(2): 145–160.

Mason, R., C. Whitehead and H. Graham (2013) 'One voice to many voices? Displaying polyvocality in an art gallery', in V. Golding and W. Modest (eds), *Museums and Communities: Curators, Collections and Collaboration.* London: Bloomsbury Academic, 163–177.

Morris Hargreaves McIntyre (2006) *Audience Knowledge Digest: Why People Visit Museums and Galleries, and What Can Be Done to Attract Them?* Manchester: MHM for Renaissance North East.

Mouffe, C. (ed.) (1992) *Dimensions of Radical Democracy: Pluralism, Citizenship, Community.* London: Verso.

Savage, M., G. Bagnall and B. Longhurst (2005) *Globalization and Belonging.* London and Los Angeles: Sage Publications.

Watson, S. (2007) *Museums and Their Communities.* London and New York: Routledge.

WEBSITES

Arts Council England (2009) *Active Lives Survey*. URL: http://www.artscouncil. org.uk/participating-and-attending/active-lives-survey

Arts Council England (2011) *Arts Audiences: Insight*. URL: http://www. artscouncil.org.uk/sites/default/files/download-file/arts_audience_ insight_2011.pdf

Arts Council England / The Audience Agency (2016) *Culture Based Segmentation*, URL: http://www.artscouncil.org.uk/participating-and-attending/culture-based-segmentation and at https://www.theaudienceagency.org/audience-spectrum/profiles

Bounia, A., A. Nikiforidou, N. Nikonanou and A.D. Matossian (2012) 'Voices from the museum: Survey research in Europe's national museums', Linköping University Electronic Press. URL: http://museumedulab.ece.uth.gr/main/en/node/377

Bunting, C., T.W. Chan, J. Goldthorpe, E. Keaney and A. Oskala (2008) *From Indifference to Enthusiasm*. Arts Council England Report. URL: http://users.ox.ac.uk/~sfos0006/papers/indifferencetoenthusiasm.pdf

Coffield, F. (2013) *Learning Styles: Time to Move On*, National College for School Leadership. URL: https://www.nationalcollege.org.uk/cm-mc-lpd-op-coffield.pdf

Farrell, B. and M. Medvedeva (2010) *Demographic Transformation and the Future of Museums*. The Center for the Future of Museums: an initiative of the American Association of Museums. Washington, DC: AAM (http://www.aam-us.org/docs/center-for-the-future-of-museums/demotransaam2010.pdf)

Kelly, L. (2009) 'Australian museum visitors: Who visits museums in general and who visits the Australian museum'. Australian Museum Blog: http://australianmuseum.net.au/blogpost/museullaneous/australian-museum-visitors

Lynch, B. (2010) *Whose Cake Is It Anyway? A Collaborative Investigation Into Engagement and Participation in 12 Museums and Galleries in the UK*. London: Paul Hamlyn Foundation. URL: http://ourmuseum.org.uk/wp-content/uploads/Whose-cake-is-it-anyway-report.pdf

Morris Hargreaves McIntyre (2010) *Introducing Culture Segments*. URL: http://mhminsight.com/static/pdfs/culture-segments/en.pdf

Museums Association (MA) (2010) 'Visitor factsheet'. URL: http://www.museumsassociation.org/download?id=165106

National Endowment for the Arts (NEA) (2012) 'National Endowment for the Arts presents highlights from the 2012 survey of public participation in the arts'. URL: https://www.arts.gov/news/2013/national-endowment-arts-presents-highlights-2012-survey-public-participation-arts

National Museum of the American Indian (NMAI) (2005) 'Smithsonian's National Museum of the American Indian Chronology'. URL: http://nmai.si.edu/sites/1/files/pdf/press_releases/2005-09-14_nmai_chronology.pdf

National September 11 Memorial and Museum (2016) 'Make history'. http://www.911memorial.org/blog/tags/make-history

Obama, M. (2015) 'Remarks by the First Lady at the opening of the Whitney Museum'. URL: https://obamawhitehouse.archives.gov/the-press-office/2015/04/30/remarks-first-lady-opening-whitney-museum

Sandahl, J. (n.d.) 'Waiting for the public to change?'. URL: http://www.slks.dk/fileadmin/user_upload/dokumenter/KS/institutioner/museer/Indsatsomraader/Brugerundersoegelse/Artikler/Jette_Sandahl_Waiting_for_the_public_to_change.pdf

Serota, N. (2016) 'The 21st-century Tate is a commonwealth of ideas', *The Art Newspaper* website 5 January 2016. URL: http://theartnewspaper.com/comment/the-21st-century-tate-is-a-commonwealth-of-ideas/

Simon, N. (2010) *The Participatory Museum.* URL: http://www.participatorymuseum.org/chapter5/

University of Cambridge (2014) 'University of Cambridge Museum of Archaeology and Anthropology access policy statement'. URL: http://maa.cam.ac.uk/maa/wp-content/uploads/2012/10/MAA-Access-Policy-Statement.pdf

Van Abbemuseum (2016) 'Queering the collection'. URL: http://vanabbemuseum.nl/en/collection-and-context/queering/

FURTHER READING

Black, G. (2012) *Transforming Museums in the Twenty-First Century.* London and Oxford: Routledge.

Bourdieu, P. (1993) *Sociology in Question.* London: Sage.

Golding, V. and W. Modest (eds) (2013) *Museums and Communities: Curators, Collections and Collaboration.* London and New York: Bloomsbury.

Hooper-Greenhill, E. (2011) *Studying Visitors.* In S. Macdonald (ed.), *A Companion to Museum Studies.* Chichester: Blackwell, 362–376.

Karp, I., C.M. Kreamer and S. Lavine (eds) (1992) *Museums and Communities: The Politics of Public Culture.* AAM: Smithsonian Institution.

Leahy, H. Rees (2012) *Museum Bodies: The Politics and Practices of Visiting and Viewing.* London and New York: Routledge.

Onciul, B., M. Stefano and S. Hawke (eds) (2017) *Engaging Heritage: Engaging Communities.* Woodbridge: Boydell & Brewer.

Macdonald, S. (2002) *Behind the Scenes at the Science Museum.* Oxford: Berg.

Marincola, P. and G. Adamson (2006) *What Makes a Great Exhibition?* Philadelphia: Philadelphia Exhibitions Initiative.

Simon, N. (2010) *The Participatory Museum.* Santa Cruz, CA: Museum 2.0.

Watson, S. (ed.) (2007) *Museums and Their Communities.* London and New York: Routledge.

4

THE BUSINESS OF CULTURE

WHO PAYS FOR WHAT, FOR WHOM, AND ON WHOSE BEHALF?

In 2013, not many people had heard of Sheika Al-Mayassa bint Hamad bin Khalifa Al-Thani, Head of the Qatar Museums Authority. Yet she reportedly spent $1 billion, each year, for eight years, on works of art – far more than Tate and MoMA combined (*ArtReview* 2014). Sheika Al-Mayassa was also rumoured to have paid $250 million for Paul Cezanne's *The Card Players* (*Forbes* 2014) and $300 million for Paul Gauguin's *When Will You Marry?* (Cascone 2015) – both sales were, at the time, record-breaking figures.

Sheika Al-Mayassa is widely considered to be one of the most influential buyers on the global art market, but she is far from the only person spending vast sums on art. Georgina Adam (2014: 1) reports that fine art auctions in 2013 totalled $12.05 billion, with the value of the art market then estimated at $67.7 billion. Similarly, the European Fine Art Foundation has suggested that the global art market grew 575% between 1991 and its highest point in 2007 (TEFAF 2012: 15). Museums and galleries have hit the headlines too. The M+ museum in Hong Kong, for example, is reported to have its construction costs capped at HK$5 billion (Chow 2014), the Abu Dhabi

Louvre is estimated to cost 2.4 billion AED (Atelier Jean Nouvel 2007), and the V&A Dundee, in Scotland, is an £80.11 million construction project (Victoria & Albert Museum 2015a), with a further £1 billion needed to update the waterfront (Victoria & Albert Museum 2015b). Culture, in many parts of the world, is now not just a business, but big business.

Yet while private acquisitions, such as those of Sheika Al-Mayassa, continue to break records, in many territories the proportion of all public funding spent on museums and galleries remains extremely small, and their acquisition budgets are often shrinking. For example, in the UK, from a total public spending figure of £694 billion between 2011 and 2012, museums and galleries were allocated £407 million – less than was spent on bus subsidies and other concessionary fares (£619 million), or on administration costs for one ministry, the Foreign and Commonwealth Office (£1.12 billion) (Rogers 2012).

Similarly, spending on museums and the arts in several European countries is decreasing rapidly. In 2013 the council of the city in which we work implemented a 50% cut in arts funding (Youngs 2013). In many European countries, problems have been similar or worse. The Prado, Spain's most important museum, had a 15% cut in its annual budgets (Kendall 2012: 25). Also in Spain, the newly built Niemeyer Centre in Aviles, which cost over £37m (44m euros) to build, closed in 2011 only months after opening, although it has now reopened. In Italy, Rome's new MAXXI Museum, designed by Zaha Hadid, was the first new major museum in the city for decades. In 2012 it was reported to face closure and was put into 'special administration' by the government, after an overspend and funding cuts took their subsidy from 11 million to 2 million euros (Rosenfield 2012). The crises of funding cuts from 2010 to 2013 have not been completely played out, as yet, even if many regions of Europe are more stable. Similarly, it would seem that the earlier "galleries glut" (Tremlett 2011), and the expectation of permanent economic growth, is over.

Certain cultural heritage venues have become entirely staffed by volunteers out of necessity. For example, following funding and staffing issues, the James Joyce Tower in Sandycove, Ireland, is now entirely staffed by volunteers (Friends of Joyce Tower Society 2012). In the Netherlands, the Dutch government, which has often been seen as an exemplary supporter of culture, reduced its culture budget by a fifth – some 200m euros – down to 789m in 2012–13. What was particularly interesting in this case was that the official explanation offered for the cuts did not mention the worldwide financial crisis or what was happening to subsidised culture in other countries, but placed blame on cultural institutions themselves and a supposed public disillusionment with subsidised culture:

> As a result of changes in society, support for funding culture has diminished and the extent of the funding has declined in society. As a result, support has also declined in the political sphere. The feeling has arisen that, when providing funding, the government has paid insufficient attention to the audience or to entrepreneurship.
>
> (Ministry of Education, Culture and Science 2013: 5–6)

This brings us to the heart of the matter. A key issue here is that museums and galleries in Europe are often built and run at public expense, on the assumption – shared in many parts of the world – that they are a 'good thing' in and of themselves, and should be free and open to everyone (theoretically at least). As discussed in the previous chapter, not everyone agrees, and as the Dutch government document outlines, some public commentators and critics have felt that more emphasis should be placed upon making institutions 'self-sustaining' and 'audience focused' – whatever that might mean or entail. Even in the UK, where state subsidies are the norm, it has long been a point of contention that museums and galleries, unlike theatres, cinemas and buildings housing any other art form, except for libraries, do not charge for entry. Why should one be considered a 'public good', and not the other? Alternatively, in the US, it has traditionally been thought that culture should pay its own way, in the form of entry fees, sponsorship and self-generated revenue. Indeed, John H. Falk and Beverly K. Sheppard (2006) recently suggested that visitors to museums might pay even more, if they received preferential treatment in return, including the ability to skip the queue, individual attention from museum staff and the use of personal, reserved equipment. This trend of offering visitors the choice of paying extra for privileged, restricted access to exhibitions is also happening in some UK museums and galleries.

This raises the question: should museums and galleries charge (or charge more) to balance their budgets if it means fewer people will benefit? Are there aspects of the museum that are not for sale, at any price? While the answers to these questions are likely to vary according to people's political beliefs and assumptions, it is clear that those employed in museums and galleries have to adjudicate on the means, as much as the ends of their business, as never before. London's major museums, including the National Gallery and Tate, will not accept money from arms manufacturers (or cigarette manufacturers) (Philips and Whannel 2013: 118). In a more extreme example, the Fitzwilliam Museum in Cambridge refused to even print the colourful logo of one of its major supporters on in-gallery labels (even though it is an arts charity) because it might look like sponsorship (*Guardian* 2009). Museums and galleries face ethical dilemmas in all aspects of their corporate behaviour and financial decision-making.

WHAT IT COSTS: CAPITAL AND REVENUE

Before we go any further, it is worth briefly pausing to ask: what does it actually cost to run a museum or gallery? And what kinds of cost are involved? This might seem strange. After all, museums and galleries come in all shapes and sizes, and have access to wildly different budgets, from the just over $1 million-per-week operating costs projected for the landmark September 11 Memorial and Museum, New York (National September 11 Memorial and Museum 2015), to the £650-per-week costs required by the East Grinstead Museum, a local history museum in the south of England (East Grinstead Museum n.d.). Yet while budgets differ, the main allocations and proportions spent can be remarkably similar.

For instance, museums and galleries are likely to incur what are referred to in the UK as '*capital*' costs. Capital costs include the permanent acquisition of long-term assets, such as artworks, period furniture and geological exhibits, as well as the construction, extension and renovation of museum and gallery buildings – schemes often referred to as 'capital projects'. Indeed, it is this kind of expenditure that museums and galleries are most commonly associated with, not least because many museums and galleries can only afford to embark upon such projects following major fundraising campaigns. A good example here is the 'Save Van Dyck's Self-Portrait' appeal, set up by the National Portrait Gallery, London and ArtFund (a fundraising charity in the UK) in 2014, which aimed to raise £10 million in order to buy Sir Anthony Van Dyck's (1640–1) final self-portrait. By far the largest share was contributed by private trusts and national funds, but, notably, over 10,000 members of the public also contributed following high-profile appeals, raising £1.44 million towards the total amount (National Portrait Gallery 2014).

The other cost commonly referred to in the UK is '*revenue*' cost, or those costs incurred 'behind the scenes' in the normal day-to-day running of the museum or gallery. Revenue costs typically include staff pay, training, holidays and pensions, as well as insurance for the collections, exhibitions and equipment, electricity and water bills, office supplies and furniture, technical support, security costs, legal fees, even the fee charged by those preparing the annual accounts. Yet while revenue costs rarely attract as much attention as capital costs, they account for a significant proportion of the operating budget. For example, in 2013–14 the Tate group (which covers Tate Britain, Tate Modern, Tate St Ives and Tate Liverpool) reported a total income of £178.1 million. Of this, £29.3 million was spent on acquiring new works for the collection. By contrast, £83.5 million, almost three times as much, went towards operating costs, including public programming (£35.8 million), support costs for charitable activities (£16.5 million) and the costs of generating funds (£3.6 million) (Tate 2014: 96–97). In 2013, the British Museum was reported to have spent 40% of its operating budget on its staff (Rocco 2013: 6).

Such high operating costs can cause alarm, particularly when it is capital costs that allow for expanded collections and new display spaces; aspects of the museum's mission that many view as integral. Yet cuts to revenue funding can have an equally serious impact upon front-line services in museums and galleries, forcing them to restrict public access, or close altogether. The Museo d'Arte contemporanea Donna Regina (MADRE) in Naples is a case in point. Facing dramatic cuts, the gallery decided in 2012 to close two floors of its exhibition space (Siegal 2013). In 2013, and faced with 10% budget cuts, Director Ian Blatchford argued that the Science Museum Group in the UK would have "little choice other than to close one of our museums" if the cuts were accepted, adding, "I would rather have three world class museums than four mediocre museums" (Kendall 2013). No closures were eventually made, but these examples highlight the difficulty of the decisions to be made by museum and gallery staff, who often have to select areas to cut back, and those to prioritise.

EXTERNAL FUNDING SOURCES: THE STATE, THE LOTTERY, CHARITIES, DONORS, BUSINESS

How then, do museums and galleries find the funding they need to remain operational? One popular solution is to look to a variety of external sources, that is, to the state, the lottery, charities, donors and/or businesses. However, these options are not equally available to all, nor do they work in the same way everywhere.

- *The State:* In the US, state funding for the arts is relatively minimal, and is predominantly distributed by the National Endowment for the Arts (NEA). Although the situation is more complicated, many public museums in China receive the majority of their funding from the state, with central government, provinces and state-owned foundations all distributing funds. Likewise, in Germany, museums and galleries receive proportionately large amounts of state funding, but do so primary at the level of the 'Länder', or region, rather than via the nation–state, because of the federal system of government in place. Many other countries, including the UK, Australia and Taiwan, make state funding available at both the national and local level, as well as through a variety of national bodies.
- *The National Lottery:* Although not all countries have a National Lottery, the funds made available for those that do can be sizeable. In the UK, the National Lottery has raised over £34 billion, or £34 million per week, since 1994 (National Lottery 2015); money which is then given to a range of 'good causes' via 12 independent organisations, including the Arts Council England and the Heritage Lottery Fund. Similarly, the BankGiro Lottery in the Netherlands generated more than 62 million euros in 2015, which it then distributed to over 60 cultural institutions (Novamedia 2015).

- *Charities:* In the US, Australia, India and most parts of Europe, museums and galleries can register as charities in their own right. In addition, a number of charitable trusts and foundations, organisations set up specifically to dispense funds, have open applications schemes to which museums and galleries can apply for grants. These often have a particular remit and geographical reach. For example, the Clore Duffield Foundation, based in the UK, "concentrates its support on cultural learning" and other, related, areas (Clore Duffield Foundation 2015), while the Rothschild Foundation makes funds available for projects that protect Jewish Heritage, across Europe (Rothschild Foundation Europe 2015).

- *Donors:* Donations are funds contributed directly by individuals and range from reasonably small 'suggested donations' (anywhere between 2 and 15 euros in Europe) from visitors, to far larger amounts. The shipping magnate and philanthropist, Sammy Ofer, for instance, donated £20 million to the National Maritime Museum in the UK in 2008 (Royal Museums Greenwich 2009). Donations might also be made over several years, in the form of a 'legacy', or 'bequest' (where the transfer takes place upon the donor's death), or consist of an object or collection. Leonard A. Lauder's donation of 78 cubist artworks to the Metropolitan Museum of Art, in 2013, transformed the institution's holdings of early twentieth-century art (Metropolitan Museum of Art 2013).

- *Business:* Corporate sponsorship is now commonplace in many museums and galleries around the world, and can be extremely lucrative. However, unlike donations, sponsorship tends to involve a contract, with the sponsor paying the museum or gallery a fee in return for certain benefits. For instance, Unilever paid Tate Modern £4.4 million over 12 years to sponsor a series of artworks in the Turbine Hall (Batty 2012), referred to, at least in principle, as the 'Unilever Series'.

As we will see later on, corporate fundraising and sponsorship can be particularly controversial, although all forms of funding suggest certain relationships, consequences and compromises. It is also important to note that very few museums and galleries are entirely funded through any one of the above channels. Even in countries that once provided nearly total state funding things are changing. The Ministry for Culture in China, for instance, announced a reduction in public subsidies in 2006 as part of a plan to prompt commercial development (H!TANG and China Creative Connections 2011). In Canada, Taiwan and many parts of Europe, the rapid decrease in state funding has led to a shortfall in finances for many museums, who must now put together a patchwork of varying funders, or cut back.

THE MUSEUM AS ENTREPRENEUR: INCOME GENERATION AND ENTERPRISE

Another possible option for museums and galleries looking to raise money is internal funding, or 'self-generated income'. This can take a variety of forms. For some museums, 'self-generated funding' is anything that does not come from the state, and so includes sponsorship, donations and charitable funds. However, in this section we will focus on the income generated through entry fees, memberships, museum shops, restaurants, and cafes, object loans, consultation, image sales, publishing, partnerships, and touring exhibitions. Particularly during periods of financial difficulty, these sources can be crucial in offsetting decreased state support. In fact, while the totals raised through this kind of activity vary, some museums and galleries are hugely successful. In 2012–13, the Tate galleries in the UK generated £56.4m from commercial activities and sponsorship. They also received £31.5 million of government funds (Tate 2013). In other words, although it is a publically funded institution, over two-thirds of the costs at Tate in that year were not subsidised.

The things that museum and galleries can charge for, as well as how much, varies considerably across the world. In the UK, the principle, and practice, of free entry for all has a long history as we have seen in earlier chapters. In the 1980s, roughly half of the major national museums, including the V&A, introduced entry charges, although the British Museum, Tate and National Gallery remained free. In 1997, the new Labour government pledged to reinstate free entry for all national museums, and did so in 2001. Yet even now, it tends to be the permanent collections that are free of charge; temporary exhibitions, and particularly big 'blockbuster' exhibitions, can charge a relatively high admissions price. In 2015, for instance, an adult ticket for 'Cosmonauts: Birth of the Space Age' at the Science Museum was £14 (Science Museum 2015), while a cinema ticket at London Leicester Square was £12.50 (Odeon 2015). It has also been suggested that of the 700 local authority museums in the UK, a "very small proportion" already charge for entry, but that many more are thinking about introducing charges in the face of funding cuts (Clark 2015).

In France and Sweden, museums and galleries regularly charge visitors, despite short experiments in offering free access (Dowd 2011). A day ticket to the Louvre, for example, is currently 15 euros (Louvre, n.d.). In the US, this figure can be much higher. Although the Smithsonian Institution in Washington notably remains free of charge (Smithsonian 2015a), and the Dallas Museum of Art offers free entry in return for personal information including names, email addresses and zip codes (Rocco 2013: 6), an adult ticket for MoMA is in the region of $25 (MoMA 2015a). In 2014 MoMA raised $31,759,000 through its entrance charge (not including membership fees which were additional) (MoMA 2014). Yet not all museums and galleries get to keep the revenue generated by ticket sales, or other self-generated incomes. In India, these are collected and placed into a common fund, managed centrally by the Ministry of Culture (British Council 2014: vi). Until relatively recently, museums and galleries in Italy also had their self-generated earnings redistributed – although special autonomy was granted to 20 national heritage organisations in 2014, as part of sweeping cultural reforms introduced by the Culture Minister, Dario Franceschini, allowing them to control their own finances for the first time (Pirovano 2015).

The mixed reactions to the changes in Italy are particularly interesting as they highlight some of the key debates and ideas surrounding the self-generation of funds. On one hand, changes such as the promised financial autonomy and an increased focus on self-generated income were widely reported in the press as opportunity to 'stop the rot' (ibid.), and transform a struggling sector by promoting self-sufficiency, resilience, enterprise and a more active relationship with visitors. Not everyone was so optimistic. Marco Pierini, Director of the Galleria Civica di Modena, resigned in protest after the centre opened a display consisting of local foodstuffs, as oppose to contemporary art, remarking in his resignation letter that the move catered for "consumer tourism, rather than thoughtful citizens" (Kirchgaessner 2014). For Pierini then, the ability to self-generate income came at the cost of accepting increasing commercialisation and ultimately a 'selling-out' of the gallery's true purpose.

FUNDRAISING, SPONSORSHIP, PHILANTHROPY AND 'THE GIFT'

As the above examples illustrate, museum and gallery professionals have to consider crucial issues such as how much funding is required, where it might be found, and what funders, of all kinds, want in return for their investment. Some returns are more explicit than others. The agreement to fund an exhibition in return for the inclusion of a company logo on published materials is likely to be discussed, and agreed upon in advance. Other returns remain largely unspoken. Both can spark ethical debates about whose money it is acceptable to take, and whose it is not.

For example, in 1988, 'The Spirit Sings: Artistic Traditions of Canada's First Peoples' exhibition, held at the Glenbow Museum in Alberta, caused an international outcry after it emerged that the exhibition was heavily sponsored by Shell Oil Canada Limited; a company simultaneously drilling for oil on land claimed by the Lubicon Lake band of Cree, a group of First Nation people (Cooper 2008: 21–23). More recently, British Petroleum (BP)'s sponsorship of the British Museum, Tate galleries, National Portrait Gallery and Royal Opera House in London – a five-year, £10 million deal (BP 2015) continues to divide opinion. Green activists strongly object to the oil company's activities and environmental record, and have staged numerous protests. In September 2015, for example, protestors occupied the British Museum, arguing against what artist and activist Mel Evans (2015) has termed the "artwashing" of BP's corporate image, and pointing out that "the money [BP] gives is not a gift, it is not philanthropy. It is part of their marketing budget and strategy [and] they expect a return" (Rawlinson 2015).

Although also viewed as 'gifts', donations, too, can come with significant strings attached. The conditions agreed upon here range, from legal specifics concerning the care and exhibition of the work (i.e. that any damage will be reported to the donor), to requests to rename particular spaces, or even the whole museum. In 2013, the Miami Art Museum was controversially renamed the Pérez Art Museum Miami after a donation of $35 million in cash and artworks by Jorge M. Pérez, despite taxpayers contributing the vast majority of funds (Pogrebin 2011). Moreover, donors' motivations are not always as philanthropic as they might first appear, and may be as much about receiving tax benefits as a desire to 'give something back' to society, or worse. It has been alleged that an exhibition concerning climate change at the Science Museum, London, was influenced by funders Royal Dutch Shell (Macalister 2015). Similarly, it has been alleged that a scientist employed by the Smithsonian museums, in the US, whose work denies the risks of global warming, failed to disclose funding from the fossil-fuel industry (Gillis and Schwartz 2015). For their part, both museums released statements refuting the accusations: the Science Museum stated that representatives from Shell had no influence upon the curatorial programme (Blatchford 2015), and the Smithsonian rejected the scientist in question's findings, and launched an enquiry to address the allegations (Smithsonian 2015b).

Public funding, too, is not immune to wanting a return of some kind. In the UK, 'key performance indicators', as set by central government, have to be met in return for public investment, resulting in what cultural commentators such as Clive Gray (2008) have termed the instrumentalisation of culture – an argument discussed in more detail below. Yet while many baulk at the returns expected by funders, the cultural historian Christopher Frayling has offered a different opinion:

> Isn't it a good thing that large corporations are giving money to the arts? They don't have to. Tobacco companies and arms manufacturers are no longer seen as respectable partners. But should an organisation turn down money from an airline because one of its aircraft has gone down? Or money from a bank because we don't like it behaving like a casino? Or money from the government because of Iraq?
>
> (Interview in *The Guardian* 2010)

In a situation where institutions are set to close or reduce their services drastically, should we then agree with Frayling, and believe that "now is not the time to get squeamish" (ibid.)? Or should museums and galleries draw a line in the sand when it comes to funding, and if so, where?

AUTONOMY AND INSTRUMENTALISATION

Concerns over the entanglements between museums and money are by no means new. Admission to European 'public' museums during the eighteenth century was not open to all, but only to those of an "appropriate social standing" (McClellan 2003: 3). The art historian Alan Wallach (2003: 102) has labelled the period between 1900 and 1960 the "robber baron" phase of American art museum development, a term referring to a number of industrial billionaires who made their fortunes by exploiting labour conditions, and then used these fortunes to bankroll, and control, museums, by becoming trustees. Even further back, the art historian Michael Baxandall (1972: 1–3) has described painting in fifteenth-century Italy as "the product of a social relationship", with the patron, or 'client', an "active, determining and not necessarily benevolent agent" who might pay by the square foot, and decide on the composition and colours to be used. Painting, in the fifteenth century, was "too important to be left to the painters" (ibid.: 3). There has never been a time when cultural institutions did not rely on patronage and funding from one source or another.

While museums and galleries have, arguably, always been at least *partly* conditioned by economic factors, it has been argued more recently that notions of value are now becoming *primarily* economic in some countries. For example, the Australian economist David Throsby (2010: 1–5) has described how, following a conference in Mexico in 1967, UNESCO published a series of monographs in which member states described what 'cultural policy' meant to them. These reports "contained few, if any, references to the economics of culture". Yet by the turn of the new millennium, Throsby argues that cultural policy had transformed into "an arm of economic policy".

To give a recent example of this, Neil MacGregor, Director of the British Museum, and George Osborne, Chancellor of the Exchequer for the UK Government at that time, wrote a joint article in the UK newspaper, *The Telegraph*, in September 2015. The article is about the British Museum sending one of its flagship exhibitions (*The World in 100 Objects*) to China to be shown in the National Museum of China in Beijing and in Shanghai. The funding for this tour was provided by the UK government as part of a £6 million package of funding for cultural activities and projects which would "showcase the very best of British culture to Chinese audiences" with translation into Mandarin (Osborne and MacGregor 2015). In the following quotations from that article, notice the mixing together of ideas of cultural exchange, education, and national pride, with economic motivations and ambitions to increase trade, tourism and investment from China into the UK:

> When people exchange goods, they exchange ideas. Trade brings us not just new products, but new discoveries, ways of thinking and understanding the world around us. Commerce and culture go hand in hand. So as the UK and China broaden and develop their commercial ties it's natural that the cultural links between the two countries should also grow closer and stronger. ... There's an economic goal behind this – strengthening ties between Britain and China will bring more valuable investment and thousands of Chinese tourists to our country. Our partnership for growth, reform and innovation is already helping to deliver record levels of investment and trade in both directions, but there is so much more we can do. That's why in this flagship year of UK-China relations – with the first ever UK-China year of cultural exchange – we are exploring new opportunities to open up new markets to benefit both economies and people. Ultimately, however, it's about more than pounds and renminbi. It's in our literature, theatre, our paintings and our museums, that we express who we are as a country.
>
> (Osborne and MacGregor 2015)

It is worth noting that at this time the UK government was negotiating with the Chinese government to play a significant role in the UK's nuclear power industry by building a new nuclear power station in the UK. This was formally agreed in 2016.

Other examples include highlighting the economic 'rate of return' (e.g. a recent report in the UK highlighted that for every £1 spent by local authorities, £4 of additional funding was raised

(Local Government Association 2013: 2). Elsewhere, 'contingent valuation', an approach recently trialled at Bolton Museum, Libraries and Archives Service in the UK (Arts Council England 2012), and Queensland Museum, in Australia (The State of Queensland, Queensland Museum 2009), involves asking members of the public how much they would hypothetically be willing to pay, for example, in tax towards the museum, in order to estimate the monetary 'value' to people of that experience. The problem with such approaches is that they start from the assumption that everything can be given a monetary value. It is particularly problematic if this monetary value becomes the primary value-system by which worth is judged. We would argue that it is more important to see museums and galleries in terms of their broader cultural, societal and public values, as others have written (Scott *et al.* 2014).

Another approach is the 'social return on investment' method, or SROI, which "aims to be a kind of "social accounting" (BOP Consulting 2012: 9). In this process, varying 'impacts' (positive and negative) are identified and assessed by stakeholders and audiences, and financial 'proxies' are then established for each 'impact' in order to arrive at a ratio between the total costs and the total benefits (ibid.). While not arriving at any kind of financial figure, other kinds of 'social return' have also been proposed, and heavily critiqued. For example, in the UK, public funding is distributed via the 'arm's length' principle, which means that the treasury distributes money to a number of independent bodies, such as the Department for Culture, Media and Sport (DCMS), who then allocate funds according to their own judgement. Since the 1980s, museums and galleries have had to justify this funding by demonstrating an ability to contribute to a host of broader strategic objectives and 'key performance indicators', including social inclusion, or the tackling of youth crime. This led to claims of instrumentalism: museums and galleries were no longer 'intrinsically' valuable (i.e. valuable in their own right), but were tools of government policy (Holden 2005). For others, such as Clive Gray (2002), museums and galleries had 'attached' themselves to such agendas in order to prove their usefulness, and stake a better claim to limited public funding. While this is certainly not the case everywhere, the result in the UK has been an attempt by those within the profession, as well as museum and gallery studies academics, to re-articulate the intrinsic, or 'cultural value', of museums and galleries, and to construct more appropriate systems of measurement (Holden 2005).

IMPLICATION OF CULTURAL POLICY

Cultural policy, or the ways that governments understand and make decisions about 'culture', more broadly, has vital ramifications for museums and galleries. It is by this mechanism that governments and the public sphere are related. However, the particular relationships, principles and responsibilities decided upon are far from the same everywhere. Jennifer Craik, a cultural policy researcher based in Australia, identifies four dominant models of cultural policy worldwide, as follows:

> **Patron**: The patron model makes state funding available to art forms considered 'excellent', either directly, or indirectly (e.g. via the 'arm's length' principle).
>
> **Architect**: Culture, in the architect model, is not the responsibility of the state, but of a dedicated ministry. As this allows for cultural policy to be aligned with social welfare, or national culture objectives, the model is considered to be 'interventionist'.
>
> **Engineer**: In the engineer model, the government owns culture, and creators are required to reflect positively on the political agenda of the state. This results in overtly political forms of culture, consistent with national priorities.
>
> **Facilitator**: This model is more 'hands off'. It aims to create the conditions that favour cultural production (i.e. by offering tax incentives), and by indirectly supporting patronage, to allow a wide range of cultural activities to survive commercially. The government here has little control over who or what is supported.
>
> (Craik 2007: 1–2, adapted from Hillman-Chartrand and McCaughey 1989)

To these four models, Craik then adds a fifth option:

> **Elite Nurturer:** Here, governments select a small number of elite organisations, which receive generous, and recurrent, subsidies.

Craik makes two further points. First, there are strengths and weaknesses associated with all of the above models – and so the 'best' way to think of, and make decisions about, culture remains open to debate. Second, cultural policy is subject to change, as economic and political contexts shift. For example, even when a country has a tradition of supporting culture (and by extension museums and galleries) in a particular format, changed circumstances can result in a 'mix and match' approach, as governments are forced to seek alternatives. Craik notes that in Australia, there now exists both an 'arm's length' patronage model (offered through the Australia Council), and an 'increasingly important architect strategy' (offered through the Department of Communications, Information, Technology, and the Arts, or DCITA), as the government tries to 'fulfil diverse expectations' with regards the role culture should play in society (ibid.: 2–3).

As such, cultural policy is both complex, and culturally, historically and geographically specific. It also has an important relationship to the activities of museums and galleries, in that it can regulate understandings of what 'culture' is, whom it is for, and who has responsibility for it. Indeed, as John Holden (2005: 26) points out, even the vocabulary used in cultural policy can be influential: in the UK, the army, agriculture, and areas of industry and transport all receive public funding, but whereas farmers receive what are described as "top-up payments", "only the arts are described as a subsidised sector".

GOVERNANCE, LEGAL STATUS AND FUNDING MODELS

There are other areas in which organisational priorities, as well as day-to-day decision-making, in museums and galleries are impacted upon by factors not entirely within their control, including the system of governance in place, the legal status obtained, and the funding model adopted. The term 'governance' here refers not to a specific body of the state (i.e. the British Government), but to the action or manner of governing. One important aspect of this, cultural policy, has been discussed above. But there are other aspects to governance. For example, since the adoption of political devolution in the UK, in 1999, there have been four governing bodies: the British, Scottish and Welsh Governments, and the Northern Ireland Executive, all of which are answerable to their respective parliaments, and the public. There are also:

- national and regional departments;
- national and regional statutory bodies;
- local authorities;
- non-departmental public bodies;
- national, regional and independent charities.

In addition, the management of museums and galleries in Scotland, Wales and Northern Ireland is different to that for the arts (e.g. by Museums, Galleries Scotland, and Creative Scotland respectively), and the UK has ratified a number of international conventions, including UNESCO's (1970) 'Convention on the Means of Prohibiting and Preventing the Illicit Import, Export and Transfer of Ownership of Cultural Property'. As a result, museums and galleries in the UK, as elsewhere, operate within a complex governance landscape, and are bound by varying rules and regulations in the course of their normal activities.

The legal status and funding model of the museum or gallery likewise come with certain conditions, and benefits. For instance, many museums across the world are charities. In the UK, charities are also 'limited companies' – meaning that, provided they act within the law, members of the governing body cannot be personally liable for the museum's activities (Hebditch 2008: 2). Charitable status in England also means that museums can benefit from an 80% statutory rate relief on premises and recover tax via Gift Aid donations (ibid.). In the US, museums usually take the form of a charitable trust, association or corporation, with different legal specifics applying to each with regards personal liability, the ability to retain property, and organisational structure, although all can be tax-exempt so long as they remain non-profit making and comply with certain additional requirements (Phelan 2014: 7–11). However, neither the concept of a 'trust' nor 'charitable status' exists everywhere, and even when they do, it is not always possible to legally register. In China, for example, private museums must register as 'private non-profit-making institutions', and so cannot claim the same taxation benefits as public museums (Lu 2014 citing Gao 2010).

Systems of governance, legal status and fundraising models are thus to some extent inextricable, and work together to shape the organisational structure and practice of the museum or gallery. It is important to note, however, that systems of this kind do not necessarily imply restriction. Indeed, many museums and galleries throughout the world voluntarily sign up to accreditation schemes, or codes of ethics, such as those provided by the International Council of Museums (ICOM 2013), in order to set minimum standards for the profession as a whole. Museums can, and have been, sanctioned for breaking these agreed upon principles. In the past 25 years, three local authorities in the UK have been barred from the Museums Association (MA), while the recent sale of an ancient Egyptian Sekhemka statue, deemed to be "financially-motivated" rather than in the public interest, prompted the MA to consider "tougher measures" (Atkinson 2014).

THE PUBLIC INTEREST AND THE PRIVATE MARKET

As we have argued, since they became 'public' institutions, museums and galleries around the world have been considered, in principle, to be a 'public good'; that is, something in the service of the public, if not owned (at least indirectly) by them. What is different today, we might say, is that these public institutions are now operating in an increasingly privatised world. This is not without some precedent. The museologist Stephen Weil (1983: 4), for example, notes that while American museums were always 'public' in the sense that they were open to the public and didn't make a profit, they were also, from the very beginning, "profoundly private" in their funds, control, and even in that their "senior staff [were] drawn from a privileged social class". More recently, the art critic Claire Bishop has argued that museums and galleries in the US now operate "without any pretence to a separation of public and private interests […] it is well known that the Museum of Modern Art in New York regularly rehangs its permanent collection on the basis of its trustees' latest acquisitions" (Bishop 2014: 9).

This blurring of the boundaries between public and private interests is a concern in many other parts of the world too. The case is particularly acute for art museums and galleries, who are dealing with an explosion in the private art market, and an astonishing rise in prices. Andy Warhol's *Liz*, for instance, sold for $2 million in 1999, but for $24 million in 2007 (Adam 2014: 1). At the same time, as we have seen, state funding in many countries is decreasing. In order to acquire new works, as well as hold onto increasingly valuable collections, museums and galleries must find new ways to inspire the public to donate or explore other options. For Philips and Whannel (2013: 1–2), the growth in commercial sponsorship is not the answer. They argue that this acts as a "Trojan horse", smuggling corporate interests into the public economy.

Not everyone agrees. J. Mark Schuster (1998: 128–9), an American cultural policy specialist, points out that very few American museums actually moved from being "purely public to purely private", and, instead, have a long tradition of operating as "hybrids". For example, the museum's building and grounds may be owned by the local council, but the collection by the state, with shop revenue classified as 'profit-making', and commercial sponsorship supporting an individual exhibition. As a consequence, Schuster argued that the binary division between 'public' and 'private', in the US and elsewhere, risks "oversimplification and misunderstanding". Museums are not "pure forms", but involve a mixture of interests pushing and pulling in all directions (ibid.).

This 'mixture of interests' can result in unusual, and controversial, solutions. For instance, in the UK, shrinking funding for local governments has led to instances of "community management", where responsibility for the operation of a local authority museum is shifted from the council, to the community (Rex 2015). In other words, whereas the state once accepted responsibility for the management of the museum on behalf of the public, it now expects members of 'the public', in the form of newly registered charities, trusts or Community Interest Companies (or CICs), to take this on. The move is suggested to be pragmatic, based on the (questionable) rationale that local people are better placed to meet local needs. It also avoids 'selling off' assets to the private sector. Yet the imperative remains financial, and has political consequences; as Rex asks, "is it now part of our civic duty to step in when councils can no longer afford to run [museums and galleries]?" (ibid.).

TOURISM, LEISURE AND MARKETING

We might not all want to accept the challenge of running a museum or gallery, but huge numbers of us do visit them each year, as saw earlier in this book. According to *Art Newspaper* (2015: 2), in 2014, 9,260,000 people visited the Louvre, France, 6,695,213 went to The British Museum, while the National Gallery, in London, attracted 6,416,724, making them the top three most visited art museums in the world.

Tourists often account for a substantial proportion of these figures. The National Palace Museum in Taipei, Taiwan, for example, organised all of the top three best-attended exhibitions of 2014, with an exhibition of paintings and calligraphic works by Tang Yin drawing more than 12,000 visitors a day. Yet only one-third of the total visitors to the National Palace Museum were from Taiwan; half came from mainland China (*Art Newspaper* 2015: 2). Similarly, a report by the DCMS demonstrates that overseas visits to the Royal Armouries museums in the UK accounted for 68% of all visits (see Figure 4.1), while DCMS-sponsored museums in London tended to attract between 40–60% of their visitors from abroad (ibid.: 9).

As the sociologist Bella Dicks (2003: 44–47) explains, this was not always the case. Global tourism is a relatively new phenomenon, while the idea of "trudging around art galleries and museums" looking at 'high culture' while on holiday until quite recently "sounded like rather hard work". However, as Dicks points out, many museums and galleries now act, and are marketed as, "leisure destinations" and "entertainment hubs", offering interactive experiences, shopping, eating and places to meet with friends. As a result, Dicks suggests that cultural visits have become "an expected part of the trip" (ibid.). Cultural tourism can also reap huge rewards for the museum that succeeds in attracting day-trip visitors, as well as those from overseas. The National Museum Directors' Council (NMDC 2011), in the UK, reported that that there were "more visitors to the museums on Exhibition Road (the Victoria & Albert Museum,

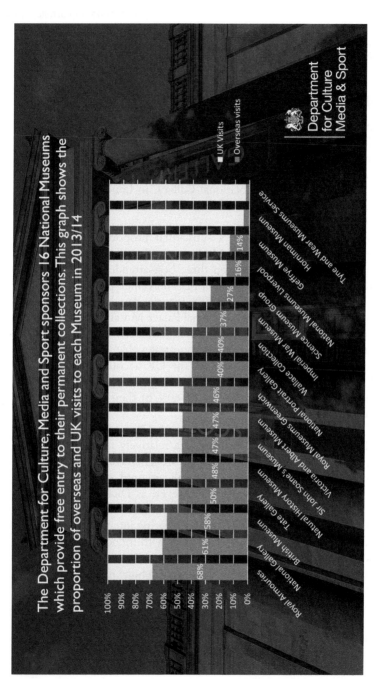

The Department for Culture, Media and Sport sponsors 16 National Museums which provide free entry to their permanent collections. This graph shows the proportion of overseas and UK visits to each Museum in 2013/14

- UK Visits
- Overseas visits

Royal Armouries, National Gallery, British Museum, Tate Gallery, Natural History Museum, Sir John Soane's Museum, Victoria and Albert Museum, Royal Museums Greenwich, National Portrait Gallery, Wallace Collection, Imperial War Museum, Science Museum Group, National Museums Liverpool, Geffrye Museum, Horniman Museum, Tyne and Wear Museums Service

68% 61% 58% 50% 48% 47% 47% 46% 40% 40% 37% 27% 16% 14%

Department for Culture Media & Sport

Figure 4.1 Proportion of overseas and UK visits to DCMS-sponsored museums in 2013/2014.

© DCMS.

or V&A, Natural History and Science Museums, all in London) each year than there are to the city of Venice", and that in 2009, UK museums and galleries "helped to secure £1 billion of inbound visitor spending".

The situation may not be entirely positive, however. Graham Black (2012: 1–15), a key figure in museum studies and heritage interpretation, has argued that museums and galleries are in fact "haemorrhaging traditional audiences" while failing to attract new ones or repeat visitors. This, Black cautions, is an "impending crisis" masked only by the continuing boom in cultural tourism (ibid.) and while national museums and "other rock stars of the tourist world" can continue to rely on tourism, small local history museums are unlikely to be able to compete (ibid.: 43). Indeed, it may that the Royal Armouries sites featured in the DCMS chart above (one in London, one in Leeds, and one in Fort Nelson) are an anomaly; both the National Museums Liverpool and Tyne and Wear Museums Service receive significantly fewer overseas visits than their London counterparts. Perhaps, as Black suggests, museums and galleries need to be "much more than tourist attractions and providers of leisure activities" (ibid.: 8) if they are to survive.

REGENERATION THROUGH CULTURE (THE 'BILBAO EFFECT')

Cultural tourism can have other effects too. One of the most famous of these is 'cultural regeneration', or the idea that culture can act as a development strategy, attracting not just visitors but invest-ment, and thus reinventing cities in economic decline. The classic example as already mentioned is Bilbao, a struggling post-industrial city in northern Spain, which, following the development of Frank Gehry's spectacular Guggenheim Museum Bilbao, in 1997, was able to rebrand itself as a 'must see' cultural destination.

The Guggenheim Museum Bilbao welcomed 1.36 million visitors in its first year, more than triple the number expected (Guggenheim Museum 1998). It also generated 198 million euros in tourism revenues, while Gehry's building is widely considered to be an architectural masterpiece (ibid.). Perhaps on account of this "phenomenal success", it quickly became a model for urban development around the world (Baniotopoulou 2001), with similar schemes hoping to recreate the 'Bilbao effect'. Yet while the Guggenheim Museum Bilbao is generally regarded as a success story, attempts to replicate it have fared less well. The newly built National Centre for Popular Music, Public, and Quad Arts Centre, in the UK, have all struggled with low visitor numbers and financial difficulties (*Economist* 2012). There are other problems too. Critics have pointed to the deployment of 'super-museums', first and foremost, as tools of economic development, and tools aimed at the international visitor, rather than the local (Baniotopoulou 2001). The prevalent focus upon displays of modern art is also a concern in these super-museums, for what then of the power of museums dedicated to anthropology, or local history (ibid.)?

Rather than a mechanism for cultural regeneration then, it appears that the legacy of the Guggenheim Museum Bilbao might instead be an increased focus on landmark or so-called 'signature' buildings, and a kind of cultural franchising. Alongside existing buildings in New York, Venice and Bilbao, the Guggenheim Abu Dhabi is currently under construction, while the Guggenheim Helsinki, in Finland, announced Paris firm Moreau Kusunoki Architects as the winning designers for a 130 million euro project, where "the potential to become a landmark and a symbol of Helsinki" was one of the key conditions of the competition (Guggenheim Museum 2015b). Not one of these key conditions made reference to a collection, or a display (ibid.), and in 2016 the Helsinki scheme was dealt a serious blow, when state funding was ruled out (Henley 2016).

An important factor here is that museums have been allocated a special importance as buildings. Museums have often become symbols of civic pride, or of progress. There are three related points. The first is that museums usually, and ideally, occupy a dedicated site, and that it is remarked upon when they do not. They seldom share premises with, say, commercial organisations not related to them. 'Public space' is 'sacred' space. There are some exceptions. The Mori Art Museum in Tokyo is only one part of a massive complex of tower blocks, for example, sitting between other functions run by other organisations.

Second, the distinction between commercial, private and public spaces is becoming less clear. Several private collectors have built museums or galleries. The Broad in Los Angeles and the Saatchi Gallery in London are two famous examples, but are distinct. The Broad is a museum with a permanent collection and subject to the same rules as other museums. The Saatchi Gallery shows work from Charles Saatchi's collection. He often sells work on, sometimes profiting from 'riding the market', albeit reinvesting funds in younger artists' work. This is a quasi- commercial operation in one sense, albeit one with enormous overheads and capital expenditure. A third point is that private museums have become a distinct and intriguing area of study, both for academics and architects, in recent years.

THE 'MUSEUM BOOM', 1980–2010: COSTS AND CONSEQUENCES

Today, it seems more urgent than ever to reconsider the purpose of building new museums and galleries. This is particularly the case when so many new museums are being built. For example, it has been suggested that, worldwide, 95% of existing museums postdate World War Two (Lowenthal 1998: 3), with the 1980s witnessing a "phenomenal growth in the building of museums across the Western world" (Aynsley 2009: 208). In Asia and the Middle East, the rate of growth has been nothing short of spectacular. In 1949, China had around 200 museums (Denton 2005: 44). By 1999, this figure had increased to 1,357 (ibid.), and by 2012, China hit its target of 3,500 museums three years early, opening a record 451 new museums that year alone (*Economist* 2013: 8). Similarly, in Taiwan, the number of museums rose from 50, in 1980, to 149 by 1997 (Chung 2005: 30). A recent "museum boom" has been reported in Beirut (Harris 2015), while the cultural district in Saadiyat Island, Abu Dhabi, lists among the five entirely new museum complexes to be built the 450,000 square-foot Guggenheim Abu Dhabi (Guggenheim Museum 2015a), and architect Jean Nouvel's Louvre Abu Dhabi, which required 21,000 cubic metres of concrete just in the base of the building (Louvre Abu Dhabi 2014). At the same time, many existing museums have undertaken comprehensive programmes of redevelopment and expansion from MoMA (2015b), Tate Modern (Tate 2016), to all five of the museums on 'Museum Island' in Berlin (Museuminsel n.d.).

There is some need for caution here, for the 'museum boom' is attributable to a variety of causes, often specific to each country, as well as to an increased range in function. Not all of the new museums are 'super-museums' costing billions to construct. Sharon Macdonald, for instance, highlights the "proliferation of small, low-budget, neighbourhood museums, often concentrating upon the culture of everyday life or local heritage" (Macdonald 2011: 5). This is arguably the case for museums in Wales, where the majority of museums were founded in the last 35 years, but in "response to local community interest" (Museums, Libraries and Archives Wales 2010: 4) rather than governmental quotas (*Economist* 2013: 8), or increased private funding (Harris 2015).

The rapid rate of building has also brought difficulties. It has been suggested that many of China's new museums lack collections and curators, leading the *Economist* to question how it planned to fill so many display spaces (2013: 8). When plans for the Louvre Abu Dhabi were announced, revealing that Abu Dhabi officials would pay 400 million euros just in order to use the "Louvre" name, 4,700 people – including "many curators, art historians and archaeologists" – signed an online petition stating that their museums were "not for sale" (Astier 2007). There are also problems with sustainability. In 2014, it was suggested that "museums that move to new, bigger homes traditionally see increased attendance" (Pes and Sharpe 2014: 6), yet by 2015 there were reports that a new generation of museum directors were struggling to keep the lights on (Halperin 2015). Perhaps most worryingly of all, there are mounting concerns about the possible "mistreatment and exploitation" of migrant workers on Saadiyat Island, Abu Dhabi (Batty 2013).

The recent 'museum boom' thus raises questions at the very heart of museum studies: what are we building, why, how and with what consequences? Are museums and galleries first and foremost houses of objects, or are they sacred spaces, educational centres, meeting places, 'signature' attractions or sites of local interest? What is the purpose of the museum in the twenty-first century?

CONCLUSIONS

As businesses in the business of culture, museums and galleries today face a range of critical questions. Who can, and should, pay for what? What might funders, of all kinds, want in return for their money? What, and who, are museums built for, and how can we continue to run them in times of economic decline? Should we? In each case, there are regulations and restrictions to consider, benefits to be obtained and, at times, unspoken obligations to be performed. What looks like a generous gift from one perspective can be seen as a cynical marketing ploy from another point of view. As we have argued, people's responses to these questions will depend on much deeper philosophical standpoints regarding what we under-stand the relationship between state(s), public(s) and culture(s) to be. Similarly, much will depend on people's and governments' broader assumptions about what should be supported publically and what should be left to market forces. Ultimately, much of what we have been discussing comes down to what individuals and societies understand the value of culture to be and how might this best be articulated, and measured. As Chapter 2 demonstrates, these issues have been around since the transformation of earlier private col-lections into public institutions. In this respect, many of the funda-mental issues are not new; what does change is the framing of the questions and the answers proposed. One thing is clear: to make a decision concerning the finances of the museum or gallery is to make a decision not only about the purpose, and possible future, of the institution itself but about the very idea of public culture.

REFERENCES

Adam, G. (2014) *Big Bucks: The Explosion of the Art Market in the 21st Century*. Farnham: Lund Humphries.

Aynsley, J. (2009) *Designing Modern Germany*. London: Reaktion Books.

Baxandall, M. (1972) *Painting and Experience in Fifteenth-Century Italy*. Oxford: Oxford University Press.

Bishop, C. (2014) *Radical Museology: Or, What's 'Contemporary' in Museums of Contemporary Art?* Revised 2nd edition. London: Koenig Books.

Black, G. (2012) *Transforming Museums in the Twenty-First Century*. London and New York: Routledge.

BOP Consulting (2012) *Measuring the Economic Impact of the Arts and Culture: Practical Guidance on Research Methodologies for Arts and Cultural Organisations.* London: Arts Council England.

British Council (2014) *Re-Imagine Museums and Galleries: UK–India Opportunities and Partnerships.* London: British Council.

Chung, Y. (2005) 'The impact of privatization on museum admission charges: A case study from Taiwan'. *International Journal of Arts Management* 7(2): 27–38.

Cooper, K.C. (2008) *Spirited Encounters: American Indians Protest Museum Policies and Practices.* Plymouth: AltaMira Press.

Craik, J. (2007) *Re-visioning Arts and Cultural Policy: Current Impasses and Future Directions.* Canberra: ANU E Press.

Denton, K.A. (2005) 'Museums, memorial sites and exhibitionary culture in the People's Republic of China', in M. Hockx and J. Strauss (eds) *Culture in the Contemporary PRC*: The China Quarterly Special Issues, No. 6. Cambridge: University of Cambridge Press.

Dicks, B. (2003) *Culture on Display: The Production of Contemporary Visitability.* Berkshire: Open University Press.

Economist (2013) 'China: Mad about museums: Special report museums'. *The Economist*, 21 December, 8–9.

Evans, M. (2015) *Artwash: Big Oil and the Arts.* London: Pluto Press.

Falk, J.H. and B.K. Sheppard (2006) *Thriving in the Knowledge Age: New Business Models for Museums and Other Cultural Institutions.* Oxford: AltaMira Press.

Gray, C. (2002) 'Local government and the arts'. *Local Government Studies* 28(1): 77–90.

Gray, C. (2008) 'Instrumental policies: Causes, consequences, museums and galleries'. *Cultural Trends* 17: 209–222.

Hillman-Chartrand, H. and C. McCaughey (1989) 'The arm's length principle and the arts: An international perspective – past, present and future', in M. Cumming and M. Schuster (eds) *Who's to Pay for the Arts? The International Search for Models of Support.* New York: American Council for the Arts Books: 54–55.

International Council of Museums (ICOM) (2013) 'ICOM code of ethics for museums'. Paris: International Council of Museums.

Kendall, G. (2012) 'Slash and burn'. *Museums Journal* November: 24–28.

Local Government Association (2013) *Driving Growth Through Local Government in the Arts.* London: Local Government Association.

Lowenthal, D. (1998) *The Heritage Crusade and the Spoils of History.* Cambridge: Cambridge University Press.

Lu, T.L.-D. (2014) *Museums in China: Power, Politics and Identities*. Oxford: Routledge.

Macdonald, S. (2011) *A Companion to Museum Studies*. Chichester: Blackwell.

McClellan, A. (2003) *Art and Its Publics: Museum Studies at the Millennium*. Oxford: Blackwell.

Pes, J. and E. Sharpe (2014) 'Expanding your space helps build an audience'. *The Art Newspaper: Special Report – Visitor Figures 2013* XXIII(256): 6.

Phelan, M.E. (2014) *Museum Law: A Guide for Officers, Directors, and Counsel*. 4th edition. Plymouth: Rowman & Littlefield.

Philips, D. and G. Whannel (2013) *The Trojan Horse: The Growth of Commercial Sponsorship*. London: Bloomsbury Academic.

Rocco, F. (2013) 'Temples of delight: Special report museums'. *The Economist* 21 December: 3–6.

Scott, C., J. Dodd and R. Sandell (2014) *Cultural Value. User value of museums and galleries: A critical review of the literature*. Leicester: RCMG and AHRC.

Schuster, J. (1998) 'Neither public nor private: The hybridization of museums'. *Journal of Cultural Economics* 22: 127–150.

Tate (2013) *Tate Report 2012–13*. London: Tate Publishing.

Tate (2014) *Tate Report 2013–14*. London: Tate Publishing.

TEFAF (The European Fine Art Foundation) (2012) *The International Art Market in 2011: Observations of the Art Trade over 25 Years*. Maastricht: The European Fine Art Foundation.

The State of Queensland, Queensland Museum (2009) *Valuing the Queensland Museum: A Contingent Valuation Study* 2008. Queensland: Queensland Museum.

Throsby, D. (2010) *The Economics of Cultural Policy*. Cambridge: Cambridge University Press.

Wallach, A. (2003) 'Norman Rockwell at the Guggenheim', in A. McClellan (ed.) *Art and Its Publics: Museum Studies at the Millennium*. Oxford: Blackwell.

Weil, S. (1983) *Beauty and the Beasts – On Museums, Art, the Law, and the Market*. Washington, DC: Smithsonian Institution Press.

WEBSITES

Art Newspaper (2015) 'Special report: Visitor figures'. URL: http://theartnews paper.com/reports/visitor-figures-2015/

ArtReview (2014) 'Power 100: 2014'. URL: http://artreview.com/power_100/ sheikha_al-mayassa_bint_hamad_bin_khalifa_al- thani/

Astier, H. (2007) 'Gulf Louvre deal riles French art world'. *BBC News* 6 March. URL: http://news.bbc.co.uk/1/hi/world/europe/6421205.stm

Atelier Jean Novel (2007) 'Louvre Museum Abu Dhabi (United Arab Emirates)'. URL: http://www.jeannouvel.com/mobile/en/smartphone/#/mobile/en/smartphone/projet/louvre-abou-dabi

Atkinson, R. (2014) 'Should there be tougher sanctions for museums that break the code of ethics?'. *Museums Journal* August. URL: http://www.museumsassociation.org/museums-journal/news/18082014-should-there-be-tougher-sanctions-for-museums-that-break-the-code-of-ethics

Baniotopoulou, E. (2001) 'Art for whose sake? Modern art museums and their role in transforming society: The case of the Guggenheim Bilbao'. *The Journal of Conservation and Museum Studies* (open access). URL: http://www.jcms-journal.com/articles/10.5334/jcms.7011/

Batty, D. (2012) 'Unilever ends £4.4m sponsorship of Tate Modern's turbine hall'. *The Guardian* 16 August 2012. URL: http://www.theguardian.com/artanddesign/2012/aug/16/unilever-ends-turbine-hall-sponsorship

Batty, D. (2013) 'Art world protest over "mistreatment" of migrants at Abu Dhabi cultural hub'. *The Guardian* 2 November. URL: http://www.theguardian.com/world/2013/nov/02/abu-dhabi-culture-guggenheim-louvre-workers-rights

Blatchford, I. (2015) 'Funders and our climate science gallery'. *The Science Museum Blog*. URL: https://blog.sciencemuseum.org.uk/funders-and-our-climate-science-gallery/

British Petroleum (BP) (2015) 'Connecting through arts and culture'. URL: http://www.bp.com/en_gb/united-kingdom/bp-in-the-community/connecting-through-arts-and-culture.html

Cascone, S. (2015) 'Paul Gauguin painting sells for record $300 million to Qatar museums in private sale'. *Artnet News* 5 February. URL: https://news.artnet.com/market/paul-gauguin-painting-sells-for-record-300-million-to-qatar-museums-in-private-sale-245817

Chow, V. (2014) 'M+ Museum adds Tiananmen images to its collection'. *South China Morning Post*. 17 February. URL: http://www.scmp.com/news/hong-kong/article/1429202/m-museum-adds-tiananmen-images-its-collection

Clark, N. (2015) 'Museums and galleries across UK planning to charge entry fees amid funding cuts'. *The Independent* 23 July. URL: http://www.independent.co.uk/arts-entertainment/art/news/museums-and-galleries-across-uk-planning-to-charge-entry-fees-amid-funding-cuts-10411329.html

Clore Duffield Foundation (2015) 'Introduction'. URL: http://www.cloreduffield.org.uk/home.htm

Department for Culture Media and Sport (DCMS) (2015) 'Sponsored museums: Performance indicators 2013/14'. URL: https://www.gov.

uk/government/uploads/system/uploads/attachment_data/file/409904/ Sponsored_Museums_Performance_Indicators_2013_14_word_doc_v2.pdf

Dowd, V. (2011) 'Museum entry fees: How the UK compares'. *BBC News* 1 December. URL: http://www.bbc.co.uk/news/entertainment-arts-15982797

East Grinstead Museum (n.d.) 'Donate'. URL: http://www.eastgrinstead museum.org.uk/support-us/donate/

Economist (2012) 'Art the conqueror', *The Economist* 17 March. URL: http:// www.economist.com/node/21550291

Forbes (2014) 'The world's 100 most powerful women: Sheikha Mayassa Al Thani'. URL: http://www.forbes.com/profile/sheikha-mayassa-al-thani/

Frayling, C. (2010) 'Crude awakening: BP in the Tate'. *The Guardian* 30 June. URL: https://www.theguardian.com/artanddesign/2010/jun/30/ bp-tate-protests

Friends of Joyce Tower Society (2012) 'James Joyce Tower saved''. URL: http://jamesjoycetower.com

Gillis, J. and J. Schwartz (2015) 'Deeper ties to corporate cash for doubtful researcher'. *The New York Times* 21 February. URL: http://www.nytimes. com/2015/02/22/us/ties-to-corporate-cash-for-climate-change-researcher-Wei-Hock-Soon.html?_r=2

Guardian (2009) 'Defying arts charity "cost museum £80,000 grant"'. *The Guardian* 5 June. URL: http://www.theguardian.com/artanddesign/2009/ jun/05/fitzwilliam-museum-loses-art-fund-grant

Guggenheim Museum (1998) 'Bilbao one year anniversary: Unprecedented success'. URL: https://www.guggenheim.org/press-release/november-2-bilbao-one-year-anniversary-unprecedented-success

Guggenheim Museum (2015a) 'Abu Dhabi'. URL: https://www.guggenheim. org/about-us

Guggenheim Museum (2015b) 'Helsinki Design Competition: About'. URL: http://designguggenheimhelsinki.org/en/about

Halperin, J. (2015) 'As a generation of directors reaches retirement, fresh faces prepare to take over US Museums'. *The Art Newspaper* 2 June. URL: http:// theartnewspaper.com/news/museums/156230/

Harris, G. (2015) 'Private fortunes drive Beirut's museum boom'. *The Art Newspaper* 7 October. URL: http://theartnewspaper.com/news/museums/ 159214/

Hebditch, K. (2008) 'Setting up a new museum'. Association of Independent Museums. URL: http://www.aim-museums.co.uk/downloads/3edb023b-f554-11e3-8be4-001999b209eb.pdf

Henley, J. (2016) 'New blow to Guggenheim Helsinki plan as Finnish party rules out state funding'. *The Guardian* 14 September. URL: https://www.theguardian.com/world/2016/sep/14/finnish-coalition-partner-rules-out-state-funding-guggenheim-helsinki

H!TANG and China Creative Connections (2011) 'How the cultural sector works in China'. URL: http://www.hitangandccc.com/blog/2011/11/financing-funding-cultural-projects-china

Holden, J. (2005) 'Capturing cultural value: How culture has become a tool of government policy'. Demos. URL: https://www.demos.co.uk/files/CapturingCulturalValue.pdf

Kendall, G. (2013) 'Science Museum group would close one site if 10% cut goes ahead'. *Museums Journal* 5 June. URL: http://www.museumsassociation.org/museums-journal/news/05062013-science-museum-group-would-close-museum

Kirchgaessner, S. (2014) 'Italy to bring private sector into its museums in effort to make a profit'. *The Guardian* 21 December. URL: http://www.theguardian.com/culture/2014/dec/21/italy-aims-to-make-museums-profitable

Louvre (n.d.) 'Hours and admission'. URL: http://www.louvre.fr/en/hours-admission/admission#tabs

Louvre Abu Dhabi (2014) 'Construction of Louvre Abu Dhabi in progress'. URL: http://louvreabudhabi.ae/en/building/Pages/development.aspx

Macalister, T. (2015) 'Shell sought to influence direction of Science Museum climate programme'. *The Guardian* 31 May. URL: https://www.theguardian.com/business/2015/may/31/shell-sought-influence-direction-science-museum-climate-programme

Metropolitan Museum of Art (2013) 'Metropolitan Museum announces gift of major cubist collection comprising 78 works by Picasso, Braque, Gris, and Léger from Leonard A. Lauder and creation of new research center for modern art'. URL: http://www.metmuseum.org/press/news/2013/lauder-announcement

Ministry of Education, Culture and Science, Holland (2013) 'The Dutch cultural system'. URL: https://www.government.nl/documents/leaflets/2013/06/17/the-dutch-cultural-system

MoMA (2014) 'The Museum of Modern Art: Consolidated financial statements June 30, 2014 and 2013'. URL: https://www.moma.org/momaorg/shared/pdfs/docs/about/MoMAFY14.pdf

MoMA (2015a) 'Hours and admission'. URL: http://www.moma.org/visit/plan/index#hours

MoMA (2015b) 'Museum history'. URL: http://www.moma.org/about/history

Museuminsel (n.d.) 'The future of the Museum Island Berlin'. URL: https://www.museumsinsel-berlin.de/en/home/

Museums, Libraries and Archives Wales (2010) 'A museums strategy for Wales'. URL: http://www.museumsassociation.org/download?id=127545

National Lottery (UK) (2015) 'Where the money goes'. URL: https://www.national-lottery.co.uk/life-changing/where-the-money-goes

National Museum Directors' Council (NMDC) (2011) '10th anniversary of free admission to national museums'. URL: http://www.nationalmuseums.org.uk/what-we-do/encouraging_investment/free-admission/

National Portrait Gallery (2014) 'News Release: National Portrait Gallery and Art Fund "save Van Dyck" appeal successful as over £10m raised thanks to Heritage Lottery Fund Grant of £6.3m'. URL: http://www.npg.org.uk/about/press/news-release-national-portrait-gallery-and-art-fund-save-van-dyck.php

National September 11 Memorial and Museum (2015) 'Facts and figures'. URL: https://www.911memorial.org/interact

Novamedia (2015) 'Charity lotteries: The Netherlands'. URL: http://www.novamedia.nl/about-charity-lotteries/the-netherlands

Odeon (2015) 'London Leicester Square'. URL: http://www.odeon.co.uk/cinemas/london_leicester_square/105/

Osborne, G. and N. MacGregor (2015) '100 objects to Help Britain and China get to know each other'. *The Telegraph* 21 September. URL: http://www.telegraph.co.uk/news/worldnews/asia/china/11878384/100-objects-to-help-Britain-and-China-get-to-know-each-other.html

Pirovano, S. (2015) 'Are Italy's museum reforms enough to stop the rot?' *Apollo* 1 June. URL: http://www.apollo-magazine.com/are-italys-museum-reforms-enough-to-stop-the-rot/

Pogrebin, R. (2011) 'Resisting renaming of Miami Museum'. *The New York Times* 6 December. URL: http://www.nytimes.com/2011/12/07/arts/design/jorge-m-perezs-name-on-miami-museum-roils-board.html?_r=0

Rawlinson, K. (2015) 'Activists occupy British Museum over BP Sponsorship'. *The Guardian* 13 September. URL: http://www.theguardian.com/business/2015/sep/13/activists-occupy-british-museum-over-bp-sponsorship

Rex, B. (2015) 'Who runs local museums and how are they surviving the funding crisis?' *The Guardian* 10 July. URL: http://www.theguardian.com/public-leaders-network/2015/jul/10/who-runs-local-museums-surviving-funding-crisis

Rogers, S. (2012) 'Government spending by department, 2011–12: Get the data'. *The Guardian* 4 December. URL: https://www.theguardian.com/news/datablog/2012/dec/04/government-spending-department-2011-12

Rosenfield, K. (2012) 'Update: Zaha Hadid's Maxxi Museum faces closure' *ArchDaily* 11 May. URL: http://www.archdaily.com/233629/update-zaha-hadids-maxxi-museum-faces-closure/

Rothschild Foundation Europe (2015) 'History'. URL: http://rothschildfoun dation.eu/about/history/

Royal Museums Greenwich (2009) 'National Maritime Museum secures £5m Heritage Lottery Fund grant towards Sammy Ofer Wing project'. URL: http://www.rmg.co.uk/work-services/news-press/press-release/national-maritime-museum-secures-%C2%A35m-heritage-lottery-fund

Science Museum (2015) 'Cosmonauts: Birth of the space age'. URL: http://www.sciencemuseum.org.uk/visitmuseum/plan_your_visit/exhibitions/cosmonauts

Siegal, N. (2013) 'Euro crisis hits museums'. *Art in America* May 2013. URL: http://www.artinamericamagazine.com/news-features/magazine/euro-crisis-hits-museums/

Smithsonian (2015a) 'Visitor information'. URL: http://www.si.edu/visit

Smithsonian (2015b) 'Smithsonian statement: Dr. Wei-Hock (Willie) Soon'. URL: http://newsdesk.si.edu/releases/smithsonian-statement-dr-wei-hock-willie-soon

Tate (2016) 'The Tate Modern project'. URL: http://www.tate.org.uk/about/projects/tate-modern-project

Tremlett, G. (2011) 'Spain's E44m Niemeyer centre is shut in galleries glut'. *The Guardian* 3 October. URL: http://www.theguardian.com/world/2011/oct/03/spain-niemeyer-centre-closes

United Nations Educational, Social and Cultural Organisation (UNESCO) (1970) 'Convention on the means of prohibiting and preventing the illicit import, export and transfer of ownership of cultural property'. URL: http://portal.unesco.org/en/ev.php-URL_ID=13039&URL_DO=DO_TOPIC&URL_SECTION=201.html

Victoria and Albert Museum (2015a) 'First major construction milestone for V&A Dundee'. 23 June. URL: http://www.vandadundee.org/news/187/First-major-construction-milestone-for-VA-Dundee.html

Victoria and Albert Museum (2015b) 'Dundee Waterfront'. URL: http://www.vandadundee.org/Dundee-Waterfront

Youngs, I. (2013) 'Newcastle Council's 50% arts cuts confirmed'. *BBC News* 7 March. URL: http://www.bbc.co.uk/news/entertainment-arts-21668498

FURTHER READING

Cooper, K. C. (2008) *Spirited Encounters: American Indians Protest Museum Policies and Practices*. Plymouth: AltaMira Press.

Craik, J. (2007) *Re-Visioning Arts and Cultural Policy: Current Impasses and Future Directions*. Canberra: ANU E Press.

Cumming, M. and M. Schuster (eds) *Who's to Pay for the Arts? The International Search for Models of Support*. New York: American Council for the Arts Books.

Dicks, B. (2003) *Culture on Display: The Production of Contemporary Visitability*. Maidenhead: Open University Press.

Evans, M (2015) *Artwash: Big Oil and the Arts*. London: Pluto Press.

Scott, C. (ed.) (2013) *Museums and Public Value: Creating Sustainable Futures*. London and New York: Routledge.

Throsby, D. (2010) *The Economics of Cultural Policy*. Cambridge: Cambridge University Press.

Weil, S. (1983) *Beauty and the Beasts – On Museums, Art, the Law, and the Market*. Washington, DC: Smithsonian Institution Press.

5

DISPLAY, INTERPRETATION AND LEARNING

WHAT DOES 'DISPLAY' MEAN IN A MUSEUM OR GALLERY CONTEXT?

Objects are everywhere. In our homes, we carefully select and arrange them on a regular basis, although we think quite differently of the photographs on the mantelpiece, the jumble of toiletries on the bathroom shelf, and the plastic bags shoved into the drawer. In our workplaces, shops, public spaces and supermarkets too, we are used to seeing objects grouped together and presented in certain ways. We know that small items placed on desks are likely to have personal value, those found in the stationery cupboard less so. We know how to scan the department store to locate certain sections, perhaps looking for changes in colour, layout, or even in the height of shelves. We know that a single, spot-lit handbag in the window of a shop is likely to be expensive, without asking the price, and that multiple objects crammed in together are likely to be cheap. To put it another way, we do more than simply 'see' objects in our everyday lives – we are constantly 'interpreting' them so as to infer their meaning, value and significance.

If some of the ways of displaying objects noted above seem reminiscent of the museum or gallery space, there is a good reason: the ways in which objects are displayed in museums and galleries has directly influenced the display of objects elsewhere. This is often done deliberately to increase the perceived worth of the object in question. For instance, Mark H. Moss (2007: 104) notes that when the retailer Nike began displaying their sports products they did so in "glass cases, with museum-like labels" set behind velvet ropes, hoping that in doing so the trainers, clothes and other accessories would be transformed into "art objects, complete with their glamorous aura". In the case of Nike, this desired-for 'specialness' is not a factor that accrues to an object in isolation, but is at least partially achieved through the way the object is displayed. Display technique, in this instance, is a crucial part of the branding process.

Financial value is not the only thing that museum display strategies convey to us. Think of a period room, such as one at The Bowes Museum shown in Figure 5.1.

Figure 5.1 Furniture in the French Second Empire style, owned by John and Josephine Bowes and used in their homes in Paris in the 1850s and 60s, now displayed in The Bowes Museum.

© The Bowes Museum, Barnard Castle, County Durham.

Rooms like this tend to have coloured walls and mix furniture, artworks and other objects together in a way that feels 'authentic' to us – that is, as we imagine they might have been encountered in the past. Here a dining table and chairs are displayed on a carpet in a functional way. By contrast, the Ardabil Carpet on display at the Victoria & Albert Museum, London (Figure 5.2), is not only isolated and surrounded by a barrier, but only lit for only ten minutes of every thirty to conserve it (V&A 2015).

Do you respond differently to this second carpet? How might we, as visitors, react to and think about the carpet if it were part of a whole environmental display? What types of difference of meaning, of historical context, and of value and importance are suggested by the two different types of display strategy?

In fact, neither form of display can claim to be entirely 'authentic'. The display in the Bowes Museum, for instance, looks like a private dining room in some kind of historic property – or grand house or even a palace perhaps – left unchanged so that we might 'step into history'. But the Bowes Museum is in fact a purpose-built

Figure 5.2 The Ardabil Carpet, by Maqsud of Kashan. Iran, mid–16th century.
© Victoria and Albert Museum, London.

museum (not a house), and the room shown in the picture is a kind of 'composite', or stage-set (de Montebello 2004: 11) designed to showcase key pieces from the collection and to give visitors an impression of what the Bowes' home in Paris *might* have looked like. No-one in the past would have encountered these objects in this specific arrangement. Similarly, the Ardabil Carpet was originally intended for a religious shrine in Iran, not a secular gallery in London. It is what Kirshenblatt-Gimblett (1998: 2) would call a "fragment" of an original whole, displayed as if it was an 'autonomous' artefact. Considering both displays together, we can see that through the particular organisation of objects, space and light, one carpet is suggested to be a historical artefact seen in its social setting, while the other is displayed as a work of art to be viewed aesthetically.

As these two examples illustrate, modes of display are a key concern for everyone working in museums and galleries. This is because display is about more than the use of a certain technique or the arrangement of certain kinds of material in a given space. To display something is an act, and the way that museums and galleries display their collections sets up and frames the visitor's encounter, not just with individual objects but with the past more broadly. Indeed, we argue here that the act of display can never be neutral, for it produces particular ways of knowing and valuing objects. This leads us to question again: what and whose stories, histories, ideas and values should curators decide to present and privilege? If display can lend 'specialness' or value to particular types of objects, and indeed types of objects owned by, or laid claim to by, particular social groups, what are the responsibilities of a public museum or gallery? And what happens when we, as visitors, misread their cues, or make sense of what we see in ways distinct from those intended by curators and exhibition designers?

CLASSIC EXHIBITION GENRES

Displays in museums and galleries often correspond to one of a number of classic 'genres', such as chronological, thematic, monographic or national. Each privileges an implied set of stories and each genre has a specific history. Specific disciplines like art, ethnography or natural history may be thought to lend themselves to particular display approaches more readily than others, although there are many examples where curators may play with these kind of assumptions to challenge conventional ways of thinking about particular topics.

Chronological displays have, aside from cabinets of curiosity and royal collections, one of the longest histories in museum and gallery studies. They are associated with the formation of the public museum in Europe, and the impetus to order collections in a 'rational', systematic way using categories that have a 'universal' applicability. By displaying objects chronologically – or via their date of production – those who worked in museums and galleries were able to situate objects within particular sequences that imply a set of causes and effects in a longer story about types of object, whether that be paintings or social history. In this format, the curator demonstrates, or claims to identify, changes over time and their causes. In the nineteenth century, this process was crucial in fulfilling public museums' new educational roles as agents of 'improvement'. Rooms that had once been crammed with a juxtaposition of objects of all kinds became surveys, sometimes encyclopaedic in scope, displaying 'types' or 'specimens' in sequence.

Chronological displays of this kind remain extremely popular around the world. Yet the kinds of history told by such formats, and even the kinds of time implied in such displays have been subject to investigation. In the 'BP Walk Through British Art' exhibition at Tate Britain, London, for example, the then Director Penelope Curtis rehung the collection focusing strictly on 'real time' rather than 'art historical time' – which tends to group objects by style, theme or movement regardless of when things were actually made (Tate 2013). As a result, Curtis and her team were able to place *Lycidas*, a sculpture often considered to be Victorian (e.g. to 'look like' things made in the mid to late 1800s) in the room dedicated to its actual date of production – in the early 1900s. This meant that the sculpture was shown alongside much more 'modern' looking artworks that were nevertheless made at the same point in time, and so disrupted traditional expectations concerning the 'proper' sequence of art history.

Even more importantly, the concept of time itself can vary significantly around the world (see also Chapter 2). For example, for Aboriginal culture 'the Dreaming' sees time not as a fixed horizontal line (e.g. past, present and future) but a complex embracing of all three, so that time can be circular, spiraling and flexible. The kinds of historical time traditionally assumed to function between European art museums and ethnographic museums have likewise come under close scrutiny in recent scholarship. It is undeniable that until relatively recently, many art museums echoed a larger story of Europe's perpetual progress, as if one continent was creating the future. Ethnographic museums, by contrast, downplayed change, as if non-Western societies were somehow 'outside' history or 'behind' industrialised ones. There is also the question of the impact of chronological displays more generally, for these can 'call up' objects to support a given narrative, or place them and the visitor on what one curator has called "the conveyor belt of history", denying both their own unique qualities, and more diverse readings (Serota 1996: 7).

Thematic displays – or displays that group and arrange objects according to key ideas, principles, questions or features – developed slightly later in nineteenth century Europe. For Marandino *et al.* (2015: 252) they mark a significant break. While chronological displays might attempt to display an "exhaustive inventory", thematic displays were more selective, choosing a limited number of items that might together, in the case of natural history at least, "illustrate certain scientific principles". Thematic displays thus continued to have "strongly educational goals" (Ravelli 2006: 3) but were designed to appeal to a "wide range of visitors" (ibid.) and not just the scholars and experts who had been museum visitors for earlier chronological surveys.

Indeed, thematic displays continue to be seen as a principal alternative to historical approaches, even being described as 'ahistorical' displays. This is not strictly true – many thematic displays incorporate some chronological element – but they do allow for different focuses. For example, 'The Value of Money' exhibition at The National Museum of American History compiled more than 400 objects from across the world, but rather than arrange these by date, the exhibition tackled key themes including "the political and cultural messages money conveys" and "new monetary technologies" (National Museum of American History 2015). Thematic displays can also be chosen for more practical, or creative reasons.

When the new, purpose-built Tate Modern, in London, opened in 2000, it made headlines for the way it re-displayed its collection. No longer organised chronologically, or with regard to art historical schools, the gallery instead offered four thematic 'blocks' (e.g. 'Landscape/Matter/Environment' and 'Nude/Action/Body') each of which juxtaposed artworks of varying time periods, styles and by very different artists.

For some, this move allowed "continuities across time and space" to be opened up and explored, and for new, exciting and flexible stories and meanings to be created (Blazwick and Morris 2000: 33). For others, it was an opportune way to hide weaknesses in the collection (Alicata 2008). We might add to this that 'continuities' and meanings of the kind noted above often rely upon large amounts of 'cultural capital' (as discussed in Chapter 3), or the ability to 'read' the juxtaposition of artworks via an application of art historical knowledge. There is therefore a danger that thematic displays remain inaccessible, even impenetrable, for certain visitors.

Monographic or *'solo' displays*, unlike chronological or thematic displays, which tend to display objects made by multiple people, present a body of work as authored by a single person or group (e.g. an artist, designer or architectural company), or biographically assemble a collection of objects as associated with a single person or group. Monographic displays tend to be prestigious, and often imply a high status for their creator or subject. A museum or gallery can likewise increase their reputation by staging the first or largest exhibition by or of a high-status individual, or by revealing new work or research (the detail and breadth of monographic exhibitions often allows for the scholarly re-examination of subjects or authors). An exhibition devoted to the fifteenth-century sculptor Nicolas de Leyde at the Œuvre Notre-Dame Museum, in France, for example, sought to "bring together the greatest possible number" of de Leyde's works and led to a reassessment of artworks' attributions, necessarily changing the picture we have of the artist (Œuvre Notre-Dame Museum 2015).

The 'honour' of receiving a monographic show is important, particularly as, in the art world at least, this continues to be divided by media (painting is often 'ranked' more highly than multi-media installations), as well as sexuality, nationality and gender. A report in *Art Newspaper* by Halperin and Patel (2015: 5), for example, analysed

590 monographic shows held in the US between 2007 and 2013 and found that there was a "disproportionate bias" towards male artists, who accounted for around 73% of the total figure. This is important, for prestigious shows do not 'reflect' an artwork's importance or value, but help to construct it – and as the Guerrilla Girls (2005) famously pointed out, "less than 5% of the artists in the Modern Art sections are [by] women, but 85% of the nudes are female". Interestingly, Halperin and Patel (2015: 5) went on to note that this bias towards male artists was not borne out in the visitor figure data, leading the authors to suggest that visitors "did not discriminate based on gender". Yet monographic shows continue to be referred to, tellingly, as 'one-man shows', and despite the history of female artists and Feminist art, explicit attempts to create a parity of gender representation are still a reasonably new development. The Elizabeth A. Sackler Centre for Feminist Art at the Brooklyn Museum, for instance, opened in 2007 (Brooklyn Museum 2015), and the Max Mara Art Prize for Women, the "only visual art prize for women in the UK", was established in 2005 (Whitechapel Gallery 2017).

It is also important to remember that although monographic exhibitions are now commonplace, they are a relatively recent phenomenon. The previously popular chronological displays required only one item of each type, for example, and so there was no need to collect multiple objects as created by a single person. Likewise, in the visual arts, exhibitions tended towards the French 'Salon'-style, with paintings of varying genre and by multiple artists covering the walls. Arguably, it wasn't until the 1980s (Serota 1996: 15) that solo shows in art museums and galleries became a "dominant convention".

National displays tell the story or stories of 'the nation', or are otherwise held to be representative of 'the nation'. National displays have a necessarily complex history. As previously discussed, the concept of a modern, European, nation-state only dates from the late eighteenth century. Moreover, the borders of every country in Western Europe changed in the twentieth century. In addition, as we have already seen, the history of museum building is very different across the globe. Thus while the British Museum, which was founded in 1753, claims to be the "first national public museum in the world" (British Museum n.d.), the National Museum of Qatar is, at the time of writing, still being built. There are also a number of ways that a display might be viewed as 'national'. For example, a display in a museum or gallery of any kind may be explicitly devised so as to represent the nation or some aspect of it, while any display within a national museum – regardless of its content – might be viewed as representative simply on account of its location.

There are also a huge number of international fairs, displays and festivals, including the Venice Biennale, where the artists involved are held to be representatives of the nation that displays or funds the display of their work. 'National' displays such as these thus decide which features associated with the nation, its politics and culture, are to be emphasised or underplayed. Their historical scope can also vary: they can lay claim to long histories associated with territorial space, rather than 'nations' in the modern sense. The distinction is important, for, as Knell warns us, "the emergence of the national museum in different national settings cannot be read as nations doing the same thing" (2011: 6). Great care must be taken when assigning or associating objects, persons or ideas to the nation, not least because ideas of what defines individual nations changes over time.

The classic display genres outlined above are by no means exclusive or exhaustive. A monographic exhibition might well be organised chronologically, within a national museum for example. There are also many other possible genres to consider. Kirshenblatt-Gimblett (1998: 3), for example, distinguishes between 'in-situ' displays that recreate certain settings (e.g. as seen in dioramas or period rooms) and 'in-context' displays, which arrange objects according to a certain frame of reference (e.g. an evolutionary sequence, taxonomy or formal relationship). What it is important to stress, however, is that no genre is a 'natural' solution to displaying any kind of material, nor can it be seen as ideologically 'neutral'. As a consequence, those who work in museums and galleries, or study them, need to be alert to the "fundamentally theatrical" (ibid.) nature of display, and to the potential consequences of their selections.

TELLING AND SHOWING HISTORIES IN SPACE AND TIME

As discussed above, each exhibition genre works to tell a particular kind of (hi)story – but how is this achieved in practice? One of the key techniques employed here is the manipulation of space, and of our gazes and bodies in that space. Museums and galleries divide collections and objects into volumes of architectural display space, and into certain zones within their buildings. Such divisions can be achieved in terms of discipline or medium, or by the geographical area of objects' producers, their key ideas and/or themes. In other words, through grouping, isolating and zoning objects and ideas, those who work in museums and galleries necessarily also spatially sequence them.

These allocations of space are often based upon understandings of value, so that the collections, key objects or displays deemed to be most significant receive the most attention (e.g. by being placed in prominent or magnificent locations, or because they are given large quantities of space). Each decision can work to suggest or reinforce that value to visitors. As Moser (2010: 25) argues, "displays in large galleries can appear more grand and thus assume more importance and authority", while displays in smaller rooms tend to be seen as "intimate" or offer a "sub-plot within the larger narrative".

Crucially, it is not just the relative amount of space that we 'read' as significant, but the ways in which multiple spaces are organised and ordered throughout a building in order to direct us. For example, The National Museum of Scotland, in Edinburgh, has seven levels, each devoted to a different key period of time and organised chronologically, so that as the visitor walks from the bottom floor to the top they take a 'journey' as if through the history of Scotland from "prehistory to the present day" (National Museum of Scotland 2016). The connotations of 'ascending' are usually positive in the West, so there is a danger inherent in such a scheme that the story becomes hierarchically understood as one of permanent improvement towards the present day.

The way that objects are arranged within a single display can also tell a particular kind of story. The sequencing of objects along a wall, or as arranged through a number of rooms, can create a linear narrative that is meant to unfold as the visitor moves through space. Alternatively, displays that encourage visitors to roam freely between groups of objects place emphasis upon visitors making their own connections, or upon individual objects' own stories, as opposed to a set framework of understanding as created by the museum.

A good example of this discussion can be found in Nicholas Serota's (1996: 8–10) distinction between displays of artworks that favoured "interpretation" or "experience". "Interpretative" approaches are here understood as those that place artworks in historical sequence, so as to "illustrate" a traditional form of art history to visitors. Displays that showed the work of a single artist only, by contrast, are suggested to allow for the visitors' undistracted, personal and intensified engagement with the work, and thus emphasise their "experience" of it.

Even the spacing between two objects, or around a single object, can tell us something. In taxonomical displays, relationships between objects are often suggested by placing things near each other to encourage understanding through comparison. By contrast, when a single object is isolated in space, we are likely to think it deserves our full attention as if 'on its own terms' alone.

In other words, the way we interpret the meanings, significance and value of objects is always 'relational': we implicitly understand objects as being part of a wider world of things. We also understand each individual object in relation to those immediately around it, as well as those we saw beforehand, and those ahead of us on our route through space. It is for this reason that space is never simply the background to display (Hillier and Tzortzi 2011: 283). Indeed the curator Robert Storr (2015: 23) argues that space is "the [very] medium in which ideas are visually phrased". We would add two qualifications. Firstly, all displays, even seemingly static ones, are created in time as much as in space – and indeed, many displays are now interactive and changing. Secondly, 'space' is not just an issue of size or volume; it is not 'empty' but always 'full' of ideas and associations, both implicit and explicit.

WORKING WITH SPACES

Space is therefore an important factor in display, but it is not always possible to manipulate buildings to suit our demands. Other factors can intervene, such as the conservation needs of an object. For example, certain types of objects, like photographs and watercolour paintings, cannot be exposed to high levels of natural light. Large sculptures cannot be made to pass through narrow doorways.

Interactive devices may require power sources, which determine where they must be sited. A large number of other factors, including the size and nature of items of furniture, audio guides, text panels and labels may also contribute to how the overall display can be designed and configured. Seating may be required to provide opportunities for a certain kind of sustained looking and contemplation of objects, or to allow visitors to rest and engage in social interaction. Similarly, required access routes for people with disabilities and regulations about the circulation of people within a given space determine whether or not and where objects can be shown.

Balancing the desired 'content' of an exhibition with the material and physical needs of objects and visitors is one of the central challenges in display. One way of thinking through this challenge concerns the 'route' or 'pathway' a visitor might take within a given exhibition. For example, Manfred Lehmbruck (1974: 224–6) developed a number of 'circulation patterns' including:

An 'arterial', or circular, pattern, where visitors walk continuously in a fixed path around a space and back out again;

A 'comb' pattern, where visitors move in one direction, but 'zig-zag' via small, optional alcoves along the way;

A 'chain' pattern, which is similar to the above but involves a series of larger, self-contained spaces that might each have their own path;

A 'star' or 'fan' pattern, where there are multiple possible areas for the visitor to explore, each connected via a central area that must be returned to, and;

A 'block' pattern, which is relatively free-choice and can be explored in multiple ways.

As noted above, the selection of any one 'pattern' will greatly influence the way that objects are approached, and understood, by visitors. It may also result in certain practical outcomes – such as 'bottlenecks' when multiple visitors try to get through a narrow space. Indeed, it is not always possible to create a 'comb' pattern, for instance, as the space available within museums and galleries is dependent on the overall architecture of the institution.

The architecture of the museum or gallery is an extremely important feature because of the way it sets up certain possibilities, while closing down others. Architecture has also been a subject of considerable attention in museum and gallery studies because of the way that it acts to convey powerful messages and values to visitors (and non-visitors) even before they step inside. For example, the traditional architecture of the nineteenth-century museum in European societies – and reproduced in many parts of the world well into the twentieth-century – was based on the design of classical temples to symbolise education, authority and tradition. These buildings were typically designed to be approached by an impressive flight of steps leading up to monumental doors (Figure 5.3), thus reinforcing the idea of being granted access to a place of importance, enlightenment and improvement. Today, most contemporary art museums deliberately avoid the 'temple' model of raising visitors up to enter and use a different set of signals – which may appear

Figure 5.3 National Gallery of Art, Washington, DC. Designed 1937 and opened 1941.

© Rhiannon Mason.

Figure 5.4 Museo Universitario Arte Contemporáneo Universidad Nacional Autónoma de México (MUAC), Mexico City. Opened 2008.

© Rhiannon Mason.

more 'open' but have their own issues (Figure 5.4). However, as we discussed earlier, not everyone has the kinds of 'cultural capital' to read such signals positively.

In the case of art museums, the last forty years have seen successive revolutions of what kinds of spaces might be 'future-proof' with regard to what artists want to create. In the 'museum boom' of the last generation, many institutions have expanded or extended their sites. The size of individual art galleries, at least until recently, has also grown to accommodate new types of artwork. Some dilemmas remain. Should gallery spaces be fixed or flexible? Should they offer intimate encounters with artworks or provide grander public spaces? Does art feel more 'at home' in reused buildings, or ones with a patina of age, than brand new ones? Should there be a clear distinction between galleries and other types of space? There is also the question of exhibition design (a field in itself). Should the permanent architecture or the materials in an exhibition be designed to be clearly 'characterful', or to be as plain and neutral as possible?

Figure 5.5 Museu d'Art Contemporani de Barcelona (MACBA), Spain. Opened 1995.

© Alistair Robinson.

Richard Meier's design of the galleries at MACBA in Barcelona included both. Rectangular rooms are offset by strange, wave-shaped galleries, whose forms protrude out of the building (Figure 5.5). As this example shows, architecture and design need to be understood as distinct elements of the display-making process, and ones with a crucial impact upon the way that an exhibition is organised and understood (Macleod *et al.* 2012).

WHAT ARE THE RELATIONSHIPS BETWEEN DISPLAY AND KNOWLEDGE?

Displays in history museums, but also all types of museums and galleries should never be seen as 'mirrors' that simply reflect society, or as "containers in which to represent truth" (Whitehead 2012: 23). Instead, modes of display construct certain kinds of knowledge and meaning. These meanings might also be unintended. Meanings certainly change: what 'counts' as scientific knowledge and accepted museum display practice is often contested over time. But the key point here is that museum and gallery staff, through the act of display, play a crucial role in the construction of knowledge and even in knowledge that we now take to be obvious. For example, it might seem 'normal' to display archaeological objects differently to artworks, yet in nineteenth-century Britain these categories ('art' and 'archaeology') were under debate. Museum staff played a crucial role in deciding what each discipline should consist of, where it should be stored, and how each should be displayed (Whitehead 2009).

Similarly, Eilean Hooper-Greenhill (1992: 7) points out that many types of classification remain flexible and varied between institutions:

A silver teaspoon made in the 18th century would be classified as 'Industrial Art' in Birmingham City Museum, 'Decorative Art' at Stoke on Trent, 'Silver' at the Victoria and Albert Museum, and 'Industry' at Kelham Island Museum in Sheffield. [In each case] the meaning and significance of the teaspoon [is] correspondingly modified.

Moreover, classificatory schemes can be incorrectly applied, For example, Goodwin *et al.* (2015) recently suggested that 58% of tropical plant specimens had been given the 'wrong' name. In natural history museums, for instance, the idea of a 'natural order' with humankind's place at the 'top' has been challenged in recent years. Aronsson and Elgenius (2015: 2) have similarly argued that national displays do not present fixed, agreed upon ideas of the nation, but rather "create models and representations of nations – their past, present and future". They do this by making decisions about where the boundaries of the nation lie, what and who 'belongs' to the nation, and that which lies 'beyond'. It is also worth remembering that most objects in museums and galleries began their lives outside of the institution, and that the act of collection might significantly alter their meaning and value. For example, Kirshenblatt-Gimblett notes that 'ethnographic objects' only become ethnographic objects when they enter the museum (1998: 2–3).

Display, in this light, is always politically and ethically charged, and potentially fraught, for "every aspect of a museum, gallery or heritage site communicates" (Mason 2005: 200). Yet despite the long history of such debates about the very serious implications of displays, certain modes of display are still commonly thought of as normal, or as presenting 'facts'.

THE GALLERY AS 'WHITE CUBE'

'White cube'-style modernist galleries are of particular interest to any discussion of the power of display, because they were originally designed to present artworks in isolation. All visual and textual 'cues' (i.e. large gold frames around artworks, coloured walls, furniture, or even the close proximity of other artworks) were stripped away, and visitors were thought to be able to now experience artworks more directly, and without interference. As the art critic Brian O'Doherty (1976: 15) famously pointed out, white cube galleries were spaces where

> the outside world must not come in, so the windows are usually sealed off. Walls are painted white. The ceiling becomes the source of light. The wooden floor is polished so that you click along clinically, or padded so that you pad soundlessly, resting the feet while the eyes have at the wall. The art is free, as the saying used to go, 'to take on its own life'.

As an important part of this, and particularly after the Second World War, 'white cube' style art galleries also presented artworks without labels or wall texts, considering these to be too 'didactic', or directive of the visitor's attention. Such ideas remain influential. Some artists and even some curators continue to resist 'imposing' labels on, or nearby, artworks, believing that this practice prevents the artwork from 'speaking for itself', or distracts attention away from the work (Figure 5.6).

Yet, as academic Christopher Whitehead (2012: xi–xvi) argues, there is no such thing as 'no interpretation', even when text is absent. Rather, interpretation includes "everything which precedes, surrounds and follows its [an object's] production and consumption" – or in other words, everything we have discussed thus far, including the space, furniture, colour of walls, as well as everything a visitor reads, feels and understands (or does not) before visiting. All displays, even those without text, 'frame' objects in particular ways.

Figure 5.6 Tate Modern: Interior gallery with visitors.
© Tate, London 2009.

This is particularly important in the case of the white cube, for, text aside, it has been argued that the style of display selected does *not* present objects without interference. Rather, white cube-style displays make a deliberate choice to isolate objects from the 'real' world, its conflicts and contests, and thus actively conceal "all social, gender, religious [and] ethical differences in the name of aesthetic autonomy" (Weibel 2007: 139). As a result, white cube–style displays have a tendency to 'consecrate' objects, as though they were religious icons, prompting silent and reverential behaviour similar to that of a church's chapel (Serota 1996).

This is key, for while the white cube style of display remains a popular choice for artworks worldwide, it actively transforms the way we understand, and respond to, artworks. More recently, artists' use of projected images has demanded all natural light be excluded from galleries as in a cinema, with this style being named a 'black box' mode of display (Figure 5.7).

Figure 5.7 Installation at Northern Gallery for Contemporary Art (NGCA), Sunderland, 2006.

© Colin Davison/NGCA.

THE 'POETICS' AND 'POLITICS' OF DISPLAY

Given the relationship between the act of display and the construction of knowledge it is important that in the museum sector we develop tools and techniques to interrogate displays of all kinds. In New Museology, discussions of this kind are often centred around two interconnected terms: the 'poetics' and 'politics' of display. Both terms are taken from the Smithsonian Institution's international conference in 1988 addressing 'The Poetics and Politics of Representation' (Stam 2005: 57).

The poetics of display was first defined as the "underlying narrative/aesthetic pattern within exhibitions" (as quoted in Weil 2004: 77). It has also been understood as "the practice of producing meaning through the internal ordering and conjugation of the separate but related components of an exhibition" (Lidchi 1997: 168). In other words, the poetics of display concerns the creative decisions about how objects are grouped, ordered and linked together, as though objects were individual words and the curator a writer telling a story and stimulating thoughts and feelings in doing so.

The politics of display was first defined as "the social circumstances in which exhibitions are organised, presented and understood" (quoted in Weil 2004: 77). This is understood to concern the role and power of the museum in relation to how 'knowledge' is constructed. Politics is always a question of who benefits. Who is being addressed? Who is expected to be paying attention and who not? Who materially owns the objects? And who 'owns' them psychologically, that is, identifies with or lays claim to the stories they tell?

To give an example: the practice of displaying indigenous people in museums, fairgrounds and World's Fairs was extremely common well into the twentieth century. One of the most famous instances of this concerns a woman who became known as Sara Baartman or the Hottentot Venus. Born in South Africa in 1770s, Sara Baartman was apparently persuaded into agreeing to come to Britain in 1810 where she was publicly displayed in universities, society parties, and museums as a curiosity because of aspects of her unusual anatomical condition (Crais and Scully 2009). Her buttocks and genitalia were considerably larger than usual. This was seen at the time by some to be evidence of the racial theory that people of African descent like Sara were more 'primitive' than European peoples, more sexualised, and half-way between animals and humans. Accordingly, Sara was exhibited in provocative clothing and later ended up with an animal exhibitor in Paris (the 'poetics' of display). She was routinely examined by scientists, academics and anthropologists, and 'objectified' by being treated as an object of enquiry and knowledge rather than as a human being (the 'politics' of display).

After her death, Sara Baartman was dissected by Cuvier, Napoleon's surgeon who pickled her brain and genitalia, made a cast of her body and wired up her skeleton for display. Baartman's remains were put on public display in the Musee de l'homme in Paris until 1974 when they were removed and put into storage. In 1994, Nelson Mandela petitioned the French government to return Sara Baartman to her homeland, South Africa. The request was initially resisted on the grounds that it might pave the way for more repatriation requests and that her remains were important for study. The request was eventually accepted by the French government and in 2002 Baartman was flown back to South Africa on National Women's Day for a state burial in a grave with a commemorative plaque. The President of South Africa, Thabo Mbeki, made a speech at her funeral.

The case of Sara Baartman makes very clear the interrelation between the poetics (the manner in which she was displayed) and politics of display (the power to claim ownership of her), and the need to interrogate both. It also demonstrates that display "not only shows and speaks, it also does" (Kirshenblatt-Gimblett 1998: 6). On this account, we need to ask questions, both of the past and the future. For example, almost every museum professional in the world now agrees it is entirely unethical to display living people as 'specimens'. But what instances of the poetics and politics of contemporary display will our successors see in a similar way?

TAKING RESPONSIBILITY?

Many of the examples presented in this chapter (and throughout this book) require us as academic and as professionals in the museum world, to ask difficult questions and consider difficult choices. But to what extent might an individual be required to take public responsibility for a given display? One way of looking at this is to consider the 'exhibition as argument'. For example, we might argue that every display is a proposition. In each profession and field (whether art or social history) there are different 'positions', each competing for status, attention and resources. To become recognised in a museum profession, you have to take a stance on a key debate of the day, or persuade others to think about a whole new argument. In doing so, all exhibitions inevitably "assert some truths and ignore others" (Lavine and Karp 1991: 1). There is also the matter of selection. Even the mere inclusion of an object within a display suggests that that it should be valued highly: inclusion promotes the work of its creator. In this sense, all displays are a call for others to agree with the valuation made by the curator.

However, as Macdonald (1998: 1) highlights, displays are usually presented as "unequivocal statements rather than as the outcome of particular processes and contexts" and "assumptions, rationales, compromises and accidents [are] hidden from public view". Thus, for example, until very recently many museums' texts were anonymous, and couched in an 'institutional', collective voice. This can be beneficial. For example, a recent survey suggested that museums and galleries in Europe continued to enjoy high levels of public trust, and that visitors wanted to "find out factual and unbiased information" without being told "what to think" (BritainThinks 2013: 6). So should the museum continue 'as normal' to avoid jeopardising this trust, or is there a need to make clear whose agency is at stake in creating a display by encouraging curators to identify themselves as authors?

This option is explored by David Dean (2005: 196–7), who believes that museum curators should personally 'sign' exhibitions, so as to treat the visitor as a "thinking being, someone worthy of taking the effort to inform fully". We have seen interesting examples of this in museums over the years. One such attempt was at the Museum of London at the entrance to its prehistory gallery and was on an interpretation panel entitled: "Politically Present and Correct?"

> This gallery is a reflection of our present. We have chosen to humanise the past by focusing on specific sites and the needs of individual people, and by giving greater prominence to green and gender issues. How will this standpoint be judged in the future? What do you think?
>
> (J. Cotton and B. Wood, Curators 1994)

This example was striking because it was unusual. The practice of naming curators as authors of exhibitions tends to be more commonly seen with temporary exhibitions, and arguably is more prevalent in the contemporary art gallery context than in other kinds of museums. Yet even here, permanent collection displays tend not to 'name' those involved. In this respect, Tate Modern, in London, is unusual. Every room of the permanent collection displays features an authored text that lays out the rationales behind individual curators' choices. Such an approach is still uncommon in most museums and galleries, and even when deployed, is not without its shortcomings. For example, while curators may now expect to have temporary exhibitions credited to them personally, the relatively recent emergence of the 'star' curator has caused some difficulties. Artists have refused to exhibit work they considered to be subordinate to the curatorial 'thesis' (Green and Gardner 2016: 34), leading many curators to downplay their own role for fear of a backlash.

COPRODUCING DISPLAYS AND SHARING AUTHORSHIP

The recognition that visitors actively participate in meaning-making processes has led to calls for visitors to become directly involved in the production of displays, or to inform and shape them. As explored in Chapter 3, the practice of participatory work and coproduction is increasingly popular in some areas of museum work, particularly in social history and community museums. In terms of the development of displays and exhibitions, participatory practices can be used to help generate themes or content. Oral histories, digital stories, film and photography are popular methods employed to incorporate audience perspectives, although this material is not always given the same status as the traditional material. The introduction of new material of this kind also speaks to another trend of recent years which is the effort by museum staff to incorporate multiple voices and contrasting perspectives. This signals an attempt to move the museum away from presenting a single, monological voice and towards poly- or multi-vocal displays.

In particular, some museums actively draw our attention to the question of self-representation and what has been described as "the problem of speaking for others" (Alcoff 1991). One of the critiques often levelled at traditional museums has been that they spoke for and about others who were themselves denied a voice within society and within its public cultural institutions. In postcolonial societies museums have often been the subject of efforts by indigenous people to change this situation and to gain the opportunity to speak on their own behalf and terms. In some cases this has led to a questioning of the traditional, institutional, anonymous and singular voice of the museum.

In certain displays it has also resulted in an approach to telling history which foregrounds competing truths. For example, in a display about treaties between the US government and Native American people at the National Museum of the American Indian in Washington, the display was organised around the perspective of the two parties presented in each text panel side by side: the Native Americans and the US government. The effect was to throw the disparity between the two accounts of history into sharp relief, to prompt the visitor to measure one against the other, and to recognise that within one country there can be acutely contrasting accounts of their shared history. History in such museums is not represented as consensual, settled or closed but as disputed, deeply unsettled, and open to debate.

This poly-vocal approach to interpretation is not confined to museums about indigenous peoples or colonialisation; it can be found more widely as part of new museological thinking and community-based museum work. It has also been put to use in other museum contexts where history is far from consensual and where a single interpretation would be politically unacceptable to communities.

One such example was developed by the Tower Museum, Derry/Londonderry, in Northern Ireland. The museum created a display relating to the period between 1968 and 1998 known as 'The Troubles' which saw violent conflict over the constitutional status of the territory of Northern Ireland (Figure 5.8). In brief, the Protestant majority in Northern Ireland wished to remain part of the United Kingdom, whereas the Catholic minority wanted to leave the United Kingdom and become part of the Republic of Ireland. In the context of this deeply divided society, any attempt at represent-ing a single historical account has highly problematic. As a result, the museum interpretation of events was organised to show both Catholic and Protestant perspectives facing each other on opposite sides of the display. In this way, the museum visitor was prompted to acknowledge the existence of radically opposed accounts of the two sides' shared history. At the same time, the museum was able to provide public recognition of the two different accounts and to create a role for itself as a 'safe space' in which both sides could find resonance. Out of this context, some museums in Northern Ireland have come to play an important social role of reconciliation.

Figure 5.8 'The Road to Partition' Gallery showing different coloured kerbstones on either side.

© Tower Museum Derry/Londonderry.

CAN OBJECTS 'SPEAK'?

Up to this point, the process of creating a display has been discussed from a particular vantage point. We might sum it up like this: those who work in museums and galleries create meaningful displays by selecting, arranging and interpreting objects. In fact, whole teams of people decide which stories objects might tell, and they make objects 'speak' through their contextualisation within the display technologies, material categories and systems of knowledge museums create and embody. This process brings objects 'to life'. It is worth thinking about why museums principally show and collect *inanimate* objects. Tate Modern claims that its 'Tanks' spaces are the first museum spaces dedicated to performance, that is, to showing animate human beings rather than inanimate artefacts (Tate 2012).

Yet, the idea that objects can 'speak' is not as strange as it might first sound. As we have seen above, the idea that artworks can (and should) 'speak for themselves' remains popular. Museum visitors often tell us that certain objects and materials caught their attention, and 'spoke' to them, at times in quite unanticipated and exciting ways. Indeed, one reason museums exist is because we 'invest' so much in material objects, through imagination, or memory. Objects can prompt us to think about past, current and future events around the world, as well as in our own lives. It is perhaps for this reason that we commonly employ objects to 'speak' for us to show others what kind of person we are and what groups we belong to or identify with. Objects tell others, and remind us, what ideas and values we hold. For Elizabeth Wood and Kiersten F. Latham (2014: 13), it is this ability of an object to act as a conduit or "mediator" between people and ideas that is so important for museums and galleries. In what they describe as the "networked museum", objects act as a point of exchange between visitors and professionals (ibid.: 18) and a means to open up new ways of thinking about the world.

And yet objects can also be intractable, both physically and intellectually, resisting being contained within particular readings or settings. For example, while those who work in museums and galleries might suggest or even create meaning through objects, they can hardly make them do or stand for anything they like. Visual and textual narratives need to convincingly illuminate an aspect of the object, seen or unseen – its appearance, history, use or context – or they place the authority of the museum or gallery at risk. Conversely, objects can provide evidence about and act as 'witnesses' to events from times or places out of sight or out of mind, and begin to make stories about them powerful and palpable.

Recent intellectual developments have developed this line of thinking, and argued that objects have a power, and agency, of their own. This approach, which is potentially very productive for museums and galleries, considers objects as akin to people: as capable of action and effects in the world. One particular strand of this development, as discussed in Chapter 2, involves thinking of objects' 'biographies', 'careers' or their 'social lives': tracing the places they pass through, their ownership or use, or roles in the world. This sometimes involves seeing the world as if from the object's 'point of view'.

Theories such as 'object-oriented ontology' go much further and propose that objects are 'actors' themselves in their own right. For example, what the theorist Jane Bennett (2010: viii) refers to as "the vibrancy of matter" demonstrates how "things" not only impede human design but act as "quasi agents or forces with trajectories, propensities or tendencies of their own". As an example, Bennett describes a power black-out in North America in 2003 that eventually affected 50 million people. She argues that various components within this power grid, such as generating plants, circuit breakers and fans, together accidentally caused a change in the flow of electrons, which led to the eventual overloading of the system and a cascade of generators (including twenty-two nuclear reactors) shutting themselves down (ibid.: 25). In other words, the blackout was not caused by human action (or error), but by a series of interacting, non-human devices. What then, are our objects, environmental devices, computer systems, and other 'things' up to in the museum?

MAKING SENSE OF WHAT WE SEE: THE ACTIVE VISITOR

Objects are not the only things to behave unpredictably in the museum. Despite the very best efforts of those who work in museums and galleries, visitors too can respond to displays in a variety of surprising, and even at times unwelcome, ways. Leinhardt and Knutson (2004: 16–17), for example, report hearing a conversation between three "conscientious" teenagers at the 'Africa: One Continent, Many Worlds' exhibition at the Carnegie Museum of National History, in the United States. The teenagers had spent some time engaging with the exhibition, but nevertheless got it "just about as wrong" as they could have – mistaking African items for Southwest Indian dream catchers, and remarking that "Africans don't get a lot of wars" and that Africa had no major government or technology.

Leinhardt and Knutson's example underlines a key point: the act of display is powerful, but it is not the whole picture. Indeed, part of the challenge for those who work in museums and galleries is that "the meaning and significance of any object is fundamentally unfixed" (Wood and Latham 2014: 11). There might be certain associations that are shared across a culture, but we bring our own memories, perspectives and assumptions as well. And as we saw in Chapter 3, visitors do not arrive at the museums or gallery as 'empty vessels' waiting to be filled with information, but instead bring a wide variety of motivations, requirements, past experiences, ideas and values to bear upon the visit. In other words, visitors actively construct meaning for themselves.

One approach to understanding how visitors make sense of what they encounter in museum and art gallery displays is the idea of 'entrance narratives'. This idea was developed by Doering and Pekarik (1996) on the basis of research they undertook at the Smithsonian Institution in the USA. They developed the term 'entrance narratives' to describe three interdependent components:

- A basic framework i.e. a fundamental way that individuals construe and contemplate the world
- Information about the given topic, organized according to that basic framework
- Personal experiences, emotions, and memories that verify and support this understanding.

(Doering and Perkarik 1996: 20)

Based on this model they argue that "the most satisfying exhibitions for visitors will be those that resonate with their experience and provide information in ways that confirm and enrich their view of the world" (Doering and Perkarik 1996: 20). This raises an important conundrum. According to the 'entrance narrative' theory, visitors will enjoy or seek out exhibitions and display that affirm their existing way of seeing the world. Because of what is described as 'confirmation-bias' – in other words, that you tend to only see what you expect to see – visitors may not even notice where museums and galleries are saying something different, unless that difference is made really explicit. At the same time, some museum and gallery professionals now say that they want visitors to be challenged, encouraged to think and to engage with debates about contemporary issues that show alternative perspectives.

Another way of looking at this issue is to consider what Cheryl Meszaros (2007: 17–18), has called the "reign of 'whatever' interpretation". Meszaros describes here a "bizarre contradiction" whereby some museums and galleries spend large amounts of money on crafting a particular story through display, but simultaneously "champion the idea that an individual's personal interpretation is the best result of the museum encounter" – even if this has nothing to do with, or even directly contradicts, the intended message. Clearly, not all museums and galleries do this, but Meszaros's point is insightful. How can museum staff engage and support visitors, while making specialist knowledge available and accessible to them, but without providing set 'answers'?

Debates of these kinds have prompted a shift in the ways many professionals think about their institutions' very purposes. Should museums and galleries be didactic and aim to show or tell the visitor things? Or should they be discursive and aim to engage with (or respond to) their visitors? On the one hand, encouraging visitors to interpret displays on their own terms may bring to light fresh perspectives or 'hidden' personal histories. It also opens up an opportunity for all visitors to engage with the museum on an equal footing, and for the visit to be personally meaningful and memorable. On the other hand, surely museums cannot champion any and all meanings generated by visitors? Or fail to encourage visitors to 'see' the world differently? How these two contrasting approaches can be reconciled is still open for debate.

VISITOR BEHAVIOUR IN GALLERY SETTINGS

A similar point might be made about the unpredictability of visitor behaviour in a gallery space. When we teach our museum and gallery students about display, we always send them into exhibition spaces to watch visitors – with the institutions' and visitors' permission. We tell them to watch what visitors do, how they behave, what routes they follow, what they pay attention to and how much they read. We ask them to sketch out a floorplan of the space and then track visitors' movements in the space, and to keep a time-log of their activities. Then we ask them what they found out. Their first response is typically one of shock and disappointment. They report that visitors do not spend nearly as much time in the exhibitions as they expected they would, and don't read everything 'properly'. Our students expect visitors to behave as they would – with keen interest and attention to detail – but for visitors the trip is much more likely to be a casual leisure activity. This does not mean that visitors are getting it "wrong" or not paying enough attention. It does mean that it is crucial to recognise that people will behave differently according to their own motivations, expectations and preferences.

This exercise is useful because it opens the students' eyes to a whole other way of thinking about visitors, interpretation and display; that of the user's perspective. This is a significant area of study; too large to cover fully here. However, we can give a few pointers to illustrate key issues. The first thing to say is that visitors typically do not faithfully follow the routes suggested by curators and designers, unless the design of the space forces them to do so (in other words if there is only one way to go around the space to get out, as in what we could call an IKEA-style layout). Although it depends on how the space is laid out and how explicitly various routes and narratives are signposted, on the whole, visitors tend to follow their own interests. We know, for example, that visitors tend to browse and graze. They do not spend equal amounts of time in all areas; they may spend longer at the outset but then speed up or slow down again. They read selectively, dipping in and out of text panels, and will tend to focus when they find something that catches their attention.

Visitor behaviour will also differ depending on whether the visitors are alone, with friends, with children, with elderly people, with little or a lot of time, whether it's their first visit or a repeat trip, whether they plan to come back or whether this is a one-off visit not to be repeated. It appears to make a difference to the length of the visit whether visitors have paid and how much, or whether it was free; it has been suggested that free admission in the UK has led to more visitors coming more frequently but for shorter visits. Presumably this is because when visitors pay there is a strong sense of needing to spend time in order to get value for their money. As one might expect, visitors' behaviour in the space and their engagement with the display depends greatly on whether they know a lot about the subject or whether they are novices. Either way, spending time in an exhibition watching how people move through the space is undoubtedly the best way to begin to understand how displays function, and how visitors do and don't behave as might be expected by professionals or researchers.

FROM 'EDUCATION' TO 'LEARNING'

The recognition that visitors actively – and at times unpredictably – engage with displays has prompted another major change in the way that we think about museums and galleries, known as the shift from 'education' to 'learning'. To go back in time very quickly: museums and galleries in eighteenth and nineteenth century Europe aimed to 'impart' information as a "means of public instruction" (McClellan 2003: 5). In this model, museums and galleries were thought to control and distribute a sanctioned and stable form of knowledge, and visitors 'acquired' the exact same knowledge by looking, reading and acting as they saw others do. But we know that visitors don't behave and respond like this. Rather, visitors bring their own experiences and ideas to bear upon the visit, and each visitor might 'take away' very different messages and understandings.

As a result, a number of academics and practitioners began to rethink the traditional 'educative' approach in the museum, and its linear model of knowledge transmission. Drawing upon educational theory, for example, George E. Hein (1998: 156–7) proposed the concept of the "constructivist museum", which argued that it was "not only difficult but almost impossible to learn something without making an association with familiar categories". Falk and Dierking (1992: 1) developed the "Interactive Experience Model", which conceptualised museum and gallery visits as involving three contexts: the personal, social and physical, while more recently, Simon (2010) has advocated for "participatory institutions", with museums and galleries as 'platforms' for coproduced activities and experiences (as discussed in Chapter 3). Many more ideas are available, but the key point here is that 'learning' in the museum and gallery is now commonly understood as an active, complex and social process, and one that might challenge, or pay no attention to, the authority of the museum. The emphasis placed upon learning has also significantly increased over time. In many parts of Europe, the US and Australia, for example, learning is now "a core purpose of museums" (MLA 2004: 24), and funding allocations have similarly increased to support this work.

Yet it is worth pointing out that there is no fixed thing that is 'learning' (Saljö 2003: 621) that we might find or test for in the museum. Rather, both 'education' and 'learning' are human attempts to define and understand what people think and do, why, and how this might change over time. Moreover, the way that individual museums and galleries decide what 'learning' is, whom it is for, how it might be encouraged or evaluated, and their overall purpose as a 'learning space', varies considerably. As a result, staff in a learning department might find themselves responsible for school trips, or adult classes and events, or family workshops, or drop-in handling sessions, or 'outreach' and engagement work (as discussed in Chapter 3). They might produce resources in varying forms (e.g. podcasts, videos and text documents), or write wall texts and access policies. Learning staff might equally have responsibility for visitors with specialist needs, for teams of volunteers, or for the 'professional development' of staff – or any combination of the above.

What we see in the above then is the opening up of a complex and multifaceted field of practice, and one that increasingly blurs 'traditional' responsibilities between display, interpretation and learning. Indeed, the recent turn towards 'socially engaged' artistic practice adopts methods and approaches commonly thought of as 'educative' – that is, socially engaged artists do not present objects for display, but rather focus directly on processes of discussion, collaboration and engagement. This is a new and important challenge for those who work in museums and galleries as they try to work out how best to benefit from varied kinds of expertise, what kind of museum or gallery they want to provide, and for whom.

CREATING ACCESSIBILITY FOR EVERYONE

We have argued throughout this chapter for the crucial importance of widely accessible interpretation, learning and display strategies if museums and galleries are to be for everyone, and not just a select few. However, we know from our own experience that this is easy to say, but can be very difficult to put into practice.

Give it a try yourself. Imagine you are responsible for the redevelopment of a collection of renaissance paintings, dating from around the fourteenth to sixteenth century. You want to make these paintings accessible to all your visitors, and not just those who already "possesses the cultural competence" or "code" (Bourdieu 1984: 2) that allows them to respond "correctly" to the symbolic and cultural cues the museum currently presents (Duncan 2005: 81). Amongst these paintings is a work by the Italian artist Sandro Botticelli (circa 1445–1510) called *The Annunciation* (Figure 5.9). It depicts a religious scene, and is famous for its use of mathematical perspective. It is also almost a metre long, includes gold leaf, and was once hung in a church in Florence but is now in the collection of the Kelvingrove Museum and Art Gallery in Glasgow, Scotland (Glasgow Museums 2008). The published description of this painting is: "The Virgin and Angel of the Annunciation within a vaulted building, beyond which

Figure 5.9 The Annunciation, by Sandro Botticelli (circa 1445–1510).
© CSG CIC Glasgow Museums and Libraries Collections.

is seen a landscape with hills. Golden rays above mark the miracu-
lous passage of the Holy Spirit from God."

If you had to display and interpret this painting, what kind of
story would you want to tell? How would you hang and position
the painting to help you tell this story? What should the painting
be next to, and in what part of the building should it be placed?
What furniture, use of colour, or multi-media devices might you
employ? What do you want visitors to learn when they see this
painting? How might you help them do this? What additional
activities and events might you design? What institutional policies
for the reading age of the labels and text panels, and their visual
presentation, might you need to consult? What terms, or fonts,
might you use, or avoid? How will you draw upon accessibility

policies, to ensure that there is enough clearance between exhibits to cater for wheelchair users, or families with buggies? How will you create interpretation for a range of audiences so that visitors with different prior knowledge and motivations can all find something of interest? And which members of staff might you call upon to help you make all these decisions?

We have used this example because between 2003 and 2006, staff at the Kelvingrove Art Museum and Gallery asked themselves precisely these questions, in relation to this artwork (among many others). As part of a major redevelopment, the staff hoped to draw upon the latest thinking with regard to display, interpretation and learning, and to "create an object-based, storytelling flexible museum that shared the wonders of the collection with as wide a range of local people and visitors as possible" (O'Neill 2007: 385). In the end, they displayed Sandro Botticelli's *Annunciation* in combination with a specially designed (and timed) light projection that highlighted the use of perspective. The projection appeared superimposed on the painting to highlight how the perspectival lines centred on the columns in the painting and converged towards a point in the background of the work. The presentation included a voiceover of the subject matter to explain what the viewer was seeing and the presentation was shown again every fifteen minutes. Elsewhere, paintings were hung lower than was usual, and labels were written in "everyday" language – all in the hope of encouraging visitors to spend longer looking at the work (O'Neill 2008: 330).

Many visitors and critics welcomed these changes, but others were furious. An editorial piece in *The Burlington Magazine*, for example, suggested that the new display revealed a "contemptuous attitude" to the collections and described the interpretation as "patronisingly simplistic", and designed to appeal to "the lowest common denominator" (*Burlington Magazine* 2007: 747). In a letter of reply, Mark O'Neill, at that time Head of Arts and Museums, refuted these claims, pointing to the institution's long history of engagement with audiences of all kinds (O'Neill 2008: 330), and not just those already in possession of considerable knowledge.

We have used this example because it makes clear that the act of display always involves always a delicate balancing act. 'New' approaches can alienate existing visitors and vice versa. Yet despite this risk, many museums and galleries worldwide continue to experiment in order to find more accessible and engaging forms of interpretation. "Cross-departmental approaches" (Whitehead 2012: xii), for example, might equally include curators, learning and marketing teams and exhibition designers, as well as museum guides and volunteers. This allows for a variety of staff to share expertise in order to identify the museum or gallery's key audiences (see Chapter 3), understand who displays and associated programmes should be 'pitched' at, and together develop accessible interpretation, in the broadest sense.

Indeed, some of the latest thinking comes straight from museum history. 'Live interpretation' may be common in museums dedicated to social history, but it is now being employed in museums and galleries of all kinds instead of, or in addition to, wall texts and pamphlets. This is both a reasonably 'new' development and an extension of a practice common at the very beginning of museum history, where wealthy patrons, "prideful of their possessions", would personally "provide all the explanation on offer to those fortunate enough to be invited in for a private view" (Schaffner 2015: 156). Sometimes, 'old' approaches can be made to work for twenty-first century visitors.

CONCLUSIONS

All displays, no matter what their content, make claims about the world. They argue that certain objects matter, that certain ideas, histories and values are important, or that we should see and think about the world in a certain way. As a result, those who work in museums and galleries need to navigate a number of fundamentally ethical and political dilemmas. Which objects should be selected? What kind of display genre might work best? What might an act of interpretation suggest, or conceal? Whose stories should be highlighted, and who should be involved in key decisions? Yet display and interpretation – no matter how well devised – form only part of the story. Visitors are always active participants, even coproducers of displays themselves in some cases. Those who work in museums and galleries need to pay careful attention to the ways that different visitors construct meanings from visitors and engage with displays, or fail or refuse to do so. These issues are arguably more important than ever as museums and galleries in many countries across the world move "away from a collections-centred identity" and towards more "visitor-centred experiences" (Wood and Latham 2014: 13–17).

REFERENCES

Alcoff, L. (1991–1992) 'The problem of speaking for others'. *Cultural Critique* No. 20: 5–32.

Alicata, M. (2008) *Tate Modern: London*. Milan: Mondadori Electa.

Aronsson, P. and G. Elgenius (2015) *National Museums and Nation-Building in Europe 1750–2010: Mobilization and Legitimacy, Continuity and Change*. London and New York: Routledge.

Bennett, J. (2010) *Vibrant Matter: A Political Ecology of Things*. Durham, NC and London: Duke University Press.

Blazwick, I. and F. Morris (2000) 'Showing the twentieth century', in *Tate Modern: The Handbook*. London: Tate Gallery Publishing.

Bourdieu, P. (1984) *Distinction: A Social Critique of the Judgement of Taste*. London: Routledge.

Burlington Magazine (2007) 'Editorial: Museums in Britain: Bouquets and brick-bats'. *The Burlington Magazine* 149(1256), November: 747–748.

Crais, C. and P. Scully (2009) *Sara Baartman and the Hottentot Venus: A Ghost Story and a Bibliography*. Princeton, NJ: Princeton University Press.

Dean, D.K. (2005) 'Ethics and museum exhibitions', in G. Edson (ed.) *Museum Ethics*. London and New York: Routledge: 196–201.

De Montebello, P. (2004) 'Introduction', in A. Peck, J. Parker, W. Rieder *et al.* (eds) *Period Rooms in The Metropolitan Museum of Art*. New Haven, CT and London: Yale University Press.

Doering, Z. and A. Perkarik (1996) 'Questioning the entrance narrative'. *The Journal of Museum Education* 21(3): 20–23.

Duncan, C. (2005) 'The art museum as ritual', in G. Corsane (ed.) *Heritage, Museums and Galleries: An Introductory Reader*. Routledge: London and New York: 78–88.

Falk, J.H. and L.D. Dierking (1992) *The Museum Experience*. Washington, DC: Whalesback Books.

Goodwin, Z.A., D.J. Harris, D. Filer, J.R.I. Wood and R.W. Scotland (2015) 'Widespread mistaken identity in tropical plant collections'. *Current Biology* 25(22): 1066–1067.

Green, C. and A. Gardner (2016) *Biennials, Triennials, and Documenta: The Exhibitions that Created Contemporary Art*. Chichester: Wiley Blackwell.

Guerrilla Girls (2005) 'Do women have to be naked update', from the series 'Guerrilla Girls Talk Back: Portfolio 2'.

Halperin, J. and N. Patel (2015) 'Museums don't know what visitors want'. *The Art Newspaper Special Report: Visitor Figures 2014*, XXIV(267), April: 5.

Hein, G.E. (1998) *Learning in the Museum*. London: Routledge.

Hillier, B. and K. Tzortzi (2011) 'Space syntax: The language of museum space', in S. MacDonald (ed.) *A Companion to Museum Studies*. Chichester: Blackwell: 282–301.

Hooper-Greenhill, E. (1992) *Museums and the Shaping of Knowledge*. London: Routledge.

Kirshenblatt-Gimblett, K. (1998) *Destination Culture: Tourism, Museums and Heritage*. Berkeley and Los Angeles: University of California Press.

Knell, S. (2011) 'National museums and the national imagination', in S.J. Knell, P. Aronsson, A. Bugge Amudson *et al.* (eds) (2011) *National Museums: New Studies from Around the World*. London and New York: Routledge.

Lavine, S.D. and I. Karp (1991) 'Introduction: Museums and multiculturalism', in I. Karp and S.D. Lavine (eds) *Exhibiting Cultures: The Poetics and Politics of Museum Display*. Washington: Smithsonian Institution: 1–10.

Lehmbruck, M. (1974) 'Psychology: Perception and behaviour'. *Museum* 26: 191–204.

Leinhardt, G. and K. Knutson (2004) *Listening in on Museum Conversations*. Oxford: Alta Mira Press.

Lidchi, H. (1997) 'The poetics and politics of exhibiting other cultures', in S. Hall (ed.) *Representation: Cultural Representations and Signifying Practices*. Milton Keynes: The Open University Press: 151–222.

Macdonald, S. (ed.) (1998) *The Politics of Display: Museums, Science, Culture*. London: Routledge.

MacLeod, S., L. Hourston Hanks and J. Hale (eds) (2012) *Museum Making: Narratives, Architectures, Exhibitions*. London and New York: Routledge.

Marandino, M., M. Achiam and A. Dias de Olivereira (2015) 'The diorama as a means for biodiversity education', in S.D. Tunnicliffe and A. Scheersoi (eds) *Natural History Dioramas: History, Construction and Educational Role*. Heidelberg, New York, London: Springer: 251–266.

Mason, R. (2005) 'Museums, galleries and heritage: Sites of meaning-making and communication', in G. Corsane (ed.) *Heritage, Museums and Galleries: An Introductory Reader*. London and New York: Routledge: 200–214.

McClellan, A. (2003) 'A brief history of the art museum public', in A. McClellan (ed.) *Art and Its Publics: Museum Studies at the Millennium*. Oxford: Blackwell.

Meszaros, C. (2007) 'Interpretation and the hermeneutic turn'. *Engage* 20: 17–22.

Moser, S. (2010) 'The devil is in the detail: Museum displays and the creation of knowledge'. *Museum Anthropology* 33(1): 22–32.

Moss, M.H. (2007) *Shopping as an Entertainment Experience*. Plymouth: Lexington Books.

Museums, Libraries and Archives Council (MLA) (2004) *The Accreditation Scheme for Museums in the United Kingdom*. London: MLA.

O'Doherty, B. (1976) *Inside the White Cube: The Ideology of the Gallery Space*. Expanded edition. London, Berkeley and Los Angeles: University of California Press.

O'Neill, M. (2007) 'Kelvingrove: Telling stories in a treasured old/new museum'. *Curator: The Museum Journal* 50(4), October: 379–399.

O'Neill, M. (2008) 'Kelvingrove defended'. *The Burlington Magazine* 150(1262), May: 330.

Ravelli, L.J. (2006) *Museum Texts: Communication Frameworks*. London: Routledge.

Saljö, R. (2003) 'From transfer to boundary crossing', in T. Tuomi-Gröhn and Y. Engeström (eds) *Between School and Work: New Perspectives on Transfer and Boundary Crossing*. Amsterdam: Elsevier Science: 311–321.

Schaffner, I. (2015) 'Wall text', in P. Marincola (ed.) *What Makes A Great Exhibition?* Philadelphia, PA: The Pew Center for Arts and Heritage: 154–167.

Serota, N. (1996) *Experience or Interpretation: The Dilemma of Museums of Modern Art*. London: Thames & Hudson.

Simon, N. (2010) *The Participatory Museum*. Santa Cruz, CA: Museum 2.0.

Stam, D.C. (2005) 'The informed muse: The implications of the "new museology" for museum practice', in G. Corsane (ed.) *Heritage, Museums and Galleries: An Introductory Reader*. London: Routledge: 54–70.

Storr, R. (2015) 'Show and tell', in P. Marincola (ed.) *What Makes a Great Exhibition?* Philadelphia, PA: The Pew Center for Arts and Heritage: 14–31.

Weibel, P. (2007) 'Beyond the white cube', in P. Weibel and A. Buddensieg (eds) *Contemporary Art and the Museum*. Ostfildern; Hatje Cantz.

Weil, S.E. (2004) 'Rethinking the museum: An emerging new paradigm', in G. Anderson (ed.) *Reinventing the Museum: Historical and Contemporary Perspectives on the Paradigm Shift*. Walnut Creek: Altamira Press: 74–79.

Whitehead, C. (2009) *Museums and the Construction of Disciplines: Art and Archaeology in Nineteenth Century Britain*. London: Duckworth Academic.

Whitehead, C. (2012) *Interpreting Art in Museums and Galleries*. London: Routledge.

Wood, E. and K.F. Latham (2014) *The Objects of Experience: Transforming Visitor-Object Encounters in Museums*. Walnut Creek, CA: Left Coast Press.

WEBSITES

BritainThinks (2013) 'Public perceptions of – and attitudes to – the purposes of museums in society.' Report commissioned for the Museums Association. URL: http://www.museumsassociation.org/download?id=954916

British Museum (n.d.) 'History of the British Museum'. URL: http://www.britishmuseum.org/about_us/the_museums_story/general_history.aspx

Brooklyn Museum (2015) 'Brooklyn Museum building'. URL: https://www.brooklynmuseum.org/features/building

Glasgow Museums (2008) 'Sandro Botticelli – The Annunciation'. URL: http://collections.glasgowmuseums.com/starobject.html?oid=166843

National Museum of American History (2015) 'The value of money'. URL: http://americanhistory.si.edu/exhibitions/value-money

National Museum of Scotland (2016) 'Discover the museum'. URL: http://www.nms.ac.uk/national-museum-of-scotland/discover-the-museum/

Œuvre Notre-Dame Museum (2015) 'Nicolas de Leyde: The first monographic exhibition dedicated to the artist'. URL: http://www.musees.strasbourg.eu/sites_expos/deleyde/en/index.php?page=exposition-1&ssmenu=ssmenu-expo

Tate (2012) 'The Tanks Go Live'. URL: http://www.tate.org.uk/about/press-office/press-releases/tanks-go-live

Tate (2013) 'Meet 500 years of British Art – Director's highlights: Penelope Curtis'. Tate Britain. URL: http://www.tate.org.uk/context-comment/blogs/meet-500-years-british-art-directors-highlights-penelope-curtis

Victoria & Albert Museum (2015) 'The Ardabil carpet'. URL: http://www.vam.ac.uk/page/a/ardabil-carpet/

Whitechapel Gallery (2017) 'Max Mara Art Prize for Women'. URL: http://www.whitechapelgallery.org/about/prizes-awards/max-mara-art-prize-women/

FURTHER READING

Falk, J.H., and Dierking, L.D. (1992) *The Museum Experience*. Washington, DC: Whalesback Books.

Hein, G.E. (1998) *Learning in the Museum*. London: Routledge.

Hooper Greenhill, E. (1992) *Museums and the Shaping of Knowledge*. London: Routledge.

Kirshenblatt-Gimblett, K. (1998) *Destination Culture: Tourism, Museums and Heritage*. Berkley and Los Angeles: University of California Press.

Macdonald, S. and P. Basu (eds) (2007). *Exhibition Experiments (New Interventions in Art History)*. Malden, MA; Oxford; Victoria, Canada: Blackwell.

MacLeod, S., L. Hourston Hanks and J. Hale (eds) (2012) *Museum Making: Narratives, Architectures, Exhibitions.* London and New York: Routledge.

O'Doherty, B. (1976) *Inside the White Cube: The Ideology of the Gallery Space* [expanded edition]. London, Berkley and Los Angeles: University of California Press.

Serota, N. (1996) *Experience or Interpretation: The Dilemma of Museums of Modern Art.* London: Thames & Hudson.

Tzortzi, K. (2015) *Museum Space: Where Architecture Meets Museology.* London and New York: Routledge.

Whitehead, C. (2012) *Interpreting Art in Museums and Galleries.* London: Routledge.

6

LOOKING FORWARD

In the run-up to the 2016 US Presidential elections, President Barack Obama responded to Republican candidate Donald Trump's comment that: "there's never been a worse time to be a Black person" in America. In a public speech Obama replied by saying that Trump had: "missed that whole civics lesson about slavery and Jim Crow" referring to the system of racial segregation which persisted in the US from the 1890s until the 1960s. Obama continued: "We've got a museum for him to visit. So he can tune in. We will educate him" (DiversityInc 2016). He was talking about the Smithsonian's new National Museum of African History and Culture in Washington which opened in September 2016 and tells the story of African American people from slavery to the present day (Figure 6.1).

The fact that a museum is part of the public discussion about race in contemporary American politics proves the point we been making through this book: museums and galleries matter. They continue to be important public institutions for societies all around the world. The stories we tell about the past and who has the power, authority and opportunity to shape public understandings of the past remain vitally important. As we have argued, we need to understand museums and galleries, not only as individual physical buildings and collections of objects, but also as a means by which all

Figure 6.1 'Game Changers' Gallery in the National Museum of African American History and Culture.

© National Museum of African American History and Culture (NMAAHC).

societies identify, value and communicate to themselves and others what matters to them about the past. This has ramifications – ethical, political and philosophical – for the ways in which 'we' understand the world and our place in it. To put it simply, the way people understand what has happened before shapes both how they understand their current position and what they imagine might happen next. 'We' will all interpret what we find in museums and galleries differently, according to our own relationship to those histories on display, our own personal histories and the various social, political and identity-based groups to which everyone belongs. 'We' will interpret them according to who 'we' are.

If we see museums and galleries in this way – as a technology for social organisation with political consequences – then we understand why museums and galleries are always bound up with questions of power, authority and the ongoing struggle to control, shape and influence public understandings of the past. Even when museum visiting seems like it is simply a leisure pursuit that people undertake on a rainy day, this is still political, if we understand politics as being about how people have come to understand their position in society relative to others. As we have shown in Chapter 3 on visitor studies, there is concrete evidence to show that what people choose to do in their leisure time is influenced heavily by assumptions (our own and others) about whether it is 'for people like us' or not.

What also should be clear by now is the extraordinary flexibility of museums and galleries as a form of social technology. At different points in time and in different parts of the world, societies and their peoples have adapted the museum and gallery format to suit their purposes, beliefs, values and present needs. Sometimes this has meant placing emphasis on preserving and protecting objects for all time, whereas sometimes, as more recently in places like Australia, this has meant accepting that certain communities believe those objects should be allowed to age and decay. Given the adaptability that museums and galleries have shown so far and the increases in visitor numbers that we have identified in earlier chapters, it seems safe to say that the form of the museum and gallery will endure, although their fortunes may vary wildly according to their size, location and funding as we have seen in Chapter 4. So, looking forward, what can we predict might be future trends and issues for museums and galleries? In this concluding chapter, we offer some suggestions.

POWER AND POLITICS

Questions of power and politics are present in all the chapters. Museums are public institutions, usually, and their special status means that whilst outside of *party* politics, they cannot avoid being 'political' in the broader sense that we have been using it in this book. This informs all our thinking about the very purposes of museums and galleries. It informs how we think about what they collect, how they might best be paid for, who does and does not visit, how they structure their displays, and how their displays communicate ideas and inform our understanding of the world.

As we have seen, for a group to be excluded from the stories told, however inadvertently, has consequences for what people think about a whole field of knowledge. For example, if women artists are side-lined in stories of museums of modern art it means their contributions are invisible. Art museums send signals to the public, and to the art market alike. Having a monopoly means you own the officially sanctioned story, in effect. Around the world new museums are still being built, often on unprecedented scales, or even canonising whole new national traditions of contemporary art, as with the MATHAF Arab Museum of Modern Art, Qatar, or M+ in Hong Kong. The apparently unstoppable spread of museums and art galleries across the world marks a continuing desire for nations to attain equal cultural recognition with dominant world cities, and a desire to play a role in international conversations. (At the same time we should recognise that these major projects do not represent the whole picture; many museums and galleries are small and facing great financial pressures.)

Despite these challenges and the burden of responsibility, museums and art galleries are an extraordinarily successful type of institution. Museums and art galleries have a highly privileged place in people's imagination: they are symbolic spaces – symbolic of cities' and nations' aspirations, and symbolic for visitors about what kind of people they are or want to be. They can also see themselves as having a responsibility to make a political comment about political controversies and events. In 2016, on the inauguration day of President-elect, Donald Trump, more than 130 artists, critics and curators came together for #J20 Art Strike, which has been described as "a semi-open-ended call for collective action in the arts" (Kornhaber 2017). Some museums and galleries will close in protest at the politics represented by the new President. The Whitney Museum in New York has decided instead to stay open and offer "civic-minded programming and pay-what-you-want admission" (ibid.).

Many museums and galleries have led and continue to shape public discussions and understandings about history, culture and identities. For those seeking to gain recognition for their position in the world, particularly at state level, it remains vitally important to have a public space within which to tell their stories. To give a recent example, on 18 May 2016, a new museum opened near Ramallah, in the West Bank of Palestine. Its website describes its purpose as follows:

The Palestinian Museum is an independent institution dedicated to supporting an open and dynamic Palestinian culture nationally and internationally. The Museum presents and engages with new perspectives on Palestinian history, society and culture. ... The Museum will focus on promoting Palestinian culture in the Arab World and internationally; creating the environment for free and innovative intellectual and creative endeavour; advocating the use of cultural tools for educational purposes; strengthening a sense of unifying national identity; and fostering a culture of dialogue and tolerance.

(Palestinian Museum 2016)

This theme of seeing museums as a means of fostering a culture of dialogue and tolerance is one that occurs again and again when people describe the purpose of museums as this next example also shows.

MUSEUMS AS A MEANS TO FOSTER MUTUAL UNDERSTANDING

As mentioned above, in Washington DC, in the US, another new museum also opened in 2016. It is the newest of the Smithsonian's extended family of museums: the National Museum of African American History and Culture (NMAAHC) (Figure 6.2). The ceremony of breaking the ground to build the museum in 2012 was led by the USA's first black President, Barack Obama. Positioned in the middle of the nation's memorial and museum complex, the new museum is the neighbour of many other historic sites of national history and government.

In his speech at the museum's ground-breaking ceremony, President Barack Obama made the following observations:

When future generations hear these songs of pain and progress, and struggle and sacrifice, I hope they will not think of them as somehow separate from the larger American story. I want them to see them as a central and important part of our shared story; a call to *see ourselves in one another*. That is the history we will preserve with these walls.

(22 February 2012; authors' italics)

Figure 6.2 Exterior view of the National Museum of African American History
        and Culture.

© National Museum of African American History and Culture (NMAAHC).

Obama's framing of the museum's purpose as building an imaginative 'bridge' between oneself and other people highlights a central
dynamic of museums: that of identification and differentiation.
Obama's vision is one where the museum allows us to understand
each other, and in doing so, understand our place in the world.
Museums are one of the very few spaces and places in which, it is
suggested, we can overcome what Obama labelled the "empathy
deficit" we face (speech on 4 December 2006), although the question of empathy is itself a complex one.

The challenge for the NMAAHC is how to speak about the
inequalities and brutalities of the past, and bear witness to the hor-
rifying histories of African-Americans' slavery, while also attempting
to connect with white Americans whose antecedents benefited from
the injustices of racial segregation and slavery. Museums such as
this are often seen as a means of making a public reparation about

past wrongs and, simultaneously, attempting to creating imaginative frameworks within which to build new collective futures for all of society. How this might, or might not, work in practice is an important question and takes us back to the realm of visitor studies and visitors as active meaning-makers as considered in Chapter 3.

This symbolically charged new building raises several questions crucial to understanding current debates about museums in many societies and which can be found throughout this book. As we have asked many times, a critical question is, who museums are for? In this instance, is this museum for the specific group which they represent and whose histories they document? Are museums primarily for dominant groups or are they for the entirety of the wider society and reach everyone equally? If created with particular groups, how do they speak simultaneously to those on the 'inside' of the community and to others? In our increasingly diverse societies how can we think about identities and communities without the apparently simplistic concepts of 'insiders' and 'outsiders'? What role do museums and other cultural heritage institutions play in addressing social issues such as prejudice, inequality, racism and exclusion?

In recent years, museum staff in many countries have grappled with issues of diversity, community cohesion and inclusion. They have increasingly worked with communities, including them in the representations they produce as institutions. In many cases this work comes from genuine commitment to social justice. It is also a political necessity and an important line of defence against accusations of elitism from both academics and communities as well as critics of public subsidy. As we have seen, these kinds of involvement range from consultation through to including community representatives in the decision-making processes. Involving communities in such processes can be fraught as well as beneficial. How identities are represented will continue to become more complex and contested in our contemporary societies, especially as many countries are witnessing a resurgence of identity-politics and narrowly defined, ethnic nationalism.

MUSEUMS AND GALLERIES AS SOCIAL ACTIVISTS

In response to a growing recognition by museum practitioners and museologists of the political nature of what museums and galleries do, some institutions have actively adopted a role as social activists (Sandell 2017). This can be around any number of issues, for example LGBTQ or gender equality, as discussed in earlier chapters. Some museums, particularly those in places with colonial histories or those relating to the slave trade, have repositioned them as institutions committed to fighting for human rights, for example, the International Slavery Museum in Liverpool, UK. Similarly, the Anne Frank Museum in Amsterdam actively monitors and publishes reports of racism, anti-Semitism and right-wing extremist violence in the Netherlands. At the same time, the counter-argument often raised by critics of the 'museum as social activist' agenda is that museums should remain outside of politics and neutral. As the preceding chapters have made very clear, in our view it is not possible for museums to be outside of politics or neutral. They are always implicated in the politics of places, be that at the level of communities, states or nations. They are always having to think about the moral and political implications of where their funding comes from and what that means for them as an institution. They are always needing to think about who they are for and how that relationship works. Last but not least, they cannot be simply 'neutral' because all representations inherently involve taking one position as opposed to another. That said, it is fair to say that there are many different ways of being 'politically engaged' and offering a balanced acknowledgement of different perspectives is different to claiming to be 'neutral'. There is a great deal more to unpack here which goes beyond the scope of this chapter. However, where one stands on the 'political activism versus neutrality' debate is an extremely important ethical question facing the museum and gallery profession at this time. It goes to the heart of the questions we raised at the outset: what and who are museums and galleries for?

Another increasingly important thematic grouping appearing in the sector is that of historical persecution, particularly around topics such as genocide and specifically the Holocaust. For example, a recent survey listed 95 museums about Jewish culture and history around the world in 32 different countries. The greatest predominance of these museums is in the USA, which has 25, followed by 13 in Germany and seven in Italy. A further 65 museums or memorial sites are dedicated to the Holocaust in 19 countries worldwide, again

24 are located in the USA with the second greatest number of eight in Germany. The geographical patterning suggests that the impulse to build such museums has two drivers. Firstly, it is closely linked to the destinations of many Jewish people fleeing from the Nazis during and after World War II. Secondly, it speaks of a need to publicly atone for a nation's historical past and complicity in persecution in the case of Germany or Italy.

Holocaust museums are part of a new genre of what has been described as 'memorial museums' which have started to become more common all around the world (Williams 2007). These museums are closely related to histories of persecution and some will be site-specific. However, some of these museums do not necessarily confine themselves to one local or ethnicity. Instead, they deal with broad themes such as genocide and the promotion of tolerance. For example, in Mexico, the Museum of Memory and Tolerance was founded in 1999 with the following mission statement:

> To transmit to broad audiences the importance of tolerance, nonviolence and Human Rights. To create awareness through historical memory, focusing on genocides and other crimes. To warn about the dangers of indifference, discrimination and violence for generating, instead, responsibility, respect and awareness in each individual.
>
> (Museum of Memory and Tolerance 2017)

These museums represent a departure from the traditional role of many museums which, as we have seen, is to place their own peoples as the central focus of their representations (insiders) and to place all other groupings as other and external (outsiders). What we are seeing with museums like the Museum of Memory and Tolerance in Mexico City is that the representational standpoint adopted by the museum is more supranational and global in orientation. In other words the viewpoint which the museum sets up for the visitor is one which looks across national boundaries and places the topic – in this case, genocide – as its centre point rather than nationality or ethnicity. In this situation the museum's representation is explicitly cross-cultural so that ethnic and national differences are less prominent than the common unifying theme which is deliberately foregrounded.

Indeed, there is a growing trend for museums to coordinate their activities internationally. In 2013 a group of liked-minded museums joined together to create SJAM: the Social Justice Alliance for Museums. Its membership has now grown to 80 museums from around the world. Its charter states:

1 We celebrate the incalculable value to society of museums and their collections.
2 We recognise that the duty of museums is to enable everyone to learn about the human and natural worlds.
3 We support the concept of social justice – we believe that the whole of the public is entitled to benefit from access to the resources museums contain and the ideas they provoke.
4 We acknowledge that many museums have for many years failed to operate for the wider public benefit, and instead have catered primarily for educated minorities. We reject this approach.
5 We pledge to lead the fight for access to museums for all – this is the essence of social justice.

(SJAM 2016)

Another example of museums joining together from around the world with a common social purpose can be found in the International Coalition of Sites of Conscience. This organisation has 200 members, many of them museums, and describes its mission as follows: "We are sites, individuals, and initiatives activating the power of places of memory to engage the public in connecting past and present in order to envision and shape a more just and humane future" (International Coalition of Sites of Conscience 2017). Their subtitle on the website is: "From Memory to Action".

Another area where some European museums have been increasingly active in the last few years is around work with migration and refugees (Whitehead *et al.* 2015). Museums in Denmark, for example, have teamed up with the Danish Red Cross to offer free cultural activities to refugees and asylum seekers in order to introduce them to Danish culture, history and contemporary society, as well as practical information about employment and welfare (NEMO 2016). The German Historical Museum in Berlin has also been offering free visits in multiple languages to introduce refugees to German's history and culture. Whereas most of these initiatives are about helping refugees to acclimatise to the new societies, one project has been taking a different approach. The "Multaka: Museum as Meeting Point" project organised in 2015 by the Staatliche Museen zu Berlin and the Deutsches Historisches Museum has been training refugees to be the guides and to give tours of the Museum for Islamic Art and the Museum of the Ancient Near East (both in the Pergammonmuseum) to other refugees in their own language (SMB 2017). As so often seems the case today, museums which started off by collecting treasures from other parts of the world now find themselves showing and accounting for those histories to the people from those 'other places' who now reside within the museum's own territory. The distinctions between us/them, national/foreign, here/there are increasingly collapsing in our global and multicultural societies.

GLOBALISATION

What we might call 'centrifugal' forces like globalisation, migration and the blurring of identity boundaries across gender and ethnicity continue to provide a spur to museums to adapt to dramatic change. The phenomenon of 'superdiversity' in many societies is challenging traditional ideas about communities and 'their cultures'. 'Superdiversity' refers to academic Stephen Vertovec's (2006) idea that in the last three decades as a result of "the changing nature of global migration" many societies have witnessed a "transformative 'diversification of diversity'". This goes beyond simply saying that societies are more ethnically diverse and complicates any attempt to categorise societies in terms of simple ethnic grouping. For example, if we use the term 'the Polish' to refer to Polish migrants in the UK we could be talking about those who migrated at the time of the second world war, or those who arrived since Poland joined the EU in 2004. We could be talking about Polish people who are working as builders or who are in the UK working as academics. They might be permanently resident or they might be commuting regularly between the UK and Poland on cheap flights. In all of these cases, the experiences of Polish people in the UK is likely to be varied. As this shows, contemporary diversity now has such great diversification within it so that old labels and categorisations cease to be adequate.

At the same time, it is important to recognise that 'superdiversity' does not exist uniformly throughout societies. Moreover, fear of diversity is provoking a backlash in some countries from those who would wish to arrest such diversification and turn the clock back by promoting an idea of a more traditional view of national culture and identity. This accounts for recent growth in so-called 'populist' and politically conservative moments across Europe and in the United States. As always, these movements are concerned with expressions of culture and identity so we can expect that these pressures will come to bear ever more strongly on museums and galleries in due course.

CHANGING PERSPECTIVES

Changes in digital technology and to fundamental perceptions of trust and knowledge are also transforming museums and art galleries in many parts of the world. Nicholas Serota of Tate has argued that Europe has become less provincial (has taken notice of more of the world), whilst having been provincialised itself (no longer being the automatic centre of things). He also notes that museums need to take the demands of twenty-first century audiences seriously, and see their role as opening dialogues *with* rather than speaking *at* visitors as if in a monologue. In his words:

> The forces that are changing the world are challenging the role of museums. Our world is different ... [because of] globalisation, increasing cultural diversity, technological and personal mobility .... We see the world in a different light and from a different perspective: our understanding of modernism and the Western historical tradition has been transformed .... We plan to move from a Western-centred, single-voiced and single-lensed perspective to the many-voiced and many-lensed viewpoints of a new internationalism.
>
> (Serota 2010)

If the museum is to flourish in the 21st century, it cannot afford to be solely a place of retreat from society. It must stimulate, provoke and engage, as well as offering a place for contemplation or consolation. It must be a place in which we can share in a commonwealth of ideas ...

The world also sees museums differently. Wide international access, directly or through digital media . . . [means that whilst] the traditional function of the museum has been that of instruction, with the curator setting the terms of engagement in the past 20 years the development of the internet . . . has begun to change the expectations of visitors, and their relationship with the curator as authoritative specialist. The challenge for museums in the 21st century is to find new ways of engaging with much more demanding, sophisticated and better informed viewers. Our museums have to respond to and become places where ideas, opinions and experiences are exchanged, and not simply learned.

(Serota 2016)

These arguments about the decentring of Europe and North America and the need for global exchange and full engagement; about acting as a 'forum' rather than a temple; about the relationship between expert and audience, and curator and community, exemplify many of the ideas we have explored above. Museums and galleries themselves are not refuges from the world but actors in a world defined by dramatic change and realignments internationally, and between groups, as well as between the state and private capital.

VALUING CULTURE

In addition to the societal and technological changes, public museums and galleries in many European countries find themselves assailed by increasing pressures towards 'marketisation' and 'financialisation'; broadly speaking, both terms refer to a widespread trend in many contemporary societies whereby all values are seen through the lens of economic value. While nineteenth-century British social reformers argued for museums as a means of social improvement for the working-classes, the discourse now around museums and galleries is more weighted towards economic benefits to society, regeneration of cities, promoting Britain abroad, and attracting tourists. Social benefits are still appreciated but even this is given a monetary value; museums and galleries, it is increasingly argued, can improve the public's health and wellbeing, thereby reducing costs to the National Health Service. While none of these proposed outcomes is individually negative, when taken collectively, there is a real problem that museums and galleries will be made to twist what it is that they do and are to fit a narrowly define economic model of value to such an extent that it conflicts with other social and cultural values. We must continue to look for ways to recognise that museums and galleries have value to the public which is not reducible to monetary terms. In many countries we have also seen since the financial crash of 2008 a trend by successive governments towards shrinking the amount of public funding available and pressurising cultural organisations to find private income. This raises all sorts of ethical, moral and practical challenges for those museums and galleries which see themselves as having a remit to be accessible and available for everyone.

If you see a museum or gallery as holding a culture's or community's collective memories in trust forever for the public benefit, then restricting access to those who can pay is philosophically and morally problematic. If, on the other hand, you see museums and galleries as primarily part of the leisure industry competing alongside private enterprises or as a means of achieving economic regeneration, then your whole ethos towards funding, programming, sponsorship and access will be different. In our experience, many public museums and galleries perform an extraordinary juggling act of balancing both ways of thinking as best they can. The Louvre, for example, charges all visitors a sizeable entry fee most days of the week but opens its doors free to anyone on the first Sunday of every month. The question is whether we are about to reach a tipping point in some countries, like the UK, where the delicate balance of funding will shift irrevocably much further towards ideas of the economic value of culture and away from the idea of civic culture for public benefit with significant effects.

VISITOR TRENDS

In addition to changes to core funding, the patterns of visitation raise questions about the future. Although we are seeing ever-increasing numbers of cultural tourists to large venues in major world capitals, it may be that, away from the tourist hotspots, the picture looks quite different. Museums and galleries in many countries find themselves competing for the leisure time of local visitors against an ever-growing range of competitors, for example, in the realm of shopping, sport, cinema and online entertainment. How successfully will museums and galleries keep pace with the explosion in social media and digital entertainment opportunities? Will they attempt to move further into that territory by incorporating more and more of those platforms in their own activities or will they instead promote themselves precisely for the ways in which they are different? Will they become popular again with some audiences because they offer 'off-grid' opportunities for stillness, contemplation and encounters with material, non-digital traces of the past? It is impossible to predict where some of these current trends will take museums and galleries in future but it does seem possible to say that the variability between institutions will increase even more and with that, their chances of continuing to exist.

These are some of the challenges for museums and galleries today; there are others. They find themselves, as they have always done, at the intersection of competing pressures and demands. They are always working to meet the needs of multiple stakeholders and always needing to think about how to define and redefine their standpoint and, ultimately, their relevance to society. As a form of cultural practice, and as a critical part of public culture and civic life, museums and galleries have proven enormously adaptable to new needs and new demands. Whatever forms they take next, museums and galleries will continue to be one of the key ways that we can think about who we are or want to be.

REFERENCES

Sandell, R. (2017) *Museums, Moralities, and Human Rights*. London: Routledge.

Whitehead C., K. Lloyd, S. Eckersley and R. Mason (eds) (2015) *Museums, Migration and Identity in Europe: Peoples, Places and Identities*. Farnham: Ashgate.

Williams, P. (2007) *Memorial Museums: The Global Rush to Commemorate Atrocities*. Oxford and New York: Berg.

WEBSITES

DiversityInc (2016) 'President Obama on Trump: "We've got a museum for him to visit": The National Museum of African American History and Culture will provide a history lesson on Black progress in America that Donald Trump needs'. http://www.diversityinc.com/news/president-obama-trump-weve-got-museum-visit/

International Coalition of Sites of Conscience (2017) 'About us'. URL: http://www.sitesofconscience.org/about-us/

Kornhaber, S. (2017) 'The tangled debate over art-world protests'. *The Atlantic* 18 January. URL: https://www.theatlantic.com/entertainment/archive/2017/01/meryl-streep-j20-art-strike-trump-protests/512675/.

Museo Memoria Y Tolerancia [Museum of Memory and Tolerance], Mexico City (2017) Homepage. URL: http://www.myt.org.mx/

Network of European Museum Organisations (NEMO) (2016) 'Initiatives of museums in Europe in connection to migrants and refugees'. URL: http://www.ne-mo.org/fileadmin/Dateien/public/Documents_for_News/NEMO_collection_Initiatives_of_museums_to_integrate_migrants.pdf

Obama, B. (2012) 'Remarks at a groundbreaking ceremony for the National Museum of African American History and Culture'. *The American Presidency Project* 22 February. URL: http://www.presidency.ucsb.edu/ws/index.php?pid=99597andst=andst1=

Palestinian Museum (2016) 'The museum'. URL: http://www.palmuseum.org/about/the-museum

Serota, N. (2010) 'Why Tate needs to change'. *The Art Newspaper* 1 May. URL: http://theartnewspaper.com/news/museums/from-the-archive-why-tate-needs-to-change/

Serota, N. (2016) 'The 21st-century Tate is a commonwealth of ideas'. *The Art Newspaper* 5 January. URL: http://theartnewspaper.com/comment/comment/the-21st-century-tate-is-a-commonwealth-of-ideas/

Social Justice Alliance for Museums (SJAM) (2016) 'Museums'. URL: http://sjam.org/who-we-are/museum-members/

Staatliche Museen zu Berlin (SMB) (2017) 'About us'. URL: http://www.smb.museum/en/museums-institutions/museum-fuer-islamische-kunst/about-us/whats-new/detail/kultur-als-integrationsmotor-multaka-projekt-ausgezeichnet.html

Vertovec, S. (2006) *The Emergence of Super-Diversity in Britain. Working Paper No. 25.* Compas: Centre on Migration, Policy and Society, University of Oxford. URL: https://www.compas.ox.ac.uk/media/WP-2006-025-Vertovec_Super-Diversity_Britain.pdf

FURTHER READING

Bishop, C. (2014) *Radical Museology: or, What's Contemporary in Museums of Contemporary Art?* Cologne: Verlag Der Buchhandlung Walther Konig.

Crooke, E. (2007) *Museums and Community: Ideas, Issues and Challenges.* London and New York: Routledge.

Marstine, J., A. Bauer and C. Haines (eds) (2013) *New Directions in Museum Ethics.* London and New York: Routledge.

Message, K. and A. Witcomb (eds) (2015) *Museum Theory: An Expanded Field. The International Handbooks of Museums Studies.* Oxford: John Wiley.

Onciul, B. (2015) *Museums, Heritage and Indigenous Voice: Decolonising Engagement.* London and New York: Routledge.

Parry, R. (ed.) (2010) *Museums in a Digital Age.* London and New York: Routledge.

Sandell, R. (2017) *Museums, Moralities, and Human Rights.* London: Routledge.

INDEX

Note: *italic* page numbers indicate tables; **bold** indicate figures.

Natural History Society of
   Northumbria, specimens **55**
Net Art 69
networked museum 189
networks and offshoots 39
neutrality 59–60, 62, 212
new media art historians 69
new museology 7, 20–2; poetics of
   display 182–3
Niemeyer Centre, Aviles 131
Nightingale, E. 19
non-visitor motivation 102–3
Northern Gallery for Contemporary
   Art (NGCA), Sunderland **182**
Nye, J. 13

Obama, B. 205, 209–10
Obama, M. 111, 125
object biographies 70–1, 190
object-oriented ontology 190
object-subject distinction 71
objects: as agents 190; animate/
   inanimate 189; classification 179;
   sequencing 173; in social relations
   71; as speakers 189–90; symbolism
   and social meaning 77–8; ubiquity
   of 164
O'Doherty, B. 180
OEuvre Notre-Dame Museum 170
Ofer, S. 136
omnivore hypothesis 110
O'Neill, M. 198
operating costs 134–5
operational museology 21
oral histories 68
origins, of museums and galleries
   22–4
Osborne, G. 141–2
Osborne, P. 65
ownership 19, 38; ethics and law 33

Paine, C. 36
Palestinian Museum, Ramallah
   208–9

Parthenon 27
participatory institutions 195
passports 26
past, vs. histories 56–7
Patel, N. 170–1
patron model of cultural policy 144
patronage 141, 145
Pérez Art Museum Miami 140
Pérez, J. 140
periodisation 57
Perkarik, A. 191–2
personal heritage 48–9
Pes, J. 154
philanthropy 139–40
Philips, D. 148
physical access 104
Pierini, M. 138–9
poetics of display 182–3
policy implications, culture business
   144–5
policy initiatives, visitors and
   audiences 113–14
political consequences 206–7
political implications, funding and
   governance 37
political motivations 15
political roles 19–20
political statements, role of museums
   and galleries 25
politics: of museum and gallery use
   206–7; and power 207–9; role of
   museums and galleries 43
politics of display 183–4
politics of time 65
poly-vocal displays 187–8
population management, role of
   museums and galleries 25
positional economy 75
positive action 113
post-medium condition 67–8
power, and politics 207–9
power relations 19
practicalities, acquisition and
   accession 71–2